# INTERSUBJECTIVITY,
# PROJECTIVE IDENTIFICATION, AND OTHERNESS

# Intersubjectivity, Projective Identification and Otherness

Maurice Apprey
& Howard F. Stein

*with a Foreword by James S. Grotstein*

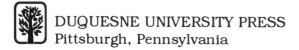
DUQUESNE UNIVERSITY PRESS
Pittsburgh, Pennsylvania

Published by
DUQUESNE UNIVERSITY PRESS
600 Forbes Avenue
Pittsburgh, PA 15282-0101

Library of Congress Cataloging-in-Publication Data

Apprey, Maurice, 1947–
  Intersubjectivity, projective identification, and otherness /
 Maurice Apprey and Howard F. Stein; with a foreword by James S.
 Grotstein.
      p.   cm.
  Includes bibliographical references and index.
  ISBN 0–8207–0247–1
  1. Projection (Psychology) 2. Interpersonal relations.
  3. Intersubjectivity. 4. Other minds (Theory of knowledge)
  5. Social groups—Psychological aspects.   I. Stein, Howard F.
  II. Title.
  RC455.4.P75A67   1993
  155.2/32–dc20                                                92-47242
                                                                    CIP

To
AMEDEO GIORGI
who teaches
Gaston Bachelard,
Maurice Merleau-Ponty,
and
Georges Politzer
with utmost care and intellectual generosity

AND TO
the memory of
the late TOM MAIN
who understood the
juxtaposition of life and death
in that precarious
process of childbirth

# Contents

Foreword (James S. Grotstein)                                    ix

Acknowledgments                                                xvii

Introduction (Apprey)                                             1

PART ONE:

*Intersubjectivity and Projective Identification:*
*Research and Clinical Observations*

1/ The Intersubjective Constitution of Anorexia Nervosa:
   A Descriptive Psychoanalytic Study (Apprey)                    7

2/ Projective Identification and Maternal Misconception
   in Disturbed Mothers (Apprey)                                 76

3/ Dreams of Urgent/Voluntary Errands
   and Transgenerational Haunting in Transsexualism
   (Apprey)                                                     102

PART TWO:

*Projective Identification and Intrapsychic*
*Stories of Parental Projects*

4/ A Prefatory Note on Motives and Projective
     Identification (Apprey)                                             131

5/ "When One Dies Another One Lives": The Invariant
     Unconscious Phantasy in Response to a Destructive
     Maternal Projective Identification (Apprey)               137

6/ Ambivalence, Rigidity, and Chaos: Integrating
     Individual and Family Therapy in the Treatment of
     Chemically Dependent Adolescents (Ehrmantraut and
     Apprey)                                                               169

PART THREE:

*Otherness: Application of Thoughts on Projective
Identification to Understanding of Groups*

7/ Clinical Decision-Making in Groups, Counter-
     transference, and Projective Identification (Stein)        187

8/ Adapting to Doom: The Group Psychology of an
     Organization Threatened with Cultural Extinction
     (Stein)                                                                207

9/ Beneath the Anger: Projective Identification in the
     Depths of Meaning of a Physician-Patient Relationship
     (Stein)                                                                243

Conclusion (Stein)                                                    257

Afterword (Apprey)                                                   263

References                                                               265

Index                                                                     280

# Foreword

*James S. Grotstein*

Drs. Apprey and Stein have written a postmodern text, "postmodern" in the sense that older values and concepts in psychoanalytic and social theory are deconstructed, questioned, and reinterpreted along newer lines of human individual and group experience. Perhaps one can conceive of the perspective of their inquiry by imagining the graphic image of a Siamesetwin, where there are two heads and one body, the former representing individuality and separation, and the latter representing normal and/or abnormal fusion (the group process). Thus, one can envision the dialectic between individual psychology (one head) and group psychology (two heads and one body). The thrust of the authors' contribution seems to be an innovative exploration of what might be called the "Möbiusstrip" of paradoxically discontinuous continuity between individuality and group process.

Each of the contributors has accumulated considerable experience in research and its clinical application, one in group organization and the other in psychoanalysis. Dr. Apprey formally conducted a longitudinal research study involving infant outcome as a result of their mothers' unconscious phantasies of projective identification, and additionally, he studied the degrees of severity of the phantasies in these mothers. The research began in the third trimester of pregnancy and continued for four years, thus giving Dr. Apprey the opportunity to study this phenomenon in depth.

Projective identification has long been known in the psychoanalytic literature but first came to prominence in Melanie Klein's (1946) now famous contribution on the subject and has ever afterwards been a mainpiece of Kleinian psychoanalysis—and now more recently in classical analysis as well. Projective identification can be seen its most sublimated form as the quality of empathy, and its most primitively defense form as the phenomenon in which the individual denies his/her emotional experience, relocates (disidentifies) it in phantasy to his/her image of another person, where it is now identified as belonging. The projecting subject now feels free of the specific pain, yet paradoxically feels persecuted by the object into which he/she projected them, as if these were the "Siamese-twinship"–"Möbius-strip" connection between them. Thus, the subject is persecuted by "nameless dread" (Bion 1962), "nameless" because the specific name of the experience was lost in the denial, relocation, and projective identification.

Klein and her followers emphasized the intrapsychic aspects of projective identification. According to them, the creation of the structure of the internal world generally, and of the superego specifically, is due almost entirely to the projective identification of aspects of the infantile self into its object. These projections transform the images of the object so that, when subsequently introjected and identified internally, they become concrete psychic structures. Thus phantasy structures concretely become psychic structures. Subsequently, there occurs a series of reprojections of these phantasy structures into the object, thereby imbuing the object with persecutory superego qualities, amongst others. The Kleinian point of view, even more than the classical Freudian, allowed us to envision that our object world was inhabited by myriads of confusions of alter egos or ghosts of our former selves which were now detached from us, inhabited others, and yet persecuted us with the déjà vu of "strange-familiarity." To be persecuted meant to be hounded by a former aspect of ourselves confused with an object, seemingly longing to return to its original self—apparently with a vengeance.

Projective identification then underwent a second phase of understanding beginning with Bion's (1962) conception of "container and contained," which postulated that a mother in a state of reverie (akin to Winnicott's primary maternal preoccupation) sustains her infant's projective identifications of its feelings of mental pain, the principal one of which, according to Bion, is that of dying. The mother sustains these projective identifications through her own partial identification with them—she, in part, feels the pain as her own. She then must distance herself from her identifications, understand them, interpret them by name, and conduct proper interventions with her infant as a result. In the clinical situation, we refer to this as therapeutic counter-transference or projective counteridentification. Roger Money-Kyrle has termed it *introjective identification* by the therapist.

Following Bion's redefinition of projective identification, in which he transcended the one-person perspective and invoked the transactional perspective, the concept was imported, as it were, into the United States and addressed principally in this latter form, mainly by Ogden and by Tansey and Burke. What is important in this second development is that projective identification was no longer seen exclusively as an intrapsychic process but as a group process. The concept of projection remained clear, but the concept of identification underwent a radical change. In the original Kleinian sense, the defense mechanism of projective identification actually involves a three-step process: (1) disidentification from the subject, (2) reidentification (relocation) of the disidentification in the object, and (3) introjection of the object and identification with it intrapsychically in its transformed alteration. The Bion modification of identification became the interpersonal way of understanding projective identification, where identification no longer applied to the projecting subject but only to the containing object. This new understanding (or as Kleinians would think—"misunderstanding") followed closely in parallel with the rising importance of countertransference in the clinical situation and with the rise of importance of the interpersonal, interactive, and intersubjective aspects of psychoanalytic theory as well. Its importance was furthered by research findings in infant development.

Dr. Apprey's studies of projective identification take yet another course—one that reverses the line of inquiry originated by Klein (of the infant's projective identification into its mother) by investigating mother's projective identification of her feelings, conflicts, painful ideas, values into her infant. By utilizing the treatment of patients' suffering from anorexia nervosa, Dr. Apprey has extended the concept of projective identification even further, so that it now embraces the transgenerational or intergenerational context. He has ingeniously demonstrated a number of invariants in this transgenerational context and has pinpointed the importance of the patient's grandmother as an important source of toxic projective identifications that traverse through her daughter (and presumably her son as well) into yet the next generation. The biblical concept of "the sins of the fathers" and the classical Greek concept of family curses, which was expressed in the background of Oedipus (the curse of the Labdacid dynasty of Thebes) and of Orestes (the curse of the house of Atreus), now finds a new psychoanalytic basis of understanding.

So far I have alluded to the intrapsychic, interpersonal, and trans-generational aspects of projective identification. There is still another aspect which is infrequently alluded to but has not yet been rigorously pursued. I am referring to the distinction between projection and projective identification. I shall refrain from getting into the debate on this issue because Kleinians in general seem to believe that there can be no distinction between projection and projective identification, and others, of more classical views, seem to believe that there is a distinction. Bion was most explicit in stating that there can be no projection without an object being suitably conceived as "worthy" of the projection to be identified with it.

The importance of this issue is more than academic because the heart of Dr. Apprey's thesis is that the grandchild is the recipient of projective identifications originating at least in the grandmother and coursing through her daughter, the patient's mother. Who is chosen to be the recipient of projective identifications, particularly archaic, violent, aggressive ones, constitutes a matter of great theoretical and clinical importance. Here I think there is an element of ambiguity or perhaps paradox. It is my impression that there is a bimodal paradox in the chosen targets of projective identification. On the one hand, we project into objects that are already conceived of as being tainted and suitable for projection—"projection into reality." On the other hand, and this theme is implicit in Dr. Apprey's work, we have a tendency to project into persons—and generations—which are as yet innocent of taint. The putative sacrifice of Isaac by Abraham and the actual attempted sacrifice of Oedipus, as well as the sacrifice of Christ, bear testimony to this need for an innocent one to be the bearer of our projections. Herman Melville's *Billy Budd* is a beautiful demon-stration of this concept.

The bimodal, dialectical twin of Christ, is of course, the devil. Insofar as the sacrificial lamb, into whom we project our guilt, transcends our projections, it evolves into higher innocence and achieves the godhead. In proportion as the sacrificial lamb is transformed by our projections, it becomes the devil, and its feet, horns, and tail are the remaining residues of its formal innocence. It then, as the devil, becomes a more appropriate target of projection, whereas its twin, Christ, becomes the facilitator of absolution through projective identification and idealization.

In establishing the parameters of his research design, Dr. Apprey has evolved as a pioneer in pregnancy psychoanalysis and has been able to locate invariants in the sequence of projective identifications that his pregnant patients experienced toward their unborn and later postnatal offspring. He has isolated three significant sequential factors in the analysis of pregnancy: (1) the "fostering of the intrapsychic story" and the emergence of the unconscious invariant pathogenic phantasy in the expectant mother, (2) the uncovering of aggression and hatred, both as identification with her mother's aggression toward her and as her own, and in her introjection of this hatred in the form of depression, and (3) a therapeutic regression with reanimation of core depressive affects comprising the superego and requiring superego analysis. One of the key features of the intrapsychic story, according to Dr. Apprey, is the universal belief, among pregnant mothers, that for someone to live, someone else must die.

Dr. Apprey traces this belief to unconscious hostility on the part of the pregnant mother's own mother. This concept is an important contribution to the psychoanalysis of pregnancy, and I can verify it from my own clinical experience. Perhaps one can recast Dr. Apprey's view in this regard as the consequences upon the mother and her infant-to-be of her lack of receiving a full, unconditional "blessing" from her own mother. Thus, the helpless mother perceives her mother's unconscious hostility partial or total curse—or at least, as a lack of blessing. Another aspect of this universal belief is the "cosmic hydraulic," by which I mean the cosmic beliefs on the part of the primitive aspect of the mind that conceives of things only in terms of "either/or." "Either/or" is a remnant of first-dimensional thinking, from the cosmic dimension where the infant dwells when it leaves the symmetry of the zero dimension of uterine existence. Thus, there is no concept of absence per se; the absence of a good mother is axiomatically the presence of a bad mother. According to Melanie Klein, the infant must achieve the experience of the depressive position, where objects can be regarded as separate and their absence can be mourned in order for them to merge into a cosmic conception in which the absence of a good mother is not axiomatically connected to the presence of a bad mother. For mourning to take place, destructive aggression toward the object must be reconciled, and ambivalence, rather than splitting, and positive and negative idealization must hold forth.

The second part of the book contains the work by Drs. Ehrmantraut and Apprey (chapter 6) and deals with newer ideas emerging from family therapy of chemically dependent adolescents. Here again, the authors have utilized the mechanism of projective identification to highlight the systems approach to the understanding of dysfunctional families. They state: "Thus, it was apparent that the family structure as it existed could not contain the negative projective identifications or the ambivalence" (p. 260). They were able to differentiate two different kinds of dysfunctional families, the rigid and the chaotic, and found that it was important, as in individual psychoanalysis and psychotherapy, to facilitate the family's transformation from either rigidity or chaos to a state of ambiguity or uncertainty in the direction of detoxifying the projective identifications located in the delegated, drug-abusing adolescent child. Interestingly, as numerous other studies have shown, they found that in none of the families studied had the father or father surrogate been available emotionally. Thus, there was a constant imbalance in these families.

In the final part, Dr. Stein undertakes to be the spokesman for the "middle ground of local, relatively small medical groups in which crucial clinical decision-making occurs." His work stands on the threshold of the revolution in health care delivery systems in our country, which have rapidly evolved from individual practitioners to group providers, behind which are often large corporations. Dr. Stein addresses the issue of decision-making and leadership and its practical consequences, group countertransference to patients, families, other medical institutions. The field of group analysis was first initiated by Freud and was later deepened by Bion's contributions, which culminated in so-called Tavistock group method in England and at the A. K. Rice Institute in the United States. It has also been addressed by Anzieu et al., Ashbach and Shermer, Coleman and Geller, and more lately by Alford, and by Volkan on the international level.

The dilemma of the group process is multifaceted, but it seems to devolve into the following: there is no such thing as a psychology of a group per se because the group is simply the sum of the individuals who comprise it. Yet, at the same time, the group behaves in invariant ways which cause us to believe that there is such a concept as "groupthink." Perhaps one can imagine the group to be not only a collection of individuals but also a collection of projected ghosts into the composite group structure, so that the context of the group, which is first formed when individuals come together to organize around the common purpose (Bion's "workgroup") and then when they work together on the common theme, develops invariant resistances to the performance of this common theme. Bion conceived of three resistant subgroups, which he termed *basic* assumption groups. They included (a) fight and flight, (b) dependency, and (c) pairing.

Dr. Stein believes that the context of the group's work is of great importance in defining a series of preconceptions that become projected into various members of the group or clients (patients) of the group and that ultimately foster misunderstandings. Specifically, he details unconscious "agendas" existent in clinical groups. Whether illustrating "generational succession" in medical residency groups or competition in identity status between rival medical specialties, the clinical examples Dr. Stein presents are telling. I can confirm his conclusions from my own experience. Reporting episodes of child abuse and child molestation, especially in the state of California, is on the brink of being out of control, according to some observers. It is mandatory for all clinicians to report even suspicions of child molestation and abuse. Invariably, such reports are taken as concrete truth. Reporting drug abuse is another process that lends itself to oversuspicion of the patient by hospital personnel, and often to undersuspicion by individual private psychotherapists.

One of the great sources of antagonism toward self psychology by other psychoanalytic schools is the fear of collusion with the patient's narcissism and omnipotence, whereas self psychology often expresses its rejection of classical and Kleinian concepts in terms suggesting that these other schools are "patient abusers," emotionally speaking.

Running through the course of the authors' whole work is the Ariadne's thread of projective identification, that schizoid mechanism which Melanie Klein associated with the paranoid-schizoid position and which is grouped with such other schizoid mechanism as splitting, idealization, and magic omnipotent denial. The defense against the attainment of its successor, the depressive position, is characterized

by a more sophisticated form of projective identification, which Klein
termed "manic defense against the sense of the reality of the dependency and of the object of that dependency."

I understand the authors of this work to be working within that
framework and extending it in a most innovative way to the intergenerational process, the family process, and to the group process,
all of which foster a group paranoid-schizoid experience of mytholo-
gies or untruths as a form of defensive protection against feared
persecutory anxiety. When the anxieties have been located, contained,
and named, the myths dissolve and ambiguous reality takes place.
Reality must be ambiguous. It is the fear of the consequences of
ambiguity that causes the regressive descent into the absoluteness of
the omnipotent paranoid-schizoid domain. Thus, what is needed is a
dualtrack, a respect for dialectics, ambiguity, paradox, and uncertainty—and for trust, hope, and faith.

# Acknowledgments

*Maurice Apprey* wishes to thank the following five journals for permission to reprint previously published material:

"Intersubjective Constitution of Anorexia Nervosa," *New Literary History* 22 (4) 1991: 1151–1069. Published by Johns Hopkins University Press, Baltimore, Maryland.

"Projective Identification and Maternal Misconception in Disturbed Mothers," *British Journal of Psychotherapy* 4 (1) 1987: 5–22. Published by Artesian Books, London, England.

"Dreams of Urgent/Voluntary Errands," *Melanie Klein and Object Relations* 10 (2) 1992: 1–29. Published at the Ontario Institute for Studies in Education, Ontario, Canada.

"A Prefatory Note on Motives and Projective Identifications," *International Journal of Psychoanalytic Psychotherapy* 11 1985: 111–116. Published by Jason Arowson, Inc., New York, New York.

"When One Dies Another One Lives: The Invariant Unconscious Phantasy in Response to a Destructive Material Projective Identification," *Melanie Klein and Object Relations* 5 (2) 1987: 18–52. Published at the Ontario Institute for Studies in Education, Ontario, Canada.

Jacqueline Rose of Queen Mary College, University of London introduced me to the work of Nicholas Abraham. Patrick Fowler of the University of Virginia School of Medicine read and provided helpful comments on chapter 2. Brenda Wood, Elisabeth Clarke and

Margaret Stein masterfully typed, arranged and rearranged the manuscript until it reached a presentable form.

I wish to thank Robert M. Carey, M.D., Dean of the University of Virginia School of Medicine for supporting the publication of this book.

*Howard F. Stein* wishes to thank the following two journals for permission to reprint previously published material, here expanded:

"Adapting to Doom: The Group Psychology of an Organization Threatened with Cultural Extinction," *Political Psychology* 11 (1) March 1990: 113–145. Published by Plenum Press, New York.

"Beneath the Anger: Depths of Meaning and Emotion in a Physician-Patient Relationship and Its Larger Group Context," *Family Systems Medicine* 9 (2) Summer 1991: 177–188, published by Family Process, Inc., New York.

I also wish to thank Dr. Maurice Apprey for over a decade of friendship and support, which here culminates in our fourth book.

# Introduction

*Maurice Apprey*

In 1975 there was a vigorous debate between Frederick Kurth, Roger Money-Kyrle, Peter Knapp, Mark Kanzer, Marjorie Brierley, and Donald Meltzer following Kurth's paper on *Projective Identification, Analyzability, and Hate* (1975). Kurth put forward the idea that there was such a mental mechanism or psychological process as "violent projective identification." In his view,

> violent projective identification, examined prismatically, reveals such elements as envy, persecutory anxiety, possessive jealousy, deficiency of trust, intolerance of separation, etc. (Meltzer 1967). It is particularly linked with the spoiling qualities of envy and the paranoid grievances external reality nurtures simply because it is there . . . (p. 315).

Meltzer took exception to Kurth's linking violent projective identification with massive projective identification. In Meltzer's view, massive projective identification had a specific meaning. It referred to the obliteration of boundaries between self and other, the confusion of one's identity with that of the other, the blurring of geographical boundaries between self and object. Although Meltzer saw some affinity between the notions of "massive projective identification" and "violent projective identification," he insisted that they were not interchangeable. Meltzer's objection was correct. It was up to Kurth to fine-tune his own notion of "violent projective identification," where ontological hate is strongly implicated in the self-other relation. Kurth explained that

1

> This *ontological hate* refers to a negative condition of being set against
> the sources of life. Put another way, this hate does not allow life to
> come into being. It positions itself behind life in order to shut off the
> wellsprings. This hate primordially repudiates any idea of being "behind"
> someone in the sense of supporting and nourishing and protecting and
> comforting. On the contrary, to be "behind" someone . . . means com-
> pletely to enter into and take over (1975, 325).

Kurth's notion of "violent projective identification" is thus about total
annihilation of the other, hence the description "violent" as opposed
to "massive." Kurth went on to suggest that besides the infusion of
ontological hate in violent projective identification, other motivational
factors intrinsic to the use of this psychical mechanism included
"consuming love." In other words, one can perish by love or freeze
with hate. One can annihilate the other as much by *smothering* the
other as by maliciously hating the other. This violent form of projective
identification which includes ontological hate and consuming passion
"annihilates *by choking off the life of the object before it ever comes
into being*" (p. 326; emphasis in original).

    In this book we make the radical departure from the traditional
use of projective identification to construct an infant's relation to the
mothering person or a patient's relation to the analyst as m(other).
Rather, we describe a variety of situations where a mother or parent
involves an infant in a state of projective identification. This radical
shift allows us to describe rather than to construct what would otherwise
be a preverbal, prelinguistic relation to an m(other). With this radical
shift we see more clearly what Kurth attempted to capture in his
notion of violent projective identification. A mother's hatred thus
becomes easier to describe. Even better, she can articulate her own
hatred rather than have it described for her by an analyst or some
other researcher. Countertransference and group relations where
projective identification is implicated can be described with greater
lucidity and conviction.

    It is not our intention to reach finality in terms of understanding
any interperceptual or interactional process or mechanism. Rather, we
accept that there are plural motivational factors which present
themselves as one form of projective identification or other. So, in
this book, we approach projective identification as a framework for
understanding how people come to embody in others disembodied
aspects of themselves. Through studies ranging from mother–anorexic

daughter relations, to mothers' attitudes toward their pregnancies and their young offspring, to group dynamics within a modern corporation, we shall explore the numerous facets of intersubjectivity, projective identification, and otherness. Thus, projective identification is not expected to unpack every interperceptual or interactional process. Rather, we allow it to appear in a multiplicity of ways: as a defensive process, as a conscious fantasy or unconscious fantasy, as a vehicle for communicating a wish, as an interpersonal maneuver to deny separation, as a strategy to annihilate in fantasy an other. We shall show how projective identification—in tandem with its internalizing counterpart, introjective identification—functions as an elemental block of dyadic, familial, group, and international relations. Furthermore, we shall show that one need not be shackled to the term *projective identification*. Rather one can discipline oneself to describe with care so that interperceptual and interrelational processes between human beings can present themselves in ways familiar to us through projective identification or in other proximal or horizonal ways. Hence, we have entitled this volume *Intersubjectivity, Projective Identification, and Otherness*. We neither want to promote any semblance of finality nor any semblance of ambiguity. Each context speaks to some phenomenon. Thus, we shall see contexts where a mother's infanticidal wishes become disclosed, where other, less noxious motives become apparent, or where self and other boundaries become blurred.

*Intersubjectivity, Projective Identification, and Otherness* recognizes that in this postmodern era, there is a departure from one all-encompassing mode of articulating our world, a flight from one authoritative reality. Instead, there are multiple essences, plural and dispersed modes of capturing different worlds. Indeed, there are multiple structures of experience where the term *structure* designates a term of knowledge. In short, we can come to know the world in which we live in more than one way.

This interdisciplinary book, coauthored by a child analyst and a psychoanalytic anthropologist, should be of interest to a wide variety of professionals in clinical, educational, and corporate fields, as well as in the social and behavioral sciences.

PART ONE

# INTERSUBJECTIVITY AND PROJECTIVE IDENTIFICATION: RESEARCH AND CLINICAL OBSERVATIONS

# 1/ The Intersubjective Constitution of Anorexia Nervosa
## A Descriptive Psychoanalytic Study

*Maurice Apprey*

Bachelard (1936/1986), the French physical chemist turned aesthetician, asserted that

> literary symbolism and *the* symbolism that is Freud's, such as they are executed in classical symbolism and normal dreamwork, are only mutilated examples of the symbolizing powers active in nature. Both present an expression that has been arrested too soon. They remain substitutes for a substance or person that desert evolution, syntheses named too quickly, desires uttered too soon. A new poetry and a new psychology that might describe the soul as it is being formed, language in bloom, must give up definite symbols or images learned merely and return to vital impulses and primitive poetry (p. 31; emphasis in original).

We must return to both vital impulses and primitive poetry because primitive and vital impulses are as much integrated in the functions they serve as are high-level symbolic behavior and poetics. For this reason, separation of primitive and higher levels of behavior can be misleading. From that viewpoint anorexia nervosa can reveal meaningful data about its sufferers and their families, whether primitive manifestations of psychopathology or higher-level functions present themselves to us. Bachelard's assertion has not been sufficiently heeded by psychoanalysts, clinical psychologists, medical scientists, or biological scientists. Although some feeble attempts have been made to study the zone between self and other, a huge cleavage still exists in the work of scientists. Artificial barriers exist between notions of past and present, conscious and unconscious, surface and deep structures. The greatest of these barriers, between the biological and the psychological, still exists in the minds and works of clinical investigators. Nowhere are these assumptions more observable than in the understanding and treatment of the pathological formation called anorexia nervosa. It is not surprising, therefore, that anorexia has made fools of endocrinologists, psychiatrists, psychoanalysts, and many other clinicians or educators for years. Today, some anorexics die, some transform their anorexia into bulimia, some go through the motions of treatment and live a sterile life of sexual asceticism, and some others recover with varying degrees of success.

In *The Structure of Behavior* (1942/1983) Merleau-Ponty tackled the problem of the cleavage between consciousness and nature. He put forth a new mode of comprehension, asserting that we needed to understand what happens in that neutral zone between the body and behavior, or between the body and existence. For Merleau-Ponty, the structure of behavior as directly perceived was this new mode of knowing, of grasping how consciousness is engaged in the world. In determining the meaning of this structure of directly perceived behavior, we would deepen our understanding of the human order—when humans behaved at the human order. In so doing, we should not treat the body as "thing" or the body as "idea." Rather, we should abandon causal thinking, introspection, and abstraction in favor of dialectical thinking. For Merleau-Ponty, complexes should have priority over isolated stimuli, and linear causality should be replaced by circular causality in ways that include other relations; for example, intentionality must be allowed to enter the inquiry. According to his thinking, the isolated phenomenon as conceived in the laboratory is pathological. Merleau-Ponty's preference for complexes, rather than isolated phenomena, his interest in the relationship between scientific consciousness and the givens of naive consciousness, and his aversion to the cleavage between the objective and the subjective will serve as a useful backdrop to this study. This backdrop is consistent with Bachelard's admonition that we graft poetics on material imagination, that we see vital impulses as continuous with symbolism.

Anorexia nervosa, therefore, presents us with very serious challenges and opportunities. Perhaps through our studies we can come to grips with those ruptures between self and other, surface and deep, biological and psychological, and other related fissures. In this descriptive study of the intersubjective constitution of anorexia nervosa, where the reciprocal perceptions of mothers and daughters are foregrounded, attempts will be made to articulate continuities, mutualities, and any other forms of shared subjectivity that present themselves in the process. We shall be interested in all other discoveries that present themselves as we follow the consciousness, perceptions, and experiences, and in all other forms of knowing and presences made available to us by anorexics and their mothers. These subjects will take us to the prior latency which modes of experience and pure description are capable of disclosing, so that we may, among other contributions, ultimately bridge the gap between vital impulses and the complexities of intersubjectivity.

To define and state the problems posed by intersubjectivity and its place in the study of anorexia nervosa, the literature review of this study will begin with a "conversation" between Husserl, Scheler, and Merleau-Ponty. This will serve as an entrée into a discussion of studies on anorexia nervosa, after which will come the conceptual underpinnings of the phenomenological praxis we will use to conduct our study on intersubjectivity.

## CONVERSATION BETWEEN MERLEAU-PONTY, HUSSERL, AND SCHELER

Husserl (1913/1931) suggested that every perception, being a consciousness that intends an actual object, possesses a perspectival horizon of before and after, among others. In this respect, a perception, referring back to that which was perceived before, can be viewed in memories. Such a perception, in Husserl's view, can be presented through memory even when the memories are not directly linked to a current perception but are separated from the respective perception by stretches of obscurity. Husserl saw another unity, one that lies at a deeper level. According to this deeper unity, when one perceives one's own past, this past is precisely one's own. One's past environment, now remembered, belongs to the same world that one now inhabits. The difference, however, is that what is remembered is presented in the form of a fragment of one's past.

Husserl's thoughts on time, including the protentional and retentional dimensions of the experience of time, were set forth clearly in *Ideas* (1913/1931). To be more precise, "protentional" and "retentional" belong to present structures of concrete experiencing rather than to memory as such, which gives direct access to the world of the past. According to Husserl (1913/1931), the essential property that "temporality" expresses does not belong in a general way to single experiences but is rather, "a necessary form of binding experiences with experiences". Thus:

> Every real experience . . . is necessarily one that endures, and with this duration it takes its place within an endless continuum of durations— a concretely *filled* continuum. It necessarily has a temporal purview concretely filled, and stretching away endlessly on all sides. And that at once tells us that it belongs to *one* endless *"stream of experience"* (p. 236; emphasis in original).

For Husserl, real experiences endure and connect with one another. Experiences that occur in the here and now persist through change, although the content of subsequent experience may vary. Here-and-now experiences are thus continuous with those that vanished moments ago. Their forms will have continuity but their contents will change— although forms can change, too, or at least be different at different levels.

And, how does Husserl link this identity of perception to intersubjectivity? Husserl (1946/1973) explains.

> To introduce the matter of intersubjectivity, what we have said also holds true if another person tells me about his past experience, communicates his memories: what is recalled in them belongs to the same objective world as that which is given in my and our common present lived experience. The remembered environing world of the other, about which he tells us, may certainly be another world than that in which we find ourselves at present, and likewise the environing world which I myself remember may be another world (p. 163).

All these remembered worlds are, however, fragments of the very same objective world. Husserl continues:

> This world is, in the most comprehensive sense, as the *life-world* for a human community capable of mutual understanding, *our earth*, which includes within itself all these different environing worlds with their modifications and their pasts . . . . In this unique world, everything

> sensuous that I now originally perceive, everything that I have perceived
> and which I can now remember or about which others can report to
> me as what they have perceived or remembered, has its place. Everything
> has its unity in that it has its fixed temporal position in this objective
> world, its place in objective time (p. 163).

According to these views, one's perception of others begins with the cogito, where there is a reference to self, or in Merleau-Ponty's (1973) phrase, with the "sphere of ownness." This sphere of ownness, however, is achieved through a reduction. From this position Husserl makes an effort to find different but originary modes of perception of others through four rubrics, which are articulated in Merleau-Ponty's discussion of the problem of intersubjectivity, and which because they are originary do not depend upon consciousness of self. Merleau-Ponty (1973) lists the four rubrics as (1) lateral perception; (2) lacunary perception, (3) perception of other people's behavior, and (4) intentional transfer.

Under the rubric of lateral perception, other people's existence is a reflection of each of our individual selves. There is an alter ego that reflects each of us. Likewise, others take their existence from us. Under the second rubric of lacunary perception, when we perceive other people in relation to ourselves, we perceive a *reflection* and *a lack* at one and the same time. According to this view, it will always be impossible for us to perceive other people in their totality and as they perceive themselves, for "there is a limit to presence in the flesh: we never occupy exactly the same place as others. By definition, if we were in their place, we would be them. . ." (Merleau-Ponty 1973, 42).

If lateral or lacunary perception fails, a further attempt to posit other people must be made through Husserl's third possibility. We must try to posit others through the perception of their behavior, and when we attest to the behavior of other people, our body becomes a means of understanding them. Our corporeality comprehends their corporeality. We grasp the final meaning of the other's behavior, because our body can achieve the same goals as the bodies of others. What is true for the observer is true for the observed. In one's perceptual style one apprehends and imitates simultaneously, even if one cannot articulate one's style.

Finally, through the process of "intentional" and "apperceptive" transfer, other people are perceived in a manner quite like "pairing," where one body meets its counterpart in another body a body that both realizes its intentions and suggests new intentions to the self. The ego of the self and other people are thus linked in a dialectical relation.

Merleau-Ponty and Husserl alike find it impossible to save the ego at the expense of the other, and vice versa, because they see the ego and others as varying in the same sense. Both continue to recognize serious problems in the apprehension of others through the perception of the self. For example, how does one reconcile the idea of other people's existence as a primordial condition with the view that their existence can be rendered explicit? Merleau-Ponty sees this reconciliation as impossible. Also, one cannot allow one's self to be constituted by the questionable acuity that lurks behind other people's conception of one's self.

Merleau-Ponty (1973) recognizes at least two persistent tendencies in Husserl's work:

> (a) the attempt to gain access to others by starting with the *cogito,* with the sphere of ownness;
> (b) the denial of this problem and an orientation toward "intersubjectivity," that is, the possibility of starting without the primordial cogito, starting with a consciousness which is neither self nor others (pp. 44–45).

Where does this second possibility lead us? We are told by Merleau-Ponty that

> while envisaging this second possibility, Husserl effectively shows that, even though it would be satisfactory, it does not hide the difficulties of the problem which remain intact for him. Thus, *at the frontier of an intersubjective conception, Husserl finally maintains an integral transcendental subjectivity* (p. 45; emphasis added).

But Husserl did not stop here at this frontier of an intersubjective conception. He came to affirm that "subjectivity is intersubjectivity (the experience that other people have of me validly teaches me that which I am)" (Merleau-Ponty 1973, 45). We are told by Merleau-Ponty that Husserl was not able to reconcile starting with the cogito and other people's experience validly teaching me that I am.

Scheler, a student of Husserl's, enters the picture, and now Merleau-Ponty pits Scheler's position against Husserl's. From the start Scheler renounces the cogito and abandons the Cartesian postulate of consciousness as primarily consciousness of the self. Scheler gives up the differentiation between self and others, and

> generalizes the idea of "inner perception" (the perception of feelings, for example), which applies as much to other people as to oneself. On the one hand, the perception of my own body or of my own behavior is as external as, and no more immediate than, the perception of objects. On the other hand, we see, we perceive the feelings of others (not only their expression); we perceive them with the same certitude as our own feelings. The differences between the diverse feelings are provided by the perception itself (Merleau-Ponty 1973, 45).

This position is what prompts Merleau-Ponty to speak of this undifferentiation between self and other people in terms of a "current or undifferentiated psychic experience." This current of undifferentiation is

> a mixture of self and others, primitive consciousness in a kind of generality, a state of permanent "hysteria" (in a sense of an indistinctness between that which is lived and that which is imagined between self and others) (pp. 45–46).

From Scheler's point of view, we are not going to perceive others by starting with the cogito, with the sphere of ownness. Rather, one's consciousness of self emerges from undifferentiation between selves and indistinctness through such expressions as acts, reactions, etc. Let Merleau-Ponty speak for Scheler once again:

> The consciousness of self cannot be given a privileged position. It is impossible without consciousness of others. It is of the same variety. Like all experience, the experience of self exists only as a figure against a ground. Perception of others is like the ground from which perception of self separates itself. We see ourselves through the intermediary of others (p. 46).

Thus, for Scheler, consciousness is not separate from expressive acts and reactions. Consciousness of self is inseparable from consciousness of others. In part, our sense of corporeality will assist us to apprehend the self or the other, but most of all the content and the intention of expressed acts and reactions can betray what one shares with other people.

> Thus, in a fire only the subject who is burned can feel the sensible sharpness of the pain. But everything that the burn represents: the menace

of fire, the danger for the well-being of the body, the *signification of the pain*, can be communicated to other people and felt by other people. It is therefore the same form, the same content which is lived through another channel [*matière*]. The signification, the intuition of the feeling (that which constitutes its essentials) is the same for the two consciousnesses. There is an isolation of the *felt* [*senti*], but not an isolation of consciousness (Merleau-Ponty 1973, 47).

While we cannot become others corporeally, we can become others through our intentions. In this sense, we can reach others through the manifest expressions which present themselves to us. Consciousness and its manifest expression are one with other, one with ourselves.

Bringing Husserl and Scheler back together for his conclusions on their differing positions, Merleau-Ponty sees Husserl as maintaining the originality of the ego, while Scheler minimizes consciousness of the self. But both Husserl and Scheler see the ego and other people linked by the same dialectical relation; their positions are strangely but intimately allied in such a way that we cannot save one from the other without cost. Merleau-Ponty does not wish to eliminate either position, insurmountable though their problems may be. For him, the self and the other can be joined by giving lived experience every primacy. Self and situation must be juxtaposed so that the ego must perceive itself in relation to, and identify with, the act in which the ego projects itself. Witness now, a terse Merleau-Ponty (1973):

> Our perception of others is a modification of ourselves. Man is a sorcerer for man. We are co-responsible for what the other does. What is in question is to know whether the insularity of consciousness must be placed in doubt. We must describe our relations with others before having reflected. In life, there is a zone of the voluntary, of the reflected knowing, but before that there is the prepersonal zone. The first level perhaps motivates my whole being (p. 49).

So, our perception of others can and does modify us. One person may be a sorcerer for another, and by Merleau-Ponty's account we are "co-responsible" for what the other does.

Husserl, Scheler, and Merleau-Ponty will not exhaust the issues involved in intersubjectivity, and they will not solve all the problems they raise, but their positions ultimately help us in our efforts to define the boundaries of intersubjectivity. For the purposes of this study we shall take a leap from philosophical arguments about intersubjectivity, and broadly treat it as a world of experience between two worlds. Yet within every experience there lies a world of perceptions, ideas, judgments, intuitions, and sensations; and within each world there will always be fragments of other worlds, each of which may be a world larger than we can imagine. So we shall be interested in what our mother-daughter pairs concretely tell us about their separate worlds and how each separate world fits into that of the other. It is reasonable to expect at this point that there will be descriptions by subjects which demonstrate both a lack and a reflection of oneself; descriptions which by their ambiguity tell us which interactions and expressive manifestations carry separate projects of the participants in that dyad, and which may or may not converge.

## ANOREXIA NERVOSA AND INTERSUBJECTIVITY

Before discussing the relatively conspicuous absence of mother-daughter perceptions of each other in the literature of the intersubjective constitution of anorexia nervosa, let us ask some of the major practitioners and researchers what anorexia nervosa is. Thomä's (1967) definition is as follows:

> The signs which distinguish anorexia nervosa from all other illnesses that result in emaciation and loss of weight are as follows: (1) the age of onset is usually puberty or post-puberty; (2) the patients are almost all female; (3) the reduction in nutritional intake is psychically determined; (4) spontaneous or self-induced vomiting occurs, usually in secret; (5) amenorrhea usually appears either before or, more rarely, after the beginning of the weight loss; (6) constipation, sometimes an excuse for excessive consumption of laxatives, speeds up the loss of weight; (7) the physical effects of undernourishment are present. In severe cases, they can lead to death (p. 21).

Wilson (1983) concurs with Thomä's delineation and, following Sours (1980), adds that 7 to 15 percent of anorexics die. Wilson (1983) extracts from the literature three further observations: extreme hyperactivity; a disproportionate loss of breast tissue in females; and the admixture of other psychosomatic symptoms or psychogenic equivalents with the clinical picture of anorexia nervosa. The psychogenic equivalents may include phobias, depressions, self-destructive and sexually impulsive behavior, accident-proneness, and stealing.

Minuchin, Rosman, and Baker (1978) organized the various

approaches to the diagnosis and treatment of anorexia nervosa into
two conceptual models: the linear model and the systems model.
According to them, the linear model focuses on the individual patient
and includes medical, psychodynamic, and behavioral models. The
systems model, while relying in part on the linear model, transcends
it to observe the anorexic in a wider context. The medical model is
broadly psychopharmacological. The psychodynamic model, relying
on the formulations of Freud used in psychosomatic studies, considers
etiological factors specific to psychosomatic pathological formations,
which include proneness to organ system vulnerability, genetically
acquired environmental transmission, the psychology of conflict, and
the nature of defense organization.

Minuchin and his collaborators (1978) reported on Bruch's (1974)
call for a more comprehensive framework for studying this disease:

> Bruch hypothesized that something had gone wrong in the anorectic
> patient's early experiential and interpersonal processes, warping her
> ability to identify hunger correctly and to distinguish hunger from other
> states of bodily need or emotional arousal (pp. 16–17).

They quote Bruch herself (1974, 56), speaking more specifically

> If confirmation and reinforcement of his own initially rather undiffer-
> entiated needs and impulses have been absent, or have been contra-
> dictory or inaccurate, then a child will grow up perplexed when trying
> to differentiate between disturbances in his biological field and emotional
> and interpersonal experiences, and he will be apt to misinterpret de-
> formities in his self-body concept as externally induced. Thus he will
> become an individual deficient in his sense of separateness, with "diffuse
> ego boundaries," and will feel helpless under the influence of external
> forces (p. 17).

Although Minuchin and his collaborators acknowledged the broad-
ening context that Bruch was advocating in her approach, they saw
her and her fellow psychodynamic practitioners as focusing invariably
on individual therapy, rather than, say, family therapy, which for them
provided a much broader and more compelling context for treatment.
They rejected the role of fantasy, conscious or unconscious, in favor
of systemic interactions between family members and the external
world.

Minuchin and his collaborators found operant conditioning and other
behavioral models equally unsatisfactory. They were not impressed

by a theory that considers anorexia nervosa as a set of contingencies that must be controlled. In their view, behaviorism, like the psychodynamic models, observed systemic factors that presented themselves in treatment, only to ignore them.

Minuchin's criticism of the medical, psychodynamic, and behavioral models serves as a preparation for the establishment of his strategic systemic approach to family therapy. The systems model postulates a circular movement of segments that affect each other. It is a system that can be activated at many points, and that has feedback mechanisms which operate at any number of these points.

Clearly there exist many theories on the definition and treatment of anorexia nervosa, and any detailed delineation of these theories belongs elsewhere. The sketches of some of the major ideas on anorexia articulated here will serve only as borders for our discussion. From this author's (Apprey's) point of view, no pure theory or tradition exists as to the diagnosis and treatment of anorexia nervosa, contrary to what Minuchin and his coauthors may say. As disparate as strategic family therapy and psychodynamic interventions may be, every individual is a system, albeit a small one, and it takes a nonpartisan view to plan a comprehensive model that can include individual, family, group, and other therapies to meet the needs of an anorexic. Palazzoli (1982) presents a psychoanalytic object relations viewpoint in her "transpersonal approach," as she calls it, to anorexia nervosa. Some critical passages will delineate her position.

> My psychotherapeutic observations of patients whose capacity to recognize, and distinguish between, body stimuli had been impaired in various ways have convinced me that only a psychodynamic theory based on object relations (particularly on relations with the negative aspects of the introjected object) can be substantial contribution to the psychopathology of body experience (p. 84).

How did she come to this conviction?

> Because all authorities are agreed that the child's original experience with the primary object is a corporeal-incorporative experience, I was persuaded that the incorporation of the negative aspects of the primary object, with the ensuing repression and defense against the return of that object to consciousness, must provide the dynamic foundations of psychopathological body experience (p. 84).

When, however, Minuchin criticized Palazzoli for not sufficiently recognizing that the locus of the pathology was between people, they missed the point of her understanding and her work with anorexics. They did not see or comprehend the convergence of clinical description and psychoanalytic object relations theory. It is worth reproducing in full the very passage they quoted to suggest that anorexia nervosa, following Palazzoli, is contained inside the patient, when that very passage amply suggests otherwise.

> From the phenomenological point of view, the body is experienced as having all the features of the primary object as it was perceived in the situation or oral helplessness; "all powerful, indestructible, self-sufficient, growing, and threatening . . ." To the anorexic, being a body is tantamount to being a thing. If the body grows, the thing grows as well and the "person" starts to shrink (Minuchin et al. 1978, 81).

> The ego defense which is thus built up is characterized by the rejection of the body as such and of food as a bodily substance. The pathological control of the body is effected by an attitude that I would describe as enteroceptual mistrust . . . . It is as if the patient says to herself . . ."I must not pay any attention to [the body's] signals: hunger, fatigue, or sexual excitement . . . I must differentiate myself from it, pretend that hunger speaks only for itself and hence is not worthy of my attention. I am here and the hunger is there. So let me ignore it." In this way though the patient feels and recognizes the body as her own, she treats it as if it were not (Palazzoli 1982, 92).

Thus, Palazzoli does not see the disease as simply located inside the anorexic. Rather, there are interactions between the body and others, the body self and whom that body represents, "a persecutor on whom it is easy to spy and impose controls" (p. 93). Palazzoli goes on:

> This type of projection thus protects the patient from *interpersonal* delusions and, in a way, preserves her ability to socialize and to relate to the world . . . (p. 93).

and,

> just as soon as the anorexic system is organized, these patients shed the depression of the premorbid phase, and begin to relate and act *against the "object": they become subjects* (p. 94).

Thus,

> The three-fold meaning of the anorexic symptom may be schematized as follows (p. 94):

| — to retain | the good | |
| — to ward off | | object (body) |
| — to control | the bad | |

Here Palazzoli comes close to capturing the private world view of anorexics. However, psychoanalytic hermeneutics, with its sometimes premature closure and relative arbitrariness, could benefit from a phenomenological study which closes at the very end of the inquiry, and not one moment too soon.

The point of view that stays most faithful to the utterances of the patient, and yet is one of depth, is that of the French clinical researcher Thouzery (1984). Thouzery suggests that anorexics destroy their actual bodies, deny time, love, and death, inter alia. However, I am troubled when these horizonal interpretations of the anorexics' subjectivity are collapsed prematurely into one vain perennial search for an "ideal cadaverous body," as he puts it; their bodies belong to their mothers and not to the anorexics themselves. That is an example of the leaps clinicians are prone to take. Are we to understand by Thouzery's (1984) position that an anorexic never comes to own her body, even if at some stage it was felt to have been her mother's? Although I disagree with the prematurely collapsed conclusion, the separate, private experiences are very plausible and only need some elaboration before suggesting how they could have been brought together to retain a faithful representation of the world of the anorexic.

To return to the topic of intersubjectivity, Thouzery and I agree as to the value of capturing the subjective constitution of mother-daughter relationships. In Thouzery's study (1984) the elements of the intersubjective constitution that are relevant to mother-daughter relationships are the experience of the sense of time, the sense that a body can be immortalized in relation to another, the sense that time can be denied, that the experience of love can be obliterated and, finally, that impending death can be denied. To be able to deny time, love, and death is a tall order, but nothing will stop anorexics from pursuing the unattainable.

Thouzery's findings from his clinical inquiry have not been rigorously grounded. We must therefore still submit comparable data to a rigorous descriptive psychoanalytic study. We may find that there are additional elements that present themselves in the findings. Or we may find that there are leaps in his reductions, where some elements are too specialized. We must temporarily suspend our thoughts, enter into the anorexics' world, and see if we can grasp the full range of meanings and experiential structures behind their sensations, thoughts, feelings, and actions. In short, what drives anorexic practices? No one study can answer this question in full. Other families of discourse on intersubjectivity exist beyond Merleau-Ponty and the phenomenologists before him. Levinas, Kristeva, and Lacan are examples of modern thinkers on the subject of intersubjectivity, speculative and theory-laden as their work may be. Their language gives us a taste of how broad our horizons can become if we study the world of anorexics in terms of intersubjectivity. We know from Merleau-Ponty's *Phenomenology of Perception* (1962), and from that one particular context in which he compares the function of loss of speech to that of anorexia nervosa, that anorexia nervosa constitutes a rejection of other people. Taylor (1987) quoting Merleau-Ponty (Merleau-Ponty 1968, 102), writes:

> "It is necessary to comprehend perception as . . . interrogative thought that lets the perceived world be, rather than posits it, before which the things form and undo themselves in a sort of slipping and sliding [*glissement*], on this side of yes and no." Just as flesh is neither subject nor object, so carnal perception is neither subjective or objective. Since perception remains open to difference, it is unavoidably marginal, liminal, interstitial—*entre deux* (p. 76).

In Merleau-Ponty, perception is indeed *entre deux*. Levinas (1974/1981) would say "*Esse* is *interesse*; essence is interest." For him the speculative subject has to return to itself by discovering its own self in every "other." For Merleau-Ponty, there is a place for ambiguity, even opacity as part of the human condition. We shall not have absolute knowledge; despite our best efforts, there will always be gaps. Even the subject does not coincide with its own self. If it could be determined that the subject never coincides with its self, the surmise that *for the anorexic her dysfunction is a premature closure in an imaginary synthesis* would be an important finding. Or, we may learn from Kristeva's (1982) archeological inquiry, informed by Lacan, that some terrifying mother, some abject mother, as it were, is a prime driving force behind the dysfunction of the anorexic.

The new notions of "abject" and "abjection," coming from the tradition of French psychoanalysis, touch on intersubjectivity and mother-daughter relationships, and provide another look at how dysfunctional interactions, such as those in which anorexia nervosa is implicated, may be rethought. Most importantly, these notions include instinctual drives in discussions of intersubjectivity, but if they are in the data they will come out anyway. Thus, whenever we think of subjectivity, we are reminded that we relate at two levels: (1) a horizontal, interpersonal level, and (2) a deeper vertical level, where influences from the past inform or plague the present, or influence future actions.

> The abject might then appear as the most *fragile* . . . the most *archaic* sublimation of an "object" still inseparable from drives. The abject is that pseudo-object that is made up *before* but appears only *within* the gaps of secondary repression. The abject would *thus be the "object" of primal repression* (Kristeva 1982, 12; emphasis in original).

What is Kristeva's specific theoretical use of Freud's notion of primal repression? Kristeva writes:

> Let us call it the ability of the speaking being, always already haunted by the Other, to divide, reject, repeat. Within *one* division, *one* separation, *one* subject/object having been constituted (not yet, or no longer yet). Why? Perhaps because of maternal anguish, unable to be satiated within the encompassing symbolic.
>
> ...................................................................................................
>
> The abject confronts us with those fragile states where man strays on the territories of *animal*. Thus by way of abjection, primitive societies have marked out a precise area of their culture in order to remove it from the threatening world of animals or animalism, which were imagined as representatives of sex and murder (pp. 12–13; emphasis in original).

When we remove the traditional notions of subject and object, we come across the abject, that which confronts us with the seamy side of our human desires and deeds. We struggle to repress and transform this seaminess so that we can live with ourselves and continue to be able to give our animal past a decent burial. It is not easy, however, to bury our animal past, because it is part of us. It is like destroying the very foundations on which we build our individual selves. This is why Kristeva (1982) calls abjection "a kind of narcissistic crisis."

Abjection, however, persists even after mother and child have negotiated that first year of life, when the mother has lent the child her narcissism at the same time she has been trying to repair her own, bruised by the birth process.

Abjection enters into such subsequent developmental processes and organizational series as separation and individuation. In this context, there is a very powerful passage in Kristeva's (1980/1982) essay on abjection that deserves to be quoted in full:

> The abject confronts us ... within our personal archeology with our earliest attempts to release the hold of *maternal* entity even before existing outside of her, thanks to the autonomy of language. It is a violent, clumsy breaking away, with a constant risk of falling back under the sway of a power as securing as it is stifling. The difficulty a mother has in acknowledging (or being acknowledged by) the symbolic realm—in other words, the problem she has with the phallus that her father or her husband stands for—is not such as to help the future subject leave the natural mansion. The child can serve its mother as token of her own authentication; there is, however, hardly any reason for her to serve as a go-between for it to become autonomous and authentic in turn. In such close combat the symbolic light that a third party, eventually the father, can contribute helps the future subject, the more so if it happens to be endowed with a robust supply of drive energy, in pursuing a reluctant struggle against what, having been the mother, will turn into an abject. Repelling, rejecting; repelling itself, rejecting itself. Abjecting (p. 13; emphasis in original).

This is the kind of struggle that fashions us as human beings, says Kristeva; a mimesis whereby a child becomes separate in its own right as a person. This view of the struggle coincides with my own view that one sheds blood, symbolically or otherwise, at the site of separation. But Kristeva has more to say on this:

> Even before being *like*, "I" am not but do *separate*, reject, ab-ject. Abjection, with a meaning broadened to take in subjective diachrony, is a *precondition of narcissism*. It is co-existent with it and causes it to be permanently brittle. The more or less beautiful image in which I behold or recognize myself rests upon an abjection that sunders it as soon as repression, the constant watchman, is relaxed (p. 13, emphasis in original).

For us to maintain our stable sense of being, we hear from Kristeva, the abject mother must be authenticated. We also hear from Green (1969/1979) that we must recreate ourselves to experience our very being:

> Being is that which requires creation of us so that we may experience it. But this creation, Melanie Klein says, is so urgent only the most

loving of mothers cannot satisfy the powerful emotional needs of the child. Thus *a symbol is a piece of flesh over its gap* (p. 87; emphasis added).

The convergence of the abject mother's need for authentication and of the child's need to summon its mother to meet its bodily and emotional requirements is quite unstable, thanks to the peremptory and instinctual urges from our animal past, and their newer ostensibly instinct-free editions.

Returning to anorexia nervosa for a moment, we find that the piece of flesh over the gap between maternal needs and infantile needs can be represented by the most curious means. The act of stealing in anorexia nervosa may thus be one symbolic expression of a child's need from its mother who is, herself, seeking authentication from her (m)other. Abstaining from eating may be one way of shrinking or killing the mental representation of the (m)other. Shifting from anorexia nervosa to bulimia may be a symbolic expression of keeping the (m)other, but poisoning her. Food or weight phobia may be an abortive metaphor of yearning for the (m)other and/or repulsion by the (m)other. Food may be a polluting object, Kristeva (1982) tells us. And,

> when food appears as a polluting object, it does so as oral object only to the extent that orality signifies a boundary of the self's clean and proper body. Food becomes abject only if it is a border between two distinct entities or territories. A boundary between nature and culture, between the human being and the non-human being (p. 75).

Food for anorexics is therefore a border guard, negotiating boundaries between self and (m)other, limiting or reluctantly allowing incursions by (m)other, constantly having conversations, as it were, between self, (m)other, the "I" within the (m)other, and whomever constitutes the mother.

It is most curious that, however useful Kristeva's notions of "abject" and "abjection" are to our understanding of anorexia nervosa, none of her publications to date (1980, 1982, 1984, 1987) includes a reference to anorexia nervosa or any other eating disorder. Nevertheless, Kristeva has broadened our horizons immensely by rejecting traditional notions of subject and object, and substituting for them the abject.

I have discussed Kristeva and her theoretical approach extensively partially because she covers both intersubjectivity and mother-daughter relationships, and for two other reasons. One is that Kristeva provides the depth and breadth that I believe should inform any discussion of human issues, so that we do not come away with idealizations of persons and human nature. Another reason is that no existing child development model includes adequate descriptions of intersubjectivity. Freud's child development model essentially deals with the body, its ownership, and its new representations as they converge to provide the developing individual with the means to arrive at final sexual organization at the end of adolescence. Piaget's child will negotiate cognitive development from the most concrete to the most appropriate level of abstraction, but like Freud's child it has no mother, so to speak. Bowlby's child has a mother, but its mother is a monkey. Mahler's child begins life out of some shell called the autistic phase, and thereafter begins the struggle to acquire self and object constancy. In my disappointment I embarked on a clinical infant development intervention study (Apprey 1987), sponsored by the National Institure of Mental Health, where I observed mothers from the third trimester of pregnancy to the third and fourth years of their children's lives. In that study I looked at the role of projective identification and maternal misperception in disturbed mothers. Following Klein (1946), I defined projective identification

> as an unconscious defensive process which exteriorizes an incompat-
> ible aspect of one's self organization into a representation of an object
> in ways which permit an unburdening of an unacceptable attribute or
> a preservation of an aspect of one's self away from hostile primary
> process presences. In the process of actualizing the delegated self
> organization one maintains a phantasied picture of control and oneness
> with the object. The result is that there is a change in the subject's
> own self representation as well as change in the perception of the object
> (Apprey 1987, 5).

I discussed in some detail how destructive projective identification is used to deal with excessive persecutory anxiety, envy, or intolerance of separation by disturbed or vulnerable mothers; and how, as a result, it militates against the child's progress towards autonomy. In contrast, I noted how relatively normal mothers use reaction formation and other ways of turning instinctual wishes around to bind anxiety and reverse negative attitudes about their children. Coming out of that same study were four way stations in the utilization of projective identification: (1) *the gathering of projective identification*, where prenatal interviews revealed the spoken and unspoken motivations about what kind of children the mothers wanted and what function those children would serve for them; (2) *the emergence of components of projective identification*, in the neonatal period, when projective identification began to separate out into projection, displacement, identification, and various forms of delegation of wanted and unwanted aspects of the self; (3) *the return/retrieval/reowning of projective identification* after about a year, when mothers began to retrieve delegations that had hitherto been exteriorized and located in their children; and (4) *the emergence of empathic projective identification*, after three to four years when we could see a transformation of intrusive, massive, or destructive projective identification into empathic, benign, or positive projective identification, so that mothers could lend unambivalent strength to their children in the service of autonomy and emancipation. My 1987 study serves as an additional backdrop for our present study on the intersubjective constitution of anorexia nervosa.

## REPRESENTATIVE RESEARCH AND CLINICAL FINDINGS ON ANOREXIA NERVOSA

From Scandinavia Brinch, Isager, and Tolstrup (1988) have reported on a detailed study of fifty mothers who had been diagnosed as anorexic. They found that these fifty women, who produced eighty-six children, had better overall functioning after a twelve-year follow-up than the ninety former anorexics who remained childless. The rates of prematurity and of perinatal death were significantly higher in anorexics than in the background population.

From England Hall, Liebrich, Walkey, and Welch (1986) disputed Crisp and Kalucy's (1974) findings that there was a family history of aberrant weight which was implicated in the causation of anorexia nervosa; Hall and his collaborators found no significant differences in aberrant weight histories between anorexics and the background population. Crisp and his students, of which Kalucy was one, have reported widely on anorexia as primarily a weight phobia (see Crisp, 1977, 1981, Crisp and Kalucy, 1974). Crisp and Kalucy (1974) related the aberrant weight histories to perceptual distortion. Crisp (1977) also related weight to aspects of adolescent growth and to biopsychosocial issues associated with the "fat/thin" syndrome. His work, by himself or with students or collaborators, has broadened immensely to include a myriad of issues, ranging from sleep disorders in anorexics to the psychosocial consequences of ileojejunal bypass surgery (Crisp, Kalucy, Pilkington, and Gazet 1977). Indeed, Crisp first became interested in eating disorders while conducting research into sleep disorders (see Crisp 1980, 19). References to this historical note are many but oblique; it is one of Crisp's favorite topics of discussion in lectures and personal communications. But, however important the biological basis of his work, Crisp relies on a comprehensive team of family therapists, psychoanalysts, art therapists, nurses, social workers, and nutritionists, to mention only a few, to carry out the treatment of his anorexic patients.

Halmi (1974) comprehensively studied ninety-four medical charts from a general hospital and a psychiatric hospital, including the pediatric age group, covering the period from 1920 to 1972. She found that parental and maternal age at the time of the birth was significantly greater for anorexics than for the general population. In addition, there were relatively high premorbid feeling problems and obsessive-compulsive traits in anorexics. She recognized family conflicts as one of the major factors leading to anorexia nervosa.

There are many findings relevant to the literature on anorexia nervosa from the psychoanalytic and psychodynamic frames of reference. Beattie (1988) spoke to the very nature of early female psychosexual development and to the problematic nature of girls having more difficulty separating from their mothers than boys. She suggested that hostile-dependent conflicts and ambivalent struggles for emancipation from the mother find a ready channel in eating disorders.

Thouzery (1984), cited above, suggested that anorexics strive to destroy the body in order to immortalize it by denying time, love, and death. Von-Wallenberg (1982) compared schizophrenia and anorexia nervosa, and saw defects in anorexia nervosa relating to ego organization and to separation from mother that were similar to weakness in "ego-feelings" and self-identity in schizophrenia.

Chediak (1977) attributed the cause of anorexia nervosa in his nineteen-year-old patient to a narcissistic overvaluation of the body and to a conflictual rapprochement crisis in the process of separation-individuation. The anorexic perceived the mother controlling the child's body and treating the child as a narcissistic extension of the mother's maternal self. Chediak (1977) cautioned that a successful treatment must acknowledge and move beyond the anorexic's belief that her mother owns her anorexic body, and that their two body selves are coextensive.

Ceasar (1977) spoke to the role of maternal identification in four anorexia nervosa cases that he treated. He found that there was a perceived loss in the anorexic of the maternal object; a loss which was repaired by a faulty identification with mother.

Working within a Kohutian psychoanalytic frame of reference, Geist (1989) has sought to understand anorexia and other forms of eating disorders as a form of self-pathology caused by a traumatic and chronic disturbance in maternal empathy for the child. Geist suggests we approach the study of anorexia nervosa in this way:

> Understanding food as archaic self-object further clarifies why it is used as a self-regulating function, as defensive stimulation, and as protection against emptiness, why narcissistic rage is so intimately connected with the use of food, and ultimately, how food as archaic self-object becomes reinvested with so much "primary childhood intensity" (Kohut 1984), that giving up the symptom is a life or death issue. Consequently, the symptomatologies of anorexia and bulimia represent neither unconscious compromises, symbolically acted out control battles with parents, nor internalized societal preoccupation with thinness; rather, they actualize life and death struggles to maintain the integrity of the self and prevent disintegration anxiety (p. 25).

Gordon, Beresin, and Herzog (1989) examined how the parents' relationship with each other, in particular in its role as model of a mature male/female relationship, affects preanorexic children. For these authors, the patterns of mother's perfectionism and self-sacrifice combine with the parents' sense of entitlement to make the prospect of sexual maturity a threat for girls in these families. These factors may also explain the greater incidence of anorexia nervosa in women as well as its "explosive incidence" in adolescence.

Chatoor (1989) reemphasized the early developmental stage of separation-individuation between six and thirty-six months. She described infantile anorexia nervosa as food refusal and failure to thrive. Refusal to eat subserves the fantasy of having control in regard to mother. But it fails because it only involves the mother more deeply, leading to mother-child battles over food, attention, and control. The result is that infant's feeding is now directed by emotional needs and fears rather than by physiological sensations of hunger and satiation. Such a child, according to Greenspan and Lourie (1981), will fail to develop somatopsychological differentiation. These authors implicate biological constitution, temperament, and maternal conflicts in the causation of infantile anorexia nervosa. They suggest that treatment focus on promoting the development of somatopsychological differentiation with a behavioral cognitive approach and/or psychotherapy for the mother to solve problems of dependence and control that are intrinsically hers.

Ross (1977) presents an overview of the clinical and research literature and concludes that conceptual approaches that focus on self-concept and self-coherence, mother-child relationships, interpersonal relationships, and psychosexual development are all important. Equally, behavior therapy, family therapy, and medical treatment all have a place in the treatment of anorexia nervosa.

## MAJOR THEMES IN THE LITERATURE ON ANOREXIA NERVOSA

The thematic issues of the past twenty years remain fairly polarized into those that are biologically informed and those that are psychodynamically informed. But there is a slowly increasing number of publications that explores the terrain between the biological and the psychodynamic. Those in the liminal sphere between the two tend to deal with family systems, strategic, and didactic methods of observing and/or treating anorexia nervosa.

The psychoanalytic literature, such as Bruch 1974, Thomä 1967, Sours 1980, and Sprince 1984, points to anorexia nervosa as a basic disturbance wherein there is an unconscious attempt to unite with the "feeding" mother, while simultaneously struggling to prevent that same union lest the self become fused and dissolved. These analysts and their many contemporaries have continued to treat this illness as a specific means of coping with developmental disharmony. Primarily a disease of adolescent women, this life-threatening illness, causes its victim to shun the sexual development of her body, rejecting the body wholesale, and makes her unable to overcome oedipal and preoedipal developmental task which reemerge in adolescence. Psychoanalysts see this illness as a specific psychic organization which is not hysteria, nor some imaginary disease, nor an endocrine disease. They see it as an adaptation that provides equilibrium for the psychological system to function.

Rizutto's (1988) work on transference, language, and affect, and Ogden's (1988) on misrecognitions and the fear of not knowing, point to why we need to take a step back from psychoanalytic leaps of interpretation. Rizutto suggests that anorexics defend against the transference, and that for them this very process of defense is in itself the transference. Why? In her view these anorexics believe that the analyst has no intention of listening to them. She suggests, further, that they do not believe that words serve the function of communicating. Instead, anorexics use words to attack their analysts or to detract from self-disclosure. Given this aversion towards words, they treat the analysts' words with sarcasm and incredulity while at the same time fearing that the analysts' words have the power of invasion into them. According to Rizutto, while the language of anorexics develops normally at the level of linguistic competence, that language is dysfunctional when it comes to making connections with affective components of their sense of self. As a result, the language that fails to connect with affect interferes with their verbalization of subjective experiences.

Ogden (1988), writing on how the anorexic identifies with both the representation of the mother and of the self as child, points out that this double representation makes it almost impossible to observe both the internal and the external worlds correctly. As a result, anorexics erect pathological substitute formations that create the illusion that they know what they feel.

If the anorexic is unable to observe her subjective experiences correctly or to verbalize them without important affects, do we need further interpretations of those same affects or lived experiences that are being misread and misspoken by the anorexics? Or do we need to take a step back to examine and to hear from the anorexics themselves what it means in their world for affects and language to be erroneously and verbalized? I submit that this propensity to misread or misspeak is precisely the reason why a study that faithfully captures meaning and experience from the horizon of the anorexic must be phenomenological. In a phenomenological study we are much less likely to arbitrarily misread or misunderstand private subjective experience. "I do not want to be seen when I am eating; it is like being found out" is an example of the private subjective experience mentioned above. Another is "I have created for myself a discipline neurosis" or "I feel like a self-hung millstone." It is very tempting to apply a variety of reductive interpretations to these utterances all too quickly.

So, considering the relative arbitrariness of the interpretative leaps in the psychoanalytic literature, I am not satisfied in my search for answers to the meaning of words spoken by the anorexic. Between the phenomenon and the concept formation there lies a relevant step contingent upon the *structure of experience of the particular patient*.

Answers from biological psychiatry to this question, concerning the personal meaning of the illness for the individual, are equally incomplete. The several papers that Crisp and his collaborators (Crisp 1981; Crisp, Hsu, Harding, and Hartshorn 1980) have accumulated on this subject point variously to weight phobia, sleep disturbance, perceptual distortion, familial dysfunction, and other biological issues as functional in the pathological formation of this illness. Brinch, Isager, and Tolstrup (1988) were interested in the reproductive lives of former anorexics. They found that there was just as much involuntary childlessness in successfully treated anorexics as there was in nonanorexic women. But the rate of prematurity and perinatal lethality was much higher in anorexics. As noted above, Hall, Liebrich, Walkey, and Welch (1986) investigated the hypothesis that weight pathology is common in families with anorexia nervosa. They disagreed with Kalucy, finding no support for his hypothesis that weight pathology, seen in terms of deviations in weight, shape, size, eating behavior, and physical activity was familial. Debates over anorexia as weight phobia, food phobia, school phobia, and so on add little to our search for understanding of the private subjective world of the anorexic. Crisp (1980) showed that he was taking a step towards intersubjectivity when he published fifteen anonymous accounts of anorexia nervosa by anorexics and four accounts by parents. But these anonymous accounts were not subjected to analysis; the verbatim texts were left without a systematic correlation to the structure of experience.

When we enter the liminal sphere between the biological and the psychodynamic, we do not fare any better in getting close to the anorexic's structure of experience. What we get is a series of atheoretical, strategic, or didactic methods which bypass private human experience. Jones (1985) instructed anorexics in "conscious connected breathing" and "rebirthing" and in the use of positive affirmations, and reported improvement in the subjects' nutrition and body awareness. Pirrotta (1984) compared two different schools of thought in family therapy in Milan. He compared one school of thought that was more strategic in its approach to developing ways to "counteract the rigid interactional games of the pathological family" to "a family training teaching approach" that was more interested in how elements of a systemic epistemology were transmitted to the family during family therapy.

So, after a search for prior work done on the intersubjective constitution of anorexia nervosa, in the context of the mother-daughter relationship, we have come full circle with little to draw on.

## JUSTIFICATION FOR LIMITING STUDY TO MOTHER–ANOREXIC DAUGHTER RELATIONS: A PSYCHOANALYTIC PERSPECTIVE

Why must the question of the intersubjective constitution of anorexia nervosa be asked primarily in the context of mother–anorexic daughter relations? First of all, anorexics are almost entirely female. Second, the earliest and most important parent-child relationship is held by traditional psychoanalytic theory and contemporary infant research (Brazelton and Als 1979; Brazelton 1980; Klaus et al. 1972; Lichtenberg 1983) to be a mother's relationship with her infant. In that early experience the infant utilizes its mother as though she were an auxiliary ego whose ministrations in regulating the child's needs would assist it to develop a functioning ego. A great deal of this activity between mother and child occurs in the context of mirroring, attachment-disengagement, departure-return, assisting the child to enjoy a sense of reverie as well as to tolerate moderate amounts of frustration, assisting it to tolerate ambivalence, and among other functions, "owning" the child's body until the child is ready to own it herself.

At puberty these experiences are rekindled so that the girl child has to incorporate into her self-representation a view of herself as one who has been cared for by, and can be separate from mother as well as a view of herself as becoming sexually mature. The result is that mother's hands which administered care and fostered ownership of the body must be transferred into a self-representation that permits the child to feel that she can independently hold, nurture, and own her body self. Laufer (1981) suggests that it is this transfer of mother's hands and care into caring for one's own self that makes some disturbed adolescent girls choose the wrist or arm as the area for self-injury. In Laufer's view cutting one's wrist or arm is an effort to control the hand by symbolically cutting it off.

Anna Freud (1936) suggested that asceticism is a mental mechanism used by the adolescent girl to deal with the strength of her impulses. In this view anorexia nervosa can be seen as a young girl's way of saying, "When my body tempts me I must starve it of feeling; and to starve it of feeling, I must starve it of food." Add the idea of asceticism to the problem of ownership of one's body and you have an anorexic girl struggling to define herself, become independent and in control of her body self, and seeking in various concrete or symbolic ways paradigms of self-coherence and actualization.

Asceticism and the problem of body ownership as well as their problematic developmental antecedents are thus some of the features that point to the mother-daughter relationship as the compelling relationship that is sufficiently circumscribed for studying intersubjectivity in mother-anorexic daughter relationships.

To study mother-anorexic daughter intersubjectivity does not mean that there are no similarities with mother-anorexic son relationships. At this stage of our knowledge it would seem that we must start by researching circumscribed subject areas that affect most anorexics and revisit inchoate developmental processes in contemporary pathological formations, such as anorexia nervosa, at the same time.

## FROM PHILOSOPHY TO RESEARCH METHODOLOGY

In his preface to *Phenomenology of Perception* (1962) Merleau-Ponty explained that

> phenomenology is the study of essences; and according to it, all problems amount to finding definitions of essences: the essence of perception, or the essence of consciousness, for example. But phenomenology is also a philosophy which puts essences back into existence, and does not expect to arrive at an understanding of man and the world from any starting point other than that of their "facticity" (p. vii).

What exactly are these "essences"? Are we back to Aristotelian essences or their revision in twelfth-century medieval Renaissance scholarship? The Latin medieval scholar Hermann of Carinthia (Burnett 1982) tells us that there are five essences: cause, motion, time, place, and condition, and indeed if we tried hard enough we would be able to fit our observation of phenomena into this framework. But then how faithful would we be to the phenomena under observation?

Without doubt our observations would be severely restricted and contaminated by these categories. Therefore, we shall utilize a praxis (Giorgi 1985) that is informed by Husserl and Merleau-Ponty—one which, most importantly, rejects premature reductions. This praxis will close only at the very end of our data-based study with discoveries that point to psychological essences which are not predetermined, and will therefore concentrate on revealing the essence of the subjective experience of the anorexic and her mother.

If we were more keenly attuned to the world and had no preconceptions about observed phenomena, but were able to describe what we found with great precision, we would capture the structure of experience of anorexics. What would be the structure of experience of our three pairs of mother–anorexic daughters? And what would be the interrelations among the separate structures? Which interrelations fit into the joint structures of experience? Which do not fit?

As a philosophy, phenomenology holds that knowledge comes from but is not necessarily caused by experience, so that individual consciousness is a part of knowledge, and knowledge presents itself to individual consciousness. Accordingly, phenomenology takes into account the individual's perspective toward an object in the real world, but only under the aegis of an example; and thus other variations, even if lacks are taken into account. Phenomenologically speaking, consciousness is directed toward an object that one desires, perceives, thinks about, and plans to do something with or about. An object of consciousness may be immanent or transcendent; in the latter case it presents itself as not belonging to the same consciousness as the act; in the former, the object belongs to the same stream of consciousness as the act. The object of consciousness seems different to different observers because each observer has had a different experience with it, although the object remains the same in physical structure or identity. The immanent object belongs to me but is other than me.

Methodical, critical, and systematic knowledge can be derived from phenomenology; methodical because we are on our way to making a discovery about something by thinking methodically about it; critical because we are testing our conclusions about the object; and systematic because our new learning about the object takes its place in an organized system of knowledge, and we are interested in finding the slot into which it fits.

The view of the phenomenological method put forth by Merleau-

Ponty (1973) is that we must marshal factual information about the object, reduce it, and describe it so as to give it meaning.

> We will have to vary the phenomenon in order to disclose a common signification for these variations. And the criterion for this method will not be a multiplicity of facts which will serve as proofs for predefined hypotheses. The proof will be in our fidelity to the phenomena, that is in the precise hold which we will have of the materials used and, to some extent, in our "proximity" to pure description (p. 8).

Graumann (1988) stresses intentional interaction between person and environment, and situational analysis of this interaction, suggesting that a complete description of anything under study must start with the observer's experience of its *material nature*. This must be correlated with the *materiality* or *spatiality* of the intentional environment. Then comes the *historicity* or *temporality* of experience—the story of the object that gives it a place in world experience or history. Then, because we are social beings, we must communicate in words to make our findings intelligible to others.

Giorgi (1985) would find Graumann's steps toward situational analysis restrictive, holding the formal categories of materiality (bodily nature), spatiality, historicity, and sociality a hindrance to naive description. These elements would not be a priori to the description, nor would they be isolated thematic analyses, but would probably emerge from a thorough contextual analysis. The attempt in this work to observe and describe the experience of the individual's situation with as much latitude as possible is influenced by Giorgi's view.

## GIORGI'S PRAXIS AS THE PREFERRED METHOD FOR DATA COLLECTION

Justification for using a phenomenological praxis, and Giorgi's (1985) four-step praxis in particular, to eliminate as much as possible any temptation toward premature analytic or explanatory interpretation. The four steps are (1) collect naive, concrete descriptions about anorexia nervosa from mother-daughter pairs who do not themselves evaluate their data and accordingly cannot contaminate their views about the condition; (2) break down each naive description into units of meaning, thus separating one trend of thought from another; (3) transform these discriminated meaning units into language with greater psychological meaning; and (4) determine from this language the structure of experience of the individual anorexico. The phenomenological praxis should then provide uncontaminated information about the experience of anorexia.

## SELECTION OF SUBJECTS AND SAMPLE SIZE

The research subject group consisted of three mother-daughter pairs. The daughters were between the ages of eighteen and thirty-five. They had been diagnosed and *treated* for anorexia nervosa. They could only participate *after treatment* and had then to be well-functioning members of the general public. They had to be adult students or employees for whom this study posed little or no risk. Their parents had to respond to the request independently of their daughters.

## DATA COLLECTION PROCEDURES

Treated anorexics were contacted through clinicians who had in the past treated eating disorders in hospital-based programs and who had followed up on these patients while they were in outpatient psychotherapy. Reaching subjects in this way reflected my belief that clinicians are more likely to know the severity of anorexia nervosa as an illness, and that such informed clinicians are able to sensitively introduce subjects to this study. After willing subjects contacted me, I set up appointments with them to provide more details about the study and to get their informed consent. Each daughter was then interviewed separately, and on a different day from her mother. The idea was to provide confidentiality and reduce possibilities for conflict and contamination by unresolved external issues between them. At the interview, the central question to the anorexic was

> What kind of person is your mother, and how does she fit into your world? or What is a concrete situation that typifies your mother?

The question beginning the interview with the mother was

> What kind of person is your daughter, and how does she fit into your world? or, What is a concrete situation that typifies your daughter?

*The anorexic quality of the mother-daughter relationship was allowed to emerge naturally so that it could be treated as an integral part of their shared subjectivity.* Any subsequent questions or comments were an elaboration of one of the above questions about the subject's personal horizon and how that horizon interacted with the other's horizon. As anticipated, one, two, or at the very most, three one-hour interviews sufficed. The most important issue here was that each interview end when there was closure, determined by the subject's grasp of the intersubjective issues inherent in the relationship between mother and daughter, and of the part anorexia nervosa had played in the self-(m)other negotiation.

## DATA ANALYSIS PROCEDURE

As stated above, the praxis from phenomenological psychology as outlined by Giorgi (1985) was utilized to collect the data. There was no major methodological deviation beyond this praxis. I stayed with this because the closure was not made until the last possible moment in the analysis. I then elaborated the findings with descriptive psychoanalytic thinking.

## CLINICAL DATA ON THE SUBJECTS INTERVIEWED

The three subject pairs interviewed were identified as 002A, 002B; 003A, 003B; and 005A, 005B. Anorexic daughters were given the A designation; their mothers, the B designation. 001A and 004A came to be interviewed but did not want their mothers included in the study and for that reason their data may be used for a future study with their consent. 001A had recently received a letter from her mother explaining why she thought they had a difficult relationship, and in it her mother had explained her infanticidal wishes toward her from early childhood. The recovered anorexic felt an interview might further stimulate her and so did not wish to participate. I accepted her reasoning, not wishing to include any subjects who equivocated about their decision. 004B had recently lost a close friend to cancer and was going through a grieving period which made it necessary for her to go back into treatment. She will be available for future study after her treatment.

Subjects 002A, 002B, 003A, 003B, 005A, and 005B were very willing to participate. I will describe the anorexics in terms of their suitability for this study.

002A, aged 22, was referred to this study by a clinical psychologist in a neighboring city. He had treated this subject for bulimia in psychotherapy intermittently since her hospitalization for anorexia nervosa which occurred at age 14 and developed into a psychosis at that time. This subject is now a college student studying to become a clinical social worker. It will be of interest to learn what will present itself in this study when the subject has switched from anorexia nervosa into psychosis in her middle adolescence, and then into bulimia in late adolescence and young adulthood. She stays in touch with her referring clinical psychologist and is considering taking some time out of her education to receive treatment for bulimia. This subject was curious about the study because she wanted to see how a former student of Anna Freud worked. Her mother hoped the interview would have a curative effect on her daughter.

003A was 18 when she had anorexia nervosa. She is 32 years old now and has a very young infant child. She was referred to me by a colleague who had worked with her. 003A was a nurse and my colleague, who is a child psychiatrist, described her as a very good nurse who always looked harassed but who did her work competently and reliably. Her mother was not only very pleased to participate, she also requested that I talk with a mother whose daughter had died from anorexia nervosa. This same mother has a niece who has anorexia nervosa but is not doing well with or without treatment. I agreed to speak to this mother's niece, but she changed her mind. She no longer wished for me to interview her niece, whose daughter died, because she was uncertain as to who she was doing this for.

005A, aged 23, was referred by a local child psychiatrist who had treated this former anorexic when she was 18. She is not in psychotherapy but has had a brief period of family therapy intervention at her mother's request. 005A is self-supporting and lives independently away from her mother and father. Although she had stayed in touch with her child psychiatrist, she has not had a relapse into anorexia nervosa or bulimia. Her mother, 005B, is a psychologist who came because she was curious and interested in the idea of anyone studying perceptions between anorexics and their mothers.

## RESULTS

As stated above, the praxis from phenomenological psychology by

Giorgi (1985) provided the steps we used to arrive at the results. These results will be presented below in the form of structures of experience: (a) the structure of experience at the level of individual typicalities; (b) the structure of experience at the level of intersubjective typicalities; and (c) the general psychological structure of experience, that is, the collapsing of individual subjective, and mother-daughter structures of experience into coherent constellations of discovery about the constitution of mother-daughter relationships in anorexia nervosa. Before considering this final outcome, let us briefly recap the operational format of this study's findings as it pertains to the central question asked and the type of description:

> **Step 1: COLLECT INDIVIDUAL CASE SYNOPSES,** where the interviewer asks the question: "Who is your *mother* and how does she fit into your world?" or, "Who is your *daughter* and how does she fit into your world?"

Here we were interested in hearing the perceptions of one or the other as to how each horizon accommodates the other. Specifically, what reveals and what is essential to each persons' accommodations of the other? Under this rubric each person's own words were audiotaped and transcribed.

> **STEP 2: BREAKDOWN SEQUENCES OF EVENTS INTO MEANING UNITS,** where we are interested in shifts in content, shifts in sequences of ideas or experiences.

Breaking the transcriptions down into smaller units helped us determine fragments of the whole, which were subsequently transformed into psychologically meaningful experiences, both in the individual and, finally, in the intersubjective context.

> **STEP 3: TRANSFORM MEANING UNITS INTO PERSONAL PSYCHOLOGICAL MEANING** in ways that reveal the existential or behavioral meaning for each subject in the mother-daughter pair.

Here we determined what was essential to personal meanings as a prelude to the determination of psychological structures in the next step.

> **STEP 4: DETERMINE INDIVIDUAL STRUCTURES OF EXPERIENCE,** where each subject's individual experience gives us insights into the psychological organization implicit in the mother–anorexic daughter relationship.

Here we learned how the separate psychological organizations impinge on, intersect, or dovetail into each other; and how this shared subjectivity reveals stable meanings about the ruptures or zones of weakness in a mother-daughter relationship struggling to come to terms with the consequences of anorexia nervosa. From the structures of experience we arrived at in this phenomenological study, a new description will emerge that will assist in the conceptualization of intersubjectivity with an anorexic and in theory making about anorexia.

Below are the structures that represent the results of the study:

## Structures of Experience as Results

### *Daughter's Structure:* 002A

Subject 002A perceives that one's world can be a three-way, three-generational enmeshment where a daughter loses herself in her mother, and her mother in her mother. For 002A, this enmeshment can result in regression whose outcome removes protective boundaries. Thus, when boundaries are precarious, taboos can be broken. Incest, rape, and other traumatic incursions can be experienced as real or vicarious, but the victim may assign herself or be assigned the role of protector of family sexual secrets, which she must guard at any cost. For 002A, the cost of this mission is high. Anorexia nervosa may be used to protest the territorial indiscretions, whereas bulimia may be used to conceal the complicity. Anorexia made her the enemy in her family, but now as bulimic, she may magically evade the possibility of being the perceived family foe.

### *Mother's structure* 002B

Subject 002B perceives that one can be a conduit between one's mother and one's daughter. Thus, 002B comes to perceive that one can also be a conduit between one's father and one's daughter. But different projects can be passed on. In one instance, grandmother's hated incompatible self can be injected into the grandchild with mother's complicity. On the other hand, a mother's cherished but lost relationship with her own father can be reproduced in her new relationship with her daughter. Who can better function as claustrum for a mother negotiating hated and loved internalized parental imagos than an anorexic daughter who can cleanse and fill her body self concurrently and alternately? For 002B, the body is, therefore, a place that can house welcome and unwelcome hosts, demons, and benign ghostly ancestors alike.

## *Interrelation of the two structures between mother and daughter*

Mother is in search for a receptacle for imagos of her parents, with their good and bad selves. These presentations are cloistered in that burdened anorexic/bulimic child. In response to this demand for a composite figure, the child ambivalently receives this project of her mother's and reconceives her own, which is to live as if she were no enemy to her family. In this conversation, there is a series of miscues, misconceptions, miscarriages. All participants are caught in a web of cross-purposes. One result is that they are ridden and immobilized by a nameless dread, a faceless enemy, an abject horror.

### *Daughter's structure:* 003A

For 003A, when one is perceived as a claustrum for forced identifications, one is embattled in one's effort toward emancipation. In this respect, the body self, as a place for harboring mother's feminine protest and father's perceived excessive control and compulsiveness, can create a composite compromise formation in the mode of anorexia nervosa; a strategy that protects one's self from perceived catastrophes and yet shackles one to pathological family ties. Here, in the body as battleground for negotiating self and (m)others, individuality is foreclosed or compromised; separation is tabooed.

### *Mother's structure:* 003B

For 003B, when a young woman is on target with her biological development, she can withstand the problems of anorexia nervosa. When her father is perceived as one who hates women, she assumes that her needs will not be recognized. Between his perceived hatred of women and depression, and her adolescent turmoil, lies a fertile ground for anorexia nervosa. Therefore, a mother need not be entirely the cause of her daughter's illness.

## *Interrelation of the two structures between mother and daughter*

When men hate women, women's needs cannot be met. A woman may therefore hate her femininity in revolt. She may ask her daughter to continue or rework the protest, and she fiercely finds new ways to disidentify with her mother's cause by becoming more sexual in her instinctual activities but more organized cognitively, until she finds that her perfectionism identifies her too closely with her father, whose rigid perfectionistic demands are perceived as aggressive and destructive. Hence, anorexia nervosa as a regressive solution that gives her "time out" from conflictual and otherwise progressive developmental moves.

| *Daughter's structure:* 005A | *Mother's structure:* 005B |
|---|---|

Subject 005A perceives that when a person's sense of self is part of transgenerational familial warfare, a person's emancipation can be impeded in costly ways. Such a person may not have an identity of her own. If she does, it may be a tenuous one between herself and her mother. Or it may be a self into which has been injected mother's and/or grandmother's dissonant self fragments. Such intrusive identifications prevent the development of multiple selves that are free of rigid structures. The body self in such a situation is but a claustrum that hosts representations of self and others to foster a sense of self-coherence. A person who owns such a body/claustrum may have a horizon whose vocabulary is restricted in ways that reflect a rigid and isolated psychical structuration.

For 005B, three generations can affect each other by how each prior generation injects a particular mission and how each succeeding generation accepts, denies, rejects, or reconciles with that mission. As this perceived injection occurs and unfolds, a mother caught between two generations, a prior and a succeeding one, can find herself caught in the prison house of failed emancipation, yet entertain the illusion that her daughter can be an object of transformation for both herself and her offspring. But the illusion of transformation is so complete that what one is or was intended to be, what one is named or was intended to be named, is anything but nominal. Under unfavorable conditions, what one is, is what one wills into existence. Under favorable conditions, one may lend one's positive narcissism to an offspring without destroying the vicissitudes of self-continuity and self-coherence in the child, so that she may be free to flexibly transact with her name in any way she wills to be the case.

## Interrelation of the two structures between mother and daughter

A primal matristic figure, represented by a grandmother, can seal the fate of succeeding generations of women, so that each one is simultaneously the object of prior coercion and a subject that coerces the next generation. The result is a life lived without boundaries, or without separate identities, or without any coherent self-definition. The destructive aggression in this transgenerational coercion is what makes the incarcerated participants of this living drama live and perpetuate isolated and self-confining lives.

Taking all our data into account, we provisionally suggest the following three way stations as one approach to collapsing the structures and interrelations between the three subject pairs. These structures and their interrelations will receive considerable elaboration in the next chapter.

1. There is a poverty of imagination in mother–anorexic daughter relations, where the body is essentially a psyche-soma barely able to conceive of errors in perception, as when a child interprets at the level of a personal meaning that anorexia expelled family secrets, whereas bulimia incorporated and concealed family secrets. On the part of the mother, the body person of the daughter can also be cathected as the host of positive and negative self and other presentations, such as new editions of her own mother and father within the composite figure of her daughter.

2. There is transformation of experience into thought, decision, knowledge, but at the cost of rigid psychical structuration, as when the daughter seeks multiple new selves but finds one that is made of stone which she cannot crack. On the side of the mother, there is a symbolic infusion of familial agenda; an aggressive infusion which meets with an equally rigid determination of the daughter to use aggression to tear away.

3. There is transformation of experience into thought, knowledge, and symbolic thinking with a flexibility that allows a new self organization or self and other organization to incorporate new and multiple self units and self descriptions. These new self descriptions can, on the part of the daughter, triumph over symbolic familial infusions or intrusive familial identifications. Thus, the daughter can shed the received burden of feminine protest from her mother and assimilate appropriate controls over her body and its temptations. With these new self descriptions, the mother can withdraw her otherwise coercive infusions and identify with her daughter as a woman amongst women who own their separate body selves.

## DISCUSSION: INTRINSIC ELABORATION OF FINDINGS

The structures of experience of the anorexics and their mothers must now be elaborated so that we may arrive at some understanding of the intersubjective constitution of mother–anorexic daughter perceptions. To accomplish this goal we must organize our findings in terms of (1) interperceptual structures across subjects, where there are, inter alia, presentations of experiences of chaos alternating with rigidity; (2) the structure of the daughter's perceptions of self and (m)other; (3) the structure of the mother's perception of self and anorexic daughter; (4) interperceptual structure of mother–anorexic daughter relations according to those that fit, and those that do not fit.

### *Abiding Interperceptual Structures Across Subjects*
### *Experiences of Chaos Alternating with Rigidity*

There are instances of subjects alternating between experiences of chaos and rigidity across subjects. The most compelling example of the alternation is subject 002A's switching from *anorexia nervosa and an accompanying psychosis* to *bulimia*. 002A associates experiences of her hospitalization for anorexia and psychosis to revealing family secrets such as her sister's victimizations by an incestuous father, her own felt but uncertain experience of incest by father, and her own experience of rape by middle-school boys at the time her own mother had abandoned her to some group home in favor of accommodating maternal grandmother. In relation to bulimia, the subject refuses to go into hospital for treatment because she fears that she may remove the lid on the now rigidly contained family secrets. Subject's concerns show us that she is just as unsettled whether her world revolves around anorexia or bulimia and that anorexia nervosa and bulimia are *essentially one illness* which reveals different profiles of a person's world. Consider these words from the subject herself:

> *Well, in my opinion, the Eating Disorder really doesn't have anything to do with food. It's like a control factor. It's like, see, I can get over on you, I can eat whatever I want and, I mean, it won't go anywhere because I can control it, be it purging with my finger, be it taking Ipecac whatever, taking water pills, you name it, or exercising, possibly or usually a combination of all of those. When I don't eat it's kind of the opposite.* See, I can beat you in this, *you aren't going to make me throw up.* Because I hate throwing up, it's kind of weird, it's like

*when you purge*, it's like the food won't control you, I won't gain weight from it, but then you feel so horrible after you purge, you think I'm not this, you get scared, it's like this disease is controlling you. So I'm not going to eat, or I'm going to eat bananas or whatever so they won't have a control on me. And so then I feel like I'm controlling the disease. *It's like when I binge and purge I have control of it*, or I have the control of the food, it doesn't make me fat, *and then if I don't eat, then it's like the disease can't control me.* It's like a power issue with me. And it's also, it's *like something I can do and nobody can catch.* And, no, I don't like it. I don't know how to control it, it controls me, but I control it. It's weird to explain it, but it's like when you're purging, you think you are controlling it, and the food won't make you fat, but then you are weak. You are as weak as can be, and so then you . . . so then, you don't eat, you don't have to purge, and it won't make you binge again or purge.

We can see here that 002A *stubbornly* controls or *obstinately* controls her food intake and output. 002A *actively* decides what and how much she takes in. In addition, she *aggressively but passively* decides how much she is not going to take in. Whether she is active and stubborn as to what she eats, or obstinate and passive-aggressive, she is manifestly in control of her situation. It is as if a bulimic state of mind is a stubborn-active one whereas an anorexic state of mind is an obstinate, passive-aggressive frame of reference for this subject. For this subject, being stubborn and obstinate are two sides of an equation that serve to control her plight. The only difference is that being stubborn is active, whereas being obstinate is passive.

There are alternations between rigidity and chaos in 002A, but her mother is mostly impressed by the presence of some demon within her child that drives the child out of control. Thus, subject 002B perceived her anorexic/psychotic pubertal child as possessed by a *demon* when the latter was stricken with terror at the sight of her parents during her hospital stay. 002B has retained this image of a demon to describe her daughter when she is *driven out of control* by purging or strenuous exercises.

In subject 003A, we learn that just before her anorexia nervosa revealed itself to her physician and herself, she had switched from being an excessive drinker to abstaining from everything, and becoming extremely rigid and "controlled" in her abstinence. Before the anorexia nervosa she had been compulsive as a person in a very stable and prolonged way. Thus, a subject who by personality was very compulsive revealed how troubled she was when she became an *excessive drinker*, and from excessive drinking went to a *rigidly controlled abstinence* that made a skeleton of her; it was this skeleton image of her which frightened her roommates into initiating her hospitalization.

Subject 003B revealed, close to the end of her interview, that although she had been *disorganized* in raising seven children, she had also been *compulsive* when 003A, her first child, was an infant.

Subject 005A spoke of her allegiance to her mother and to gymnastics where she perceived that she was stuck in a world where "quitting" was unacceptable to her. 005A perceived that she should create a *crisis* to unsettle such a *fixed* posture. For her, anorexia nervosa and the predictable demands of gymnastics had become a safe world, although a painful one. She saw that crisis, in the form of physical illness, could potentially lead to change. Crisis for her became synonymous with change because it unfroze a fixed posture, once safe but now conflictual. She perceived that she could create a sense of self which could accommodate "quitting" without its original connotation of failure in her anorexic world. She intended to create a new connotation which said that when one is sick and in crisis, one must let oneself change without submission to external expectations. A fixed vocabulary represented a fixed sense of self: a fixity that had an intention. To change she had to unsettle an embedded and ossified structure, first and foremost, and then create a new meaning that was compatible with perceived external expectations. For this subject, change from a destructive rigidity to crisis was seen as an "upgrade."

Subject 005B's rigid organization shows in the way she wanted to perceive her daughter only as aggressive, arrogant, insightful, and intelligent. She would not allow herself to know that her daughter could be aggressive and intelligent but anxious as well. If 005B mentioned her daughter's anxiety, it was only in the context of what some psychiatrist had told her. It was not until almost the end of the interview that 005B revealed that she thought the aggressive and insightful part of her daughter was her daughter's true self and the part 005B liked better.

In these anorexics and their mothers, forms of rigid organization alternate with chaos or vice versa. Often the shift from one level of organization to the other shows when a subject perceives another in a painful light. A subject may refer to another as "a demon" or as an entirely different person, or some aspect of the other may be treated as though it did not exist. In all these subjects, whether a person shifted from anorexia nervosa to bulimia, from drinking to abstaining, or from knowing to not knowing, there was a *split* in the perception of self or the other, so that an aspect of an individual was imagined to be separate when in fact it was only one among other aspects of a person or behavioral set. Thus, one aspect of self or the other could be acknowledged, while another aspect remained thoroughly concealed or rigidly protected.

## STRUCTURE OF DAUGHTER'S PERCEPTIONS OF SELF AND (M)OTHER

**002A.** Subject locates her true self in some distant era and her false self in the present. In her view, the true self was heavier, shy, and introverted and must remain concealed, whereas the false self, which is extrovert, has many friends and can date attractive men. 002A wants to keep her true self, which she perceives to be bad, thoroughly hidden because it made her feel bad. In her effort to preserve the opposite but desired view of herself, 002A has come to equate bad with fat, fat with lazy. For her, bad amounts to unmet standards and a self-description as misfit, one who produces insult and dirt.

While 002A has this split view of herself she also sees herself and her mother as *two people* who *mirror* each other. This subject says that she *sees herself in her mother and her mother in her*. She sees further that their *connectedness exists irrespective of good or bad ties between them.* She recognizes *the blurring of their boundaries* when she is able to speak to their shared naivety in their attitudes toward sex, in her weekly exercising of her mother. When 002A speaks to their shared naivety, we see how that ignorance is part of a strategy to control what she found painful, conflictual, or incompatible. For example, when she was raped, she felt as though someone else was raped, and because she did not know much about sex, she could not even identify that forced sexual act as rape. It was as though it was something some "bad" girl went through. Someone other than her must tell her she had been raped.

This subject acknowledges that she confuses boundaries with her mother and acknowledges further that she has *ingested her grandmother "wholesale"*; the grandmother with whom she has a shared sense of organization. Even though grandmother is hated by her, 002A finds that she is tied to the aggressive, meticulous, perfectionist standards that they share.

In her helplessness, this subject resorts to "a *control* factor" which she sees as *ambiguous* because sometimes she is in control and at other times not in control. She feels in control when she perceives that binging would rid her of some unpleasant experience, but no sooner has she begun than she notices that she is the one controlled, weak, and impoverished, at the mercy of her illness or the enemy within that must yet again be rid of. Perhaps this energy within is in part *the hated grandmother* who has been *appropriated and must now be got rid of.*

**003A**. Subject perceives her mother as disorganized, but she understands this disorganization in her mother in two ways: first, she perceives her mother is disorganized because her mother's mother was "a mean, nasty woman who was an alcoholic and substance abuser" and, by implication, her mother could not possibly have had the preparation necessary to organize her life as a person; second, and in relation to the first, 003A saw her mother, and still sees as a "reluctant" mother who had seven children but did not wish to have them. A result of this background, in 003A's view, is that her mother's development was impeded by conflicts for which she was unprepared to find solutions. Likewise, 003A could not have benefited from her mother's knowledge. This anorexic subject came to feel that her mother was a reluctant mother who divorced affection from sex, perceived sex as bad, and yet, when 003A did not have sex, she was perceived by her mother as homosexual.

**003A** perceived that the way to survive was to be different from her mother, whom she adored, but whose personality she disliked. For this subject it is axiomatic that a mother cleans, cooks, and organizes, and yet her mother failed to do that. To succeed in becoming a different woman, 003A joined forces with her organized father against her mother. Thus, she would effect a counteridentification that would enable her to become a woman in her own right, and different.

When, however, 003A's father suffered from depression, she perceived that her father was rather hurtful in his demandingness, hostile with the standards he set, and generally unpleasant. She saw then how much her mother had had to tolerate; a situation that made her shift allegiance to her mother. Now father was the perceived enemy, and mother the ally.

003A perceived that her father's depression and the ensuing deidealization that followed was implicated in her anorexia nervosa, and
resulted in the shift in allegiance to the mother. But this shift was
not decisive until the subject completed her treatment, got married,
and conceived a child. Now she was a mother, too, a woman capable
of having a child—fertile, not homosexual, but a capable mother in
her own right.

This subject's perceptions of her mother as a disorganized, unprepared, and reluctant woman enabled her to seek a counteridentification
from her mother in the first instance, and then with the deidealization
of her father that followed his depression, 003A perceived that her
mother was stronger in the face of crisis and quite able. Guilt and
subsequent pregnancy coalesced to make her see her mother's strength
and her own emergence as a capable woman. Let me add parentheti-
cally that if these processes of counteridentification and deidealization
seem like a generic solution to a developmental pathology, it is not
by accident. I surmise that 003A's ability to successfully utilize these
strategies is not inconsistent with my observation that she is the
healthiest of the three anorexics interviewed. Perhaps she is the only
one who fully recovered from her anorexia nervosa. This subject can
now create a family of her own away from her original family that
saw her as "crazy." There is further motivation here to grow away
from her family of origin.

**005A.** One way to make sense of one's world and how one's mother
fits into it is to examine relationships across generations so that one
may compare one's relationship with mother with the relationship to
her mother. For 005A, these two relationships are close to being the
same, especially when mother's efforts to tear away from her own
mother have failed. *When grandmother has historically played the
role of a martyr, aggression in one's family is concealed.* In such
a family, *closeness is contrived* in mother-daughter relationships across
generations. Messages and precepts are communicated indirectly, and
one is lured into accepting or appropriating them. For 005A, one not
only appropriates precepts, but also criticisms and fear of disapproval,
from one's mother. For this subject, it is this fear of disapproval and
the guilt for aggressively tearing away that impede one's efforts to
be one's own person. Guilt and other human affects are the means
of transmission of a message or a behavior. Thus, a child can interpret

the message that she should be good at one thing, rather than mediocre at a lot of things, by choosing gymnastics as a means of losing her self in a project with her mother. In such a project she can be her mother's star pupil, whose success is her mother's, too. When one loses one's self in such a project, one can lose one's very being and become a person who depends on external praise and affirmation for one's very existence. Thus, one can feel empty, bad, unworthy, silly, stupid, blank, lonely, and needing to hibernate until one makes the decision to break away from that contrived old self.

The way to break away from that contrived empty self is to "fill one's self with a self," not just a new self but a self. The creation of self, for 005A, begins with the naming of that activity, that is, "filling one's self with self." But there are impediments to this project of creating a self-in-embryo. As much as one needs to "get one's fill" by talking to others and enjoying the thrill of new relationships, one must not rely solely on the fill coming from outside. One must neither stick rigidly to a particular way of defining one's self nor be lost in the potential chaos of many attractive and new learning situations, for one is not centered in either situation. Indeed, one must not stay in that "time warp" that confines one to a barren world where there is no available time, no energy to think about anything else. For 005A, a time warp is not only a temporal situation, but one that also forbids regeneration or change.

Although anorexia nervosa was created out of necessity and developed to provide a background of safety, subject nevertheless has to find a way out of that same world which has now become confining; a world that excises the word "quitting" out of her vocabulary. *The way to alter this confining world is to create a new crisis.*

For 005A, crisis provides the potential energy for change. Crisis potentially upgrades one from a fixed world with a fixed vocabulary and a fixed sense of self. Crisis unfreezes. To change, one first has to unsettle an embedded or ossified structure and, second, create new intentions for the same vocabulary, but one which is endowed with new meaning and that can still meet the expectations of the world that is out there; a compromise indeed. For 005A, physical illness is the propeller for crisis and change, and for that reason she can tell others and herself that illness took gymnastics as a sport, and as a carrier of a confining mode of living, away from her. As a carrier of a confining life, gymnastics was a vehicle for *vicarious living between mother and daughter*, one that allows them to make *destructive sacrifices for each other in a world where self and other become interchangeable*. One easily became a confidante for one's mother, where one should have received her care. *One should have received her mother's care rather than become interchangeable with her.* For 005A, the protest against this kind of neglect comes when she reconstructs her early childhood from how her mother currently treats people who depend on her. 005A's construction is that just as her mother hates her clients who depend on her, just so did her mother hate her as a dependent infant, who not only summoned her for care but interrupted her life.

## Structure of Mother's Perceptions of Daughter

**002B.** Subject sees a *duality* in her daughter's behavior which intrigues her. On the one hand, she sees her daughter who is resilient and intelligent, and yet fails to feel like a person when she is unattached to a man. 002B also sees in a daughter another *duality*. The young daughter who is raped and might therefore be expected to hate men is the same one who seeks the affection of men such as her father's. In her daughter, 002B sees a mature, capable, adaptable, and responsible person, yet one who has a brittle sense of self.

This subject perceives her daughter as one who can have an idealized view of the world when she is not troubled. But this idealized view fails to be concretely grounded because of 002B's anxiety about growing up and becoming independent. This subject perceives that when her daughter is tested the little girl in her returns and detracts from her progressive steps away from home.

Implicating herself in her daughter's failure to develop, 002B sees her daughter as unable now to function without advice. She states that because she was fat as a teenager and had to resist weight gain all her life, it is likely that she and not the father, has passed on to her daughter her overweight problems. In subject's view, her child has so imbibed the mother's weight problems, that even an aggressive sexual attack on the daughter takes second place to humiliation and selfconscious feelings which result from weight gain. Subject sees her daughter punishing herself and subject with strenuous exercises which lead to subject's calling her daughter bulimarexic. Thus, 002B sees her daughter's hostile treatment of her own body as an expression of ambivalence towards the mother's body. In 002B's view, her daughter is preoccupied with aggressively feeding her body, or aggressively ridding that body of its contents, or else feeding it with something unacceptable.

In "going beyond" a respectable treatment of her body, the anorexic must be driven by some other being, some demon, as it were, and when she is so driven, she is prone to not knowing accurately who controls whom. It is 002B's view that her daughter is trying to clean out her past, her abandonment, anorexia nervosa, psychosis, all those things that make the daughter act like someone other than herself; a greatly traumatized animal that makes little sense to its/her mother.

For this reason subject is full of regret as to her part in her daughter's illness. Having imported the best of subject's father to her daughter, who is also named L. K. after her kind, gentle, loving father, there is little subject can do now to erase the harm she caused when she replaced her daughter with her ailing mother by sending the child instead of her widowed mother to a group home. 002B realizes now that the cost of capitulating to her mother was her daughter's neglect, and *a daughter's abandonment is a costly way to reconcile with one's own mother*.

**003B.** Subject perceives her daughter as a compulsive child who did not benefit from subject's disorganization in the home. Subject saw herself as someone who grew up outside the close relationship her parents had between them, whereas her daughter grew up closer to her, but in a disorganized home. Subject recalls that one cost of her sense of disorganization was that her daughter was neglected when her seventh child was born, and the mother did not notice. For 003B, when teenage troubles began and the father set no limits, that failure constituted neglect on his part, too. Subject perceives her daughter as a young woman who has suffered at the hands of men like her father who hate women, but also as one who has benefitted from obstetricians who do like women, and are thus able to sensitively notice and address the needs of women. Subject's perception of her daughter's anorexia nervosa, then, is that when her daughter suffered at the hands of negligent or women-hating men, it remained for those obstetrician/gynecologists who love women to correct the daughter's emotional highs and lows. For when a woman's physiology is out of balance, she cannot feed herself; when she is amenorrheic, her body functioning goes "off kilter." Subject's overriding perception of her anorexic daughter is that the latter was essentially victimized by a father who hates women, by psychiatrists who were too confidential to be helpful to her, by her daughter's own dieting, which she could not stop, and by the consequences of the birth of her last born, who is now depressed like his father. 003B perceives now that her daughter's compulsiveness will put her in good stead as she parents her own child.

**005B.** One can see in one's daughter a *paradoxical* set of behaviors, where the daughter is outwardly confident, verbal, independent, sensible, and angry, yet anxious and frightened inside herself. This latter behavior shows when she finds it difficult to leave home and, when she is home, wants to recognize her mother's world by rear-ranging her drawers and playing protector for her mother. For 005B, the failure to set limits comes from the misperception that limit setting is synonymous with rejection of one's daughter. One must protect one's daughter, and even if one feels driven to neglect her by not wishing to set limits, one must find another way to protect her. The way to protect her can be a way that one would use to protect one's self. Thus, when a mother wants to protect her self from painful feelings she must protect her daughter from the very same feelings at the same time. *Mother must therefore protect her daughter from death*, other *losses*, and *disappointments* in general. For 005B, *when she lied to her daughter, she lied to herself, too*. Thus, if a pet died and subject herself was grief-stricken, she would lie to her daughter as to what happened in order to spare her daughter from disappoint-ment. In 005B's world, disappointment must be concealed. Hence, it is a new experience to own that the loss of human beings and the pain it brings are quite foreign to her, when, in contrast, the loss of pets brings her the experience of guilt as to what she might have done to save them.

For 005B, this tendency to shield one's self from pain, and by extension one's daughter from pain can generalize into shielding her from the consequences of her actions in general. She perceives there is a great deal to protect self and others from, perhaps a nameless dread, perhaps depression, as abyss which she survived.

But it is important to know how the mode of protection of one's daughter is communicated, as well, quite apart from recognizing the proneness to protect one's offspring. The way to communicate protection, at least as 005B learned from her mother, is to spare one's child pain by not setting limits or rules and by providing protection from disappointment or anger. For 005B, certain body gestures and silence came to stand for discomfort in the family, so that it was as if what was not spoken did not happen or will not happen in the future. In this, now-settled way of dealing with incompatible feelings, old fears and old ways of preventing them could be passed on from one generation to the next through behaviors a mother would accept and those she would not.

There is a price to pay however, for being an agent who passes on a behavior from one generation to the next. Because subject was special and was her mother's creation, her mother created the most "beautiful," "perfect," "little gorgeous child" whom the mother treated in a possessive way, and intended to be possessive in subject's turn. For 005B, *an overvalued child*, such as herself, *becomes a neglected child because when one is tied to the mirror image of one's mother, one does not get the opportunity to be prepared for the world out there where one is expected to function autonomously*. A special child is neglected when she is not equipped to face today's problems because that special child, and especially what she represents for her mother, is tied to an historical situation.

In such a situation, subject's mother may be relating to the infant that survived meningitis and death; the child for whose survival she performed heroic acts to ensure her survival. Such a story may become a family legend that can be a vehicle for how a mother and her daughter can overvalue and be special to each other in other than helpful ways. For 005B, this unhealthy tie to one's mother keeps one from becoming independent and must be avoided.

The trouble is that when one has been raised in one way, one does not have the tools to raise one's child in another way. Hence, one can be "caught" by one's history. The best one may be able to accomplish is to create a child who is *free and independent on the outside* but *anxiously shackled to her mother in some other way*. For 005B, the sense of bondage to one's mother is a prison home of coercion and responsibility to one's other. For 005B, this sense of coercion may not abate with age, for she may still feel controlled and manipulated in subtle ways.

What one can do in such a situation is to *consciously* teach one's daughter to beat the trap in various ways that include teaching her how to be loving, gentle, and nurturing, how to be an independent woman who is not an appendage to her husband, how to be a woman with a single but exemplary skill, how to speak with pointed clarity and not compromise one's position. But when one perceives, as does this subject, that a daughter's first name is one that was once meant to be given to oneself, one comes to acknowledge and to understand that if there is a project that did not get accomplished in a previous generation, subject could "pick up the gauntlet and accomplish it" as an appropriated goal among others.

For 005B, one precept stands out in her family—a paradoxical one, a condensed one, perhaps one that is impossible to fulfill: "Be a chameleon, you should please people." When a mother wants to change such a precept for her daughter by getting her to be verbally aggressive, and yet quietly injects into her child the obedience with which she was raised, what is to become of her daughter? How is she to evaluate her daughter's progress? 005B resolves that her daughter is a *paradox* to her: outspoken externally, but anxious and frightened underneath; and by dubbing her daughter's behavior a paradox, 005B does not have to face the full impact of her bifurcated creation.

## Interperceptual Structure of Mother-Daughter Relations

Mother-daughter relations of the subject pairs divide into those which explicitly fit: 002A and 002B, 005A and 005B; and those which do not explicitly fit: 003A and 003B.

**002A and 002B.** Subjects agree in their interperceptual structure that grandmother played a principal role in the deterioration of mother-daughter relations. 002A and 002B both acknowledge that grandmother had weight problems and that they, too, had weight problems and yet grandmother chided granddaughter for the very weight problem grandmother wanted to get rid of in herself. Both 002A and 002B perceive that the replacement of granddaughter by grandmother in mother's home was an error in mother's judgment. Both agree, too, that granddaughter had appropriated overly demanding attitudes from grandmother, so that granddaughter is now severely self-critical and self-punishing in standards she set for herself.

002B sees herself as the mother who imparted self-consciousness about weight to her daughter to the point where even rape takes second place to 002A's experience of humiliation with regard to weight problems.

In this interperceptual structure it seems that *mother is the conduit of grandmother's destructive aggression*, which the *anorexic daughter has appropriated "wholesale."*

**005A and 005B.** Subjects agree in their interperceptual structure that mother felt she was raised by a possessive mother and that 005B made every conscious effort not to repeat her mother's experience of being hemmed in when 005B became a mother. Both subjects agree in their perception that mother had limited success in her effort not to repeat her prior difficulties with her mother in her own parenting of the anorexic child. 005A sees that they have physically separated, but her guilt for being outspoken towards her mother and the mother's skepticism about her daughter's independence keeps them still connected in some ambivalent way. 005B recognizes that this interview drew her attention to the reality that her mother intended to name her A. R. but she changed her mind, and yet 005B uncannily named her own daughter by the same name. 005B sees in this transfer a coercive intermingling she has not entirely been able to shed. In this interperceptual structure it seems that mother was a carrier of a project transferred from grandmother to anorexic daughter.

**003A and 003B.** Subjects do not fit in decisive ways in terms of the interperceptual structure of mother-daughter relationships. When there is a fit, it is only nominal. For example, they both mention the youngest child, who is depressed and underachieving. 003B mentions him as the one who conveyed, through his taunting, that until she got married and had a baby, the family thought of her as "the crazy one." On the other hand, 003A sees the two children as close. 003B does perceive, however, that the birth of the youngest was traumatic for her now-anorexic daughter but, as mother, she noticed it too late to be helpful. Both subjects see the anorexic's father as problematic, but for different reasons. In the mother's perception, he hated women unless they were attractive, intelligent, and independent: and his hatred of women made him unsympathetic towards women as to what they needed. In her view, the father's *hatred of women* contrasted with his *love of men* like obstetricians and gynecologists who, because of their liking of women, could offer precisely what an anorexic girl needed to recover. 003A, however, sees her father as one who, because of his depression and her consequent deidealization of him, made her see how strong her mother was in coping with his demandingness, inter alia.

Otherwise, there are several misperceptions between the subjects. For example, the daughter thought that not dating or not having sex would be perceived by her mother as being a good girl. In contrast, her mother perceived her daughter as homosexual when the mother thought the daughter did not date. Mostly, the interperceptual structure of mother-daughter relations betweem 003A and 003B is an assembly of misconceptions or misperceptions.

The grandmother does not feature decisively in this interperceptual structure. The mother saw her mother as one who had a close relationship with her husband and who was served hand and foot by her husband. The granddaughter, however, perceived her grandmother as a "mean, nasty woman who was alcoholic and substance abuser." Although granddaughter does not present herself as mean and nasty, it is interesting that just before the anorexia nervosa showed itself, granddaughter, too, used alcohol excessively. Thus, we see a small feature here of grandmother's place in the anorexic's life. The very person perceived to be the one the granddaughter must disidentify with is the one recreated wholly or in part in the grandchild.

## DIALOGUE WITH CLINICAL AND RESEARCH LITERATURE

The clinical presentation of anorexia nervosa in our subjects is manifestly very consistent with that of mainstream clinical thinkers (Thomä 1967; Bruch 1974; Palazzoli 1982; Minuchin, Rosman, and Baker 1978; Crisp 1980; Wilson 1983). Thus, we see no need to contradict their observations about anorexia nervosa: problematic early experiential and interpersonal processes between mother and daughter; psychical determination of reduction in nutritional intake; problems of fusion between mother and child; child's oral-incorporative experience of mother; weight phobia; distortion in sense of time; and omnipotent denial of death. These and other well-known features of anorexia nervosa are not in question. A second look at these same clinical descriptions and research findings, however, suggests that they are, at best, headlines that require a great deal of elaboration. Research findings from data that are phenomenologically collected but psychoanalytically elaborated, as in this study, promise to supply some of the details in question. In this study, we are interested in one profile of anorexia nervosa—that of intersubjectivity—which taps the range of perceptions that mothers and anorexic daughters have of each other.

Such a profile, dependent as it is on perceptions of bodily selves and their situatedness in the world, has suggested that the range of perceptions is virturally inexhaustible and that the details from our study can fill in some gaps in our current understanding of interperceptual relations between mothers and daughters in anorexia nervosa.

Hogan (1983) has commented on the role of projection and projective identification. In general, these modes of delegation to, and appropriation of, selves or self units have not received the amount of attention they deserve in the literature. As clear as Hogan is, even his observations appear to be headlines or fleeting references. These mechanisms will receive definition and attention in the theoretical section of our discussion. For the moment it is sufficient to say that our six subjects have provided clarifying details that are paradigmatic of anorexia nervosa sufferers with respect to intersubjectivity. Our results are new in the sense that they furnish details which do not exist in the current literature. For example, the nature of maternal grandmother's role in anorexia is not sufficiently known or appreciated. Nor is her impact on the imprecise boundaries between mother and daughter known.

"There is a range of interperceptual styles in the descriptions of our subjects and in the psychological transformations of their text data. There are transgenerational interperceptual relations, and there are complex interpersonal perceptions and misperceptions, with concrete and metaphorical expressions of self-other confusions, and so on.

## COMPLEX OF INTERPERCEPTUAL RELATIONS

Let us sketch some representative paradigms of perception, interperception, misperception, and the ambiguities that impact self-other relations into schemata, proceeding from the complex to the relatively clear and simple:

> 1. *Horizontal distinctions* between what is lost in memory and what is retained; (e.g. what is one's old self and what is one's new self); or *vertical distinctions* between what is consciously owned and what is disowned in one's perception of self or other, (e.g., between an aspect of one's daughter's behavior one acknowledges knowing about directly and another aspect of her behavior one claims to know about only through a third party, such as a doctor).

2. *Interchangeable selves* as in confusion over who protects whom; *blurred boundaries* as in "shared naivety"; *confidantes* (as opposed to mother and child) who contrive to obliterate painful experiences.

3. Thanks to a distinction, horizontal or vertical, a dissonant part of the self can become dislodged and translocated in another person with whom one now shares blurred boundaries. This blurring creates *ambiguity and exclusivity of union* between two selves whose boundaries are permeable, as in a child who puts her mother through exercises. An ambiguous "control factor" now operates which distorts perception as to who controls whom, mother or daughter, or what controls whom, anorexia nervosa controlling the anorexic and the anorexic person controlling anorexia nervosa.

4. With ambiguity or misperception, or doubts about self and other coherence, comes a *breakdown* in *the sense of order* with *pangs of anxious guilt* about "living-a-lie," feeling "crazy," and having anxiety over lack of control. The contrived misperception about one's actual reality is intended to avoid real pain, which is authentically motivated in the first instance, and then becomes further elaborated into a stable and abiding method for dealing with perceived or anticipated danger situations. Thus, "what one cannot define clearly will not hurt" becomes the unspoken message. But the ambiguity of self and other coherence leads into such feelings as numbness even in the sexual act, as if one does not know or own one's body, or as if one were another person.

This breakdown of sense of order can in turn be broken into two sets of experiences within the same horizon: a *locked-in-control* factor that keeps self and other anchored in place and yet interchangeable with; and a *loose control factor* that keeps self and other in constant interactions, so that separation or differentiation is obliterated, and for that reason, dissonant parts of one or (m)other can cross boundaries and induce one's own original dissonant self or behavior in the other. But what is truly critical perhaps is that these two factors are not centered in objective reality.

Complex interperceptual relations such as those described are above reduced by Palazzoli (1982, 94) into the three-way meaning of anorexia nervosa, which she schematizes as follows:

| — to retain | the good | |
| — to ward off | | object (body) |
| — to control | the bad | |

According to this schema, the anorexic may retain the good object or the bad object. She may ward off the good object or the bad object. Or she may control the good object or the bad object. These three variants, of course, must be understood in a particular clinical context.

In Palazzoli's schema we miss the process whereby the anorexic separates out, horizontally or vertically, good and bad parts of the self. The process is treated as if it were given and the considerable range of shifts as to owned and disowned tasks, and as to defined but imprecise boundaries is not there.


## INTERPERCEPTUAL RELATIONS ACROSS GENERATIONS

When our subjects function as though boundaries are imprecise, they do not only create diffuse borders between mother and child, they yield to or participate in interperceptual relations across generations, so that a dead father can be replaced by a daughter, who is literally given the same name (L. K.) and nurtured to become loving and caring, such as the original L. K. was. 002A got her name L. K. from her mother's father, who died a few months before she was conceived. Likewise, when a daughter is pushed out, grandmother can stay. The irony is that when mother's (002B's) father dies, her symbolic substitute is created (002A), and yet his death heralded in reality 002A's rejection. One grandparent brings her in, and another pushes her out.

002A appropriated the loving, caring, nurturing maternal grandfather, and also appropriated the rejecting, complaining, perfectionistic maternal grandmother. It was as if, wittingly or unwittingly, 002A were an incarnated symbolic compromise of the mother's father and mother.

005B understood, quite independently, in the course of her research interview that there must have been some unfinished project from her mother that she was expected to carry out in the context of the current relationship with her daughter.

The interperceptual relations across generations in the case of 005A and 005B can thus be represented:

O  grandmother
|
O  mother
|
O  anorexic  daughter

This is a relatively clear transmission from a matristic figure in one generation to a second in another generation, and then to a third in the generation of the anorexic.

There is another form of transmission of project, clearly defined or otherwise, where the anorexic becomes a receptacle of loved and hated parts of her mother's parents. This mode of transmission can thus be represented:

## Mode of Creation of Anorexic as
## Composite Figure

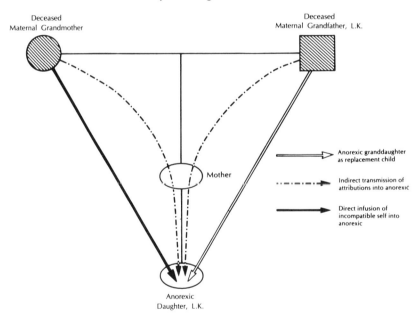

Anorexic granddaughter is thus a composite of compatible and incompatible parts of maternal grandparents. Why is such an anorexic a suitable container for the other's compatible and incompatible selves? Sperling (1983) holds the view that anorexic patients have a deep-rooted feeling of being rejected by mother, which in part is due to a projection of their own hatred, and in part is founded on reality, at least on the unconscious feelings (psychic reality) of the mother. Their mothers are ambivalent toward them and usually identify them with some rejected parts of their own personality. These mothers also suffer from unresolved infantile conflicts, particularly in regard to their sexual identities and impulse control. Such feelings are reinforced in the daughter, who may develop anorexia nervosa later under certain precipitating conditions (p. 75).

The deep fear of being rejected makes the anorexic quite willing to please even if the behavior she is subtly or blatantly coerced to appropriate is dangerous for her. Thus, a mother who is ambivalent about her femininity may inject her conflict about her femininity through how she treats her daughter. Sperling (1983) had a patient in such a situation who felt she must close up her throat so that she could not swallow her mother's food. This adolescent girl would only close up her throat when her mother served her with foods that she liked because she knew that if she did not close up her throat she would eat practically everything on the table. She felt, further, that her mother never liked her to eat what the daughter liked. In the daughter's words: "She never wanted me to do things I wanted to do. She controlled my life" (p. 75). Sperling summed up the adolescent girl's feelings:

> The pervasive feeling was "my mother never wanted me." Later in the analysis it was uncovered that she had felt rejected because of her female sex. . . . In addition to the struggle against eating, there is a struggle against accepting the female role and identification in the anorexic girl. Because of the hatred and murderous impulses towards the mother, the female role and genital sexuality are dangerous and are shunned by the anorexic patient (pp. 75–76).

In our subjects, and in Sperling's patient, the anorexic person's world is a theater where she and other participants dramatize a range of life struggles and goals. 003A, for instance, experienced some of the conflicts that Sperling's patient went through. She always felt that her mother was a "reluctant mother" and to her "*a reluctant mother is a reluctant female.*" Not surprisingly, when 003A's mother wondered why she did not date, she voiced the suspicion to the anorexic's sister that the anorexic daughter must be homosexual. The anorexic subject came to identify with her mother's reluctance to be a female and, for a while, thought she would never get married or have children. She had, albeit temporarily, appropriated the reluctance to be a mother and transformed it into reluctance as to femininity. 003A, however, resolved that she would rid herself of such a barren identification.

## ASCETICISM AND THE RELUCTANCE TO BE A MOTHER

003B is the mother who was dubbed by her anorexic daughter as a reluctant mother. This mother views anorexia nervosa as an illness that could be cured by some pill. For her, such a pill would make her daughter fertile. For that reason a gynecologist, and not a psychiatrist, is the treatment agent of choice and not a psychiatrist. As absurd as this mother's view of anorexia nervosa may sound, a certain native intelligence lurks behind her presupposition. 003B knows that if her daughter remained anorexic, she would not be psychologically able to have a child and is very much relieved that her daughter has recovered from anorexia nervosa and been able to have a child. It is also her view that not to have a child implies a perversion, which she views homosexuality to be. We also know from the daughter (003A) that the austerity with which the daughter pursued anorexia nervosa made her psychiatrist suggest, in jest, that she would be a good nun.

The relation between the austerity of anorexics and nuns is not new in the literature. In his 1985 essays, *Holy Anorexia*, historian Bell describes

> the 261 holy women officially recognized by the Roman Catholic church as saints, blesseds, venerables, or servants of God (included in the Bibliotheca Sanctorum) who lived between 1200 and the present on the Italian peninsula. For about one-third of this number the historical record is so meager that nothing of consequence can be concluded about them. . . . Of the remaining 170 or so, more than half displayed clear signs of anorexia (p. x).

Bell provides an account of those medieval women who starved themselves in search of saintliness. But as child psychiatrist Davis, writes in the epilogue to *Holy Anorexia*, starvation "is also a significant attempt to document a relationship between gender, conflict, and anorexic behavior patterns" (p. 183). This connection between gender conflicts and asceticism in nuns and in anorexia is not new, and I do not wish to enter into a debate on the correctness or incorrectness of the assumptions involved. I am interested in what is conspicuously absent or left unsaid. *Nuns do not have children. Anorexics do not have children*, at least until they are cured. In the context of this study, where there is now some question as to what anorexia nervosa does to the continuity of generations, asceticism becomes more than physical or spiritual austerity, more than self-denial or an implied feminine protest. Asceticism has to be seen as a means of not having children. *Seedlessness is implicated in ascesis or asceticism*. Asceticism in anorexics or in nuns facilitates a dead end, an aporia, where no new generation is created. In this context, Bachelard's (1936/1986) admonition that we return to vital impulses and not resort to "mutilated examples of the symbolizing powers active in nature" is apropos. It is apropos because this observation of nuns and anorexics not having children, whether by choice or as a result of psychopathology, is a concrete observable reality, a reality that is so obvious that the absence of its elaboration in the literature is itself of interest.

## TOWARDS A DESCRIPTION OF INTERSUBJECTIVE CONSTITUTION OF ANOREXIA NERVOSA

A description of the intersubjective constitution of anorexia nervosa may now proceed as follows:

1. Mother and anorexic daughter perceive and relate to each other as though each were the other's face; that face which reflects the other. At the same time they perceive and treat each other as though each were a mask, a representation and a stand-in for the other. The Greek word *prosopon,* which means "face," "person," "character," "mask," assists us to see one way that the anorexic and her mother perceive each other. Each one is a *prosopon* for the other. Each one perceives the other as a composite figure of face, mask, representation, character, and person at one and the same time. In addition, however, the anorexic may be a stand-in for a lost grandparent, and/or a claustrum for an incompatible and disagreeable grandparent.

2. Grandmother, mother, and anorexic daughter have a relationship whose borders are both shared and separate; present and de-ferred; juxtaposed and yet appositive—in the very fundamental sense of being "explanatory equivalents." Thus, each one is not simply a subject or an object; rather each of the three can

be subject and object at the same time. Each can be a subject that receives a project, passes it on to the other, who then becomes the subject, who in turn picks up the "gauntlet" and passes on the task at hand to the next generation.

3. Imprecise borders exist both in contemporary relations and across generations.

4. Across generations, there is/are unfinished project(s) that each generation must embrace as if the project(s) were its own. This project is simultaneously feared and appropriated but it never comes to be identified for what it is. It appears to be some *nameless dread* that can only be articulated through concrete events. For example, a mother's fear that her daughter would die is followed by heroic efforts to deceive hospital staff so that the mother can enter the hospital to see her daughter. Such a story can become a *legend* in the family, and its endurance points to a psychological rigidity, whose opposite must be investigated. In other words, when a mother's heroics become a legend, the fear of death must be investigated as to the coexistence of an opposite wish/fear: the wish or fear that one may kill one's own daughter.

5. A mother of an anorexic is not only a mother but also a daughter who capitulates willingly or otherwise to the mission of her mother.

6. The anorexic is the daughter whose world serves as the dead-end (*aporia*) where a compromise is made. In other words, she fulfills the mission by flirting with death or appropriating the lethal project *and* at the same time strives to flee. The result is that she lives a living death through the pathological formation called anorexia nervosa or bulimia as its counterpart.

7. There is no bridge that connects mother, grandmother, and daughter. Transfers are complete and unmediated between grandmother and mother, or between mother and daughter. No illusion, that is, no stepping stone, is entertained or processed, so that *fear of death* is confused as *real death* and heroic efforts are made to transform or transfer that fear.

8. The transformation is made with such psychological rigidity that the experience of uncertainty is transformed into certainty, chaos is transmuted into a false but rigidly presented sense of order, violence is turned into protection, alcoholism into anorexia

nervosa, anorexia nervosa into bulimia, and, inter alia, *fantasies of a child's death* are embedded and thoroughly *concealed into a fettered protection.*

Briefly, a plural intersubjectivity exists in anorexia nervosa; an intersubjectivity that has a story to tell. It is a story about a mother and a daughter without precise boundaries between them, and who are equally impacted on by an anterior mother in the person of a grandmother. Between these three persons an ominous task must be performed. This task has to do with carrying out or avoiding some nameless dread. It is the anorexic whose struggle helps us determine and articulate this otherwise nameless dread as fear of death.

Let us now graphically represent our findings:

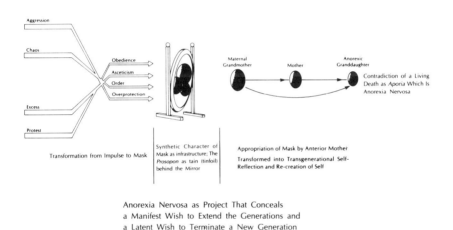

Anexoria Nervosa as Project That Conceals
a Manifest Wish to Extend the Generations and
a Latent Wish to Terminate a New Generation

Let us elaborate the contents of the sketch. Psychological rigidity is foregrounded to show what elements are transformed in the mother–anorexic daughter interpretation. We know of *rigidity* and how it may alternate with the experience of *chaos*. We know of anorexics' and their mothers' need to protect one another with every vehemence. Some describe this protection as "living a lie." And, we know how rigidly fixed this experience of "living a lie" is for them. Merleau-Ponty (1964) suggests that this "psychological rigidity" is only a *mask*:

> Beneath this rigidity one could easily find *real chaos* or at least *a divided personality*. Psychological rigidity . . . is what Freudians call a "reaction formation"; that is, a *facade* interposed by the subject between his psychological reality and others who are there to examine [her]. The principle of this formation is well known. If the individual is very aggressive he conceals his aggression under *an acquired veil of politeness*, and often the most apparently polite people are, at bottom, the most aggressive (p. 101; emphasis added).

Thus, there are features of a person that are separated so that one side acts as a mask, or screen, for the other side. One kind of behavior can be a *reaction* to the other. Borrowing from and transforming the work of an experimental psychologist named Frankel-Brunswick, who studied rigidity and its correlation with types of perception, Merleau-Ponty provides further descriptions of rigid subjects: "If they [rigid subjects] are questioned about their families in general they reply with *categorical affirmations*. Either the family is perfection itself . . . or it is horrible. In any case there are never nuances" (p. 101; emphasis added).

Following Merleau-Ponty, these categorical affirmations may be polarized as follows: concern with inessential, external traits as opposed to fear of detail and recognition of imperfection in important others; positive descriptions of parents as opposed to negative experiences of them; mild descriptions of parents as coercive or punitive as opposed to explicit or lively parental aggression. In Merleau-Ponty's view, these categorical affirmations constitute a mask with which they can avoid having to admit too much or having to accommodate ambiguity. The mask, therefore, puts a lid on the volume or extent of painful experiences and assists subjects to deal with confusion and ambivalence. In dichotomizing authority and obedience, cleanliness and dirt, good and evil, masculinity and femininity, the subject spares herself the anguish of having to negotiate or appropriate two related modes of existence.

In his articulation of ambivalence and how it is negotiated in rigid subjects, Merleau-Ponty (1964) appropriates and transforms the views of Melanie Klein, a child and adult psychoanalyst, quite successfully. Let us quote him in full to capture the impact of the connection he makes between *psychological rigidity* and *ambivalence*:

> Psychological rigidity can be found occasionally in all subjects, but it is only in an especially authoritarian environment that it becomes a

constant conduct, of which the child cannot rid himself. In this kind of authoritarian atmosphere the child divides the parent figure in half. On the one hand there is a kindly image of his parents that is willingly avowed, and on the other there is the image he is struggling against. As Melanie Klein has said, two images (the "good mother" and the "bad mother"), instead of being united in relation to the same person, are arranged by the child with the former prominent and the latter completely concealed from himself. When questioned, the child overtly recognizes only the favorable image, and is what, according to Melanie Klein, defines ambivalence. *Ambivalence consists in having two alternative images of the same object, the same person, without making any effort to connect them or to notice that in reality they relate to the same object and the same person* (pp. 102–103; emphasis added).

Having suggested what it means for the subject to separate the two images, good and bad, Merleau-Ponty borrows yet again from Klein in order to separate ambiguity and ambivalence:

As opposed to ambivalence, ambiguity is an adult phenomenon, a phenomenon of maturity, which has nothing pathological about it. It consists in admitting that the same being who is good and generous can also be annoying and imperfect (p. 103).

For Merleau-Ponty, therefore,

*ambiguity is ambivalence that one dares to look at face to face.* What is missing in rigid subjects is the capacity to confront squarely the contradictions that exist in their attitudes towards others (p. 103; emphasis added).

And,

emotional ambivalence is what demands the denial of intellectual ambiguity. In subjects whose intellectual ambiguity is strong, it often happens that the emotional foundation is much more stable than in other subjects (p. 105).

Our anorexics and their mothers are full of emotional ambivalence and resort to rigid categorizations. They are also weak in terms of their tolerance of ambiguity. It is for this reason that the mother of an anorexic may infuse in her daughter the precept that it is better to be outstanding in one subject area or goal than to attempt many others. A responding anorexic daughter may then become an outstanding gymnast and weak in her academic work. Hence the statement of one such child, "I became a star for my mother." Here a mother's project and a child's psychological rigidity converge to dismiss ambiguity and/or ambivalence. They cannot tolerate doubt, chaos, or conflict. They must focus and accomplish their mutual project brilliantly.

It is true, as Merleau-Ponty recognizes, that psychological rigidity can be found in many subjects and that it becomes a constant conduct under particular circumstances. He suggests the authoritarian environment as the seed for psychological rigidity. In our anorexics and their mothers there are authoritarian matriarchs, but the matriarchs are not the mothers of the anorexics; rather, the matriarchs are the maternal grandmothers. The anorexic and their mothers variously and repeatedly refer to these maternal grandmothers as "a mean, nasty woman, an alcoholic and drug abuser"; "a horrible mother," "a possessive mother," and so. It seems that clinicians have erred in locating pathogenesis in the mothers of anorexics and/or in the anorexics themselves, thus missing the observation in this study that *intersubjectivity is radically plural and not dual*.

It is an understandable error to think of intersubjectivity as dual because anorexics and their mothers imply it or suggest it when they speak or act as though they mirror each other. In the words of 002A, who sees her mother and herself reflecting each other:

> *I see myself in her and I see her in me.* Right now my illness affects her. She takes it as personally as I do. I see her watch for signs as to if I purge, then she takes it personally, and I on the other hand, find that when I have purged and I have made a mistake I feel like a little girl with her still, when I feel like she is disappointed in me . . . I can't lie to her. And I disclose entirely too much to her.

No sooner has this anorexic begun to describe how she and her mother mirror each other than we hear echoes of merger. From the point where she admits that she discloses "entirely too much" to her mother, she recognizes how much deeper the disclosure goes. She loses herself in her mother: "I guess I go over the boundaries sometimes."

In the same view, one mother, 005B, perceives the mirroring but we no longer have a twosome mirroring each other. Rather, we have a threesome mirroring each other through a shared subjectivity. This mother speaks to this issue:

> The lesson that I learned from my mother was being pleasing to other people. Please people first, that is the important thing, and the way

you do that is, you come in and *you assume whatever color and mood and opinion that is there*. In that way you will win friends and influence people. Of course you'd get lost in the process.

Or simply,

Be a *chameleon*; you should please people.

So sometimes the mirroring is observable in how an anorexic perceives her mother and in how she thinks her mother perceives her. At times they disappear into each other. At other times the twosome becomes a threesome which shares a familial and transgenerational view that one should teach one's child to be a chameleon. But there is yet one other kind of mirroring, as seen in 005A, where the daughter appropriates the role of a mother, becomes like her mother and coerces her mother into a role reversal. The reversal is also facilitated by the non-distinctness between inside and outside. The mother, 005B, mildly protests that her daughter is out of line:

She has a very parental kind of an attitude. She more often times will come over and *rearrange my cupboards and my cabinets.* . . . It's like a mother checking on her daughter rather than the opposite.

Whether anorexics and their mothers mirror each other in word or in deed, and lose themselves in each other, there is a dynamic and evolving process going on. Each person has a body and is a self. The anorexic, even with nondistinct boundaries, has a self. So does her mother, and so does mother's mother. Each is a subject. Each is a person for the other, and yet they have a shared subjectivity of one kind or another. Implicit in the subjectivity is that one should behave in a particular way to achieve or avoid some anxiety-laden issue. Through the shared anxiety-laden subjectivity, which may be named or nameless, they position themselves in relation to each other as figures of apposition. Ironically, the very individuals who dread ambiguity end up creating an appositional relatedness that is no less ambiguous than the original anxiety-provoking situation.

Having gathered instances of blurred boundaries or shared boundaries, instances of how self and other are compromised by anorexics and their parents, let us now examine these through a psychoanalytic lens to comment on interperception/interrelation and anorexia nervosa. Specifically, how is projective identification, that interpersonal mental mechanism and mode of unconscious communication which serves the function of obliterating boundaries between self and other, related to anorexia nervosa?

## PROJECTIVE INDENTIFICATION AND ANOREXIA NERVOSA

Projective identification (Klein 1946; Apprey 1987, 1988; Kulish 1988) is a composite mechanism that has the following elements: splitting, so that an individual may translocate an incompatible part of one's self or one's conflictual wishes; the subject's control of another individual or that individual's mental representation since such a claustrum or container holds a part of the subject's self; and including or retrieving that same incompatible self or behavior which had hitherto been translocated into another subject. In this study, we are told of subject 002A that she had swallowed her grandmother wholesale because subject was as critical of herself as her grandmother had been of subject when she came to live with the anorexic and her mother. We also learn from 002B, the mother, that the very fatness the grandmother hated in herself was indirectly injected into the anorexic grandchild by the way the grandmother taunted the grandchild, whose response was to become fat. My understanding of this transaction is that the grandmother, through behaviors she would or would not accept from her granddaughter, managed to transmit the very same parts of herself that she hated into her granddaughter—but with the mother's complicity.

This element of transmission of some incompatible part of self into the granddaughter with the mother's complicity comes out very clearly in subject 005A, who becomes named with the name that her grandmother originally intended for subject's mother. This name was not given to the mother because the grandmother became conflicted with "ethnic" names.

The function of projective identification is to obliterate boundaries and inject incompatible self units into others, in ways that control and immobilize the others, who are suitable targets or containers. Projective identification comes through as a fertile pathogen in anorexia nervosa. From Kristeva (1982) and from our subjects we can see that these pathogenic transmissions have a long history.

In short, our entire civilization is shadowed and foreshadowed by one story behind another. Deep within the universally woven fabric of maternal love, there persists a primordial strand of destruction. The confluence of anorexia nervosa and projective identification can be seen as a paradigmatic shuttle in this weaving between manifest maternal love and the primordial strand of destruction.

The shuttle between manifest maternal love and primordial destructive impulses is an aspect of Freud's death instinct, but it is much more sacrilegious. Here, mother's extension of this self-destructive impulse toward the bodily person of the other, with whom she shares imprecise boundaries, represents simultaneously hostile investments in others, who are her own body self, and in her own child, who is both a representative self and a composite figure for her forebears. Thus, derivative new editions and facsimiles of parental destructiveness underlie human development, illness, and clinical stories.

In anorexia nervosa, in particular, the shared subjectivity between mother and daughter carries discreet or overt amounts of hostility, where death is violently willed, originally by an ancient familiar, then transmitted through the anorexic's mother, and finally owned by the anorexic. However, since the murderous wishes now belong to all three, these wishes are vehemently held in check. The cost, though, to all three is that no one grows, or grows away. The anorexic lives a living death, as it were, for the others. Sadly, not all anorexics can survive this balancing act of living for oneself and living-in-death for others. Some capitulate to the transmitted whims of their ancient *mater*. They die. For this reason, I strongly disagree with Geist (1989), who insists that the symptomatology of anorexia nervosa represents neither unconscious compromises—in which control battles with parents are acted out—nor internalized societal preoccupation with thinness. For Geist, anorexia nervosa actualizes *only* life and death struggles to maintain self-coherence and integrity. This study provides results which Geist found and those which he rejects. Anorexics and their mothers, in our descriptive psychoanalytic study of perceptions between mother and daughter, reveal both unconscious compromises that are remembered in action, as well as struggles to maintain self-coherence in the face of disintegration anxiety.

## IMPLICATIONS OF FINDINGS FOR CLINICAL PSYCHOANALYTIC PRACTICE

Let us return now to descriptive psychoanalysis to identify some areas in the treatment of anorexia nervosa where our findings might be inserted. Four areas present themselves: (1) the history-taking process, which is a significant part of the data collection phase of treatment; (2) the diagnostic work, which allows us to process salient features from the history in ways that assist in eliminating competing diagnoses; (3) the formulation of treatment plans; (4) the implementation of treatment plans.

In the history-taking process we shall no longer be solely interested in the milestones of the adolescent anorexic and the genetic-developmental issues which intersect. In our attempts to come to grips with the possible environmental circumstances as to the causation of anorexia nervosa and the internal world which has rendered stable anorexic modes of adaptation, we shall remember that intersubjective factors play a crucial part in how this pathology takes hold upon its victims. Specifically, we shall remember that there are relations and perceptions that go beyond generations. This means that the mother of the anorexic must be seen not only as *the mother* but also, as *the child of her mother*. In other words, we must ask what unresolved issues between the mother and her mother carry over into the relationship and interperceptual world between the mother and the anorexic daughter. We shall remember that intersubjectivity is radically plural and that this plurality may account for the transmission of destructive projects from one generation to another.

In the diagnostic phase of treatment, we now have available to us possibilities as to the meaning of aggression and its implication in anorexia nervosa. Typically, a metapsychological diagnostic profile (Freud 1965) investigates before treatment the following: (a) the *quality* of manifest expressions of aggression, which include such tools of enactment as words, feet, sticks, and so on; (b) the quality of aggression as to whether it is barely or suitably modified, and if modified, its availability for sublimations; (c) the direction of aggression as to whether it is mainly inwardly directed or outwardly directed. In the diagnosis of anorexia nervosa we may no longer submit that aggression is thoroughly concealed and, as such, not investigate its derivative expression and the variations of meaning that present themselves. When we perceive *obedience*, we should wonder about *protest*. When we perceive *asceticism,* we should wonder about *fear of excess*. When we perceive *order*, we should wonder about *chaos*. When we perceive *overprotection*, we should wonder about *destructive aggression*. Furthermore, we should wonder what the vehicle of destructive aggression is in the family and what modes of transformation exist for its members. We should investigate the personal meanings of aggression for our clients. We should attempt to grasp what motivates their expression, as well as what motivates the concealment of aggression.

In the formulation of treatment plans we should investigate how particular treatment plans, particular forms of psychotherapy, particular forms of hospital treatment, and the like can accommodate activities or interventions that provide freedom or mental space for the patient to describe her intentional horizons. Specifically, we may have to consider modes of intervention that provide the anorexic and her family members *the freedom to describe* in favor of premature interpretations and constructions or reconstructions.

Finally, during treatment the anorexic daughter must be treated along with her mother. This is by no means a new recommendation. What is a new is that the mother of the anorexic must be treated in ways to suggest that she, too, is a victim. This reduces the possibility of the mother of an anorexic being blamed for "causing" her daughter's illness. Rather, the mother of an anorexic can now be empathized with because she, too, is part of a transgenerational struggle, where destructive aggression has constantly been nurtured and/or transformed.

When we approach our findings in this way, that is, as additional tools in the diagnostic and treatment processes, our recommendations can be inserted into any number of treatment models within psychoanalysis and outside psychoanalysis. They are intended to supplement rather than replace existing treatment methods. Where some of these tools are already in use, we suggest their consistent use until their efficacy is undermined by particular cases that require modifications. In any case, the question of who owns the body of the anorexic, which is an invariant issue in the treatment of this illness, is considerably broadened. It is now broadened to include variants of the following: Who am I, and who is my host? Who is my mother and how does she allow me to enter or stay in her world? Who is my mother and how is her world occupied by her mother and others? How do the guest and the host come to occupy the same body in the particular way that they do? Which of the two is a person and which is a figure? How many conversations are going on between the anorexic and her ancestors and what is presumed to be asked of one another in this transgenerational dialogue? These questions do not

exhaust the modes of entering the interhorizonal world of the anorexic
and her mother and grandmother. Nevertheless, they point a way to
clinical interventions that are more descriptive than constructed.

## SUMMARY

A data-based descriptive psychoanalytic study was conducted to
determine the nature of the reciprocal intersubjective perceptions and
relations between anorexic daughters and their mothers. Three mother–
anorexic daughter pairs were interviewed to provide the data base for
this discovery-oriented study. The praxis from phenomenological
psychology, as developed by Giorgi, was used to assemble the text
data, separate the text into meaning units, transform these meaning
units into psychologically meaningful data, and finally determine the
structure of experience of each subject. The structures of experience
of all six subjects were collapsed to give us the intersubjective
constitution of mother-daughter relationships in anorexia nervosa.
Having utilized a phenomenological praxis to analyze the data,
psychoanalytic thinking was used to elaborate the findings. According
to this study, we may no longer think of the shared subjectivity between
mother and daughter in terms of subject and object. Rather, it may
be more fruitful to consider the anorexic daughter, her mother, and
her mother's mother as each being both a subject and an object of
another person in that three-way relationship. Each is, therefore, an
appositive figure, a subject in her own right, yet potentially an object
who represents both self and (m)other. Each may be a conduit for
an anterior mother, and yet a perpetrator with projects of her own.

Psychoanalytic interpretation of the contents of these projects suggests that deep within mother-daughter transactions there persists a
prior agenda that includes a primordial strand of destruction. Anorexia nervosa combines so powerfully with destructive interperceptual
relations that destructive wishes and impulses may be injected into
an anorexic granddaughter with her mother's complicity. Consequently,
no individual grows into an individual in her own right. No one is
emancipated from those destructive and intrusive identifications. The
anorexic vicariously carries out an untenable balancing act for herself
and for the (m)others. She strives to live for herself and yet strives
to carry out the destructive wish infused into her by the anterior

maternal figure. The result is that, without treatment, she lives a *living death*.

With all these infusions, the interperceptual process between the anorexic and her mother goes beyond this dyad. Intersubjectivity in anorexia nervosa is thus radically *plural*, not dual. The mother's mother is an adhesive (m)other who independently of and/or collaboratively with her daughter shares an intersubjectivity with the anorexic granddaughter. In addition, this intersubjectivity, which goes beyond the anorexic's mother, may include relations with the anorexic's mother's father, where the latter may in part be "reborn" in the anorexic. The anorexic, then, is a composite figure, whose configurative world includes perceiving (m)other and being perceived in turn as a mask, a face, a mirror, a representation, and a real person. She stands in place of others, she reflects others, and replaces selective others, *at one and the same time*. She is a *prosopon*, (Greek for face, mask, character, person), as it were, for her mother and is in turn perceived as such.

# 2/ Projective Identification and Maternal Misconception in Disturbed Mothers

*Maurice Apprey*

The term *projective identification* has been used in many ways since Melanie Klein introduced it in 1946. I use it here to study intolerance of separation and motives such as envy, mistrust of dependency, and persecutory anxiety. In terms of motives we can differentiate it from other forms of delegation like projection and externalization; it is a defense set in motion after regression in the third trimester of pregnancy, especially during therapeutic regression, and after the physical separation of delivery. It entails the mother's retrieval of delegations when her child begins to move away, and can be transmuted by intervention into exploratory and empathic modes useful for the child's development.

This chapter reports a longitudinal study of women from the third trimester of pregnancy to four years after delivery. Interviews were designed to tap the subject's preoccupations and projects for her child that she developed preconsciously, unconsciously, or consciously.

I suggest that destructive projective identification is used to deal with excessive persecutory anxiety, envy, or intolerance of separation by disturbed or vulnerable mothers, militating against the child's progress toward autonomy. Relatively normal mothers use reaction formation and other ways of turning instinctual wishes around to bind anxiety and to reverse negative attitudes about their children. Thus, maternal misperception can be seen clinically in the context of

76

projective identifications; it may be reversed proactively when the clinician can use projective tests or clinical interviews to gather and classify projective identifications in order to help the mother retrieve them and keep her from impeding her child's development.

Projective identification is a unique mechanism of defense. I have argued elsewhere (Apprey 1985) that it involves the principle of multiple function. As a defense it mitigates anxiety. It is often a psychic representation of instinctual drives and related wishes. The analysand's unconscious wish for altering not only the subject's self representation but also the object's bespeaks urgency and omnipotence. The study of projective identification makes it possible to identify much unconscious behavior.

We may now define *projective identification* as *an unconscious defensive process which exteriorizes an incompatible aspect of one's self organization into a representation of an object in ways which permit the unburdening of an unacceptable attribute or the preservation of an aspect of one's self away from hostile primary process presences.* In the process of actualizing the delegated self organization, one maintains a phantasied picture of control and oneness with the object. The result is that there is a change in the subject's own self representation as well as a change in the perception of the object.

The term *projective identification* has so many meanings that it is difficult to establish a meaningful consensus, particularly since analysts adhere to various schools of thought. In discussing a paper by Kulish (1985), I held that we would gain more from exploring the function of projective identification—and the analysand's unconscious motives for using it—than from quibbling about defining it (Apprey 1985). At the descriptive phenomenological level we might be simply replacing one problematic definition with another. However we define it, we must describe its use. The motives for using projective identification explored here are the obliteration of differences between self and other, the intolerance of separation, and the aggressive control of the object.

Seeking to avoid debate on definition, I would simply like to base my study on Kernberg's definition. Kernberg (1984) suggested that projective identification has the following constituent factors: (1) the projection onto an object of an unacceptable part of the self; (2) empathy between the self and the recipient of the projection; (3) a wish to control the object; and (4) an unconscious wish to induce in the object what is projected. He indicated that although there is empathy between self and object in projective identification, there is none in projection. Kleinians, however, have invariably been aware that what is translocated from the self to the other need not always be a bad or incompatible part of the self. Sometimes, a whole self representation can be housed in another for safekeeping.

Thus, in projective identification good parts of the self can be delegated to the object, impoverishing the self and idealizing the object. If we now unpack Kernberg's definition, the mother under study here can be seen using projective identification in relation to her baby as follows:

(1) Delegating unacceptable parts of her self onto the object, her infant:
  the baby is mean = I am mean
  she is spoiled = I am spoiled
  she bites people
(2) Empathizing with the object:
  my baby is quiet = I am quiet
  my baby is attractive = I am attractive
(3) Controlling:
  I can't bear her to be away from me
(4) Inducing in the object what has been projected:
  I fear that her temper, like mine, will get between us
  I fear that her stubbornness, like mine, will get between us.

Yet the mother unconsciously injects into her baby the original spite, meanness and aggression in her own self organization. The result is that her own self representation and that of her baby undergo alteration. These factors are empirically examined to follow the vicissitudes of projective identification in pregnancy psychotherapy.

According to James Grotstein (1981), *projective identification* is:

> a mental mechanism whereby the self experiences the unconscious fantasy of translocating itself, or aspects of itself, into an object for exploratory or defensive purposes. If projective identification is defensive, the self may believe that through translocation it can rid itself of unwanted, split off aspects; but it may also have the phantasy that it can enter the object so as to (actively) control it, or disappear into it (passively) in order to evade feelings of helplessness (p. 123).

He distinguishes projective identification, which follows the principle of generalization, from splitting, which follows that of distinction. In a departure from Melanie Klein (1946) Grotstein suggests that:

> in its more positive sense, projective identification is responsible for vicarious introspection and, in its most sublimated form, for empathy. . . . As a primitive mechanism of communication it exists *first between preverbal infants* and their mothers, but is also residual in adult life as a form of affective communication. . . . Employed defensively primitive identification rids the contents of one's mind or, when the experience is severe, the mind itself. An object, hitherto separate, becomes either *the container for the alienated and mediated contents, or confused with it through identification emphasis added* (p. 124).

Thus, a prime motive for using projective identification is to lose the sense of separateness. Grotstein speaks of its *empathic* or *exploratory nondefensive* use, but I hold that it can become nondefensive when used empathically or for exploring an external object.

The descriptive phenomenological use of the term *externalization* should be separated from the metapsychological use of the term *projective identification*. What is most relevant is that both may help us see the unconscious motives behind a particular defense against a particular unacceptable idea, or the separation of one source of anxiety from another. Projection indicates instinctual anxiety, but externalization bespeaks fear arising from outside. Projective identification obliterates separation and promotes dedifferentiation.

Although the mechanisms of defense that use delegation, exteriorization, or the relocation of aspects of the self onto another can easily be confused (referred to interchangeably as *projective identification, projection*, and *externalization*), we can identify each according to what unconscious motives dictate its use. Meltzer (1967) suggests that the major "motives underlying the tendency to massive projective identification" (p. 14) can be "intolerance of separation; omnipotent control; envy; jealousy; deficiency of trust; excessive persecutory anxiety."

> Intolerance to separation can be said to exist where there is present an absolute dependence on an external object in order to maintain integration. This can be seen in autistic and schizophrenic children in whom the need for physical contact, or constant attention, or to be held

in constant verbalization, reveals the absence of the psychic equivalent
to the skin. They require an external object to hold together the parts
of the self so as to form an area of life space inside the self which
can contain the objects of psychic reality (p. 14).

Here intolerance of separation is a primary motive for projective
identification, but the others noted are inseparable from it. The mothers
studied showed their projective identification primarily through intolerance of separation, but the other motives were present in their
intrapsychic negotiations with themselves and their babies.

> Laplanche and Pontalis (1973) suggest that projective identification which
> is closely associated with the paranoid-schizoid position, consists in the
> fantasied projection of split-off parts of the subject's own self—or even
> his whole self (not just partial bad objects) into the interior of the
> mother's body, so as to injure and control the mother from within. This
> phantasy lies at the root of such anxieties as the fear of being im-
> prisoned and persecuted within the mother's body (p. 356).

In another mode, however, "projective identification may result in
introjection being experienced as a forceful entry from the outside
into the inside, in retribution for violent projection" (Klein 1946).
Laplanche and Pontalis (1973) see it "as a mode of projection" and
add that "if Klein speaks of identification here it is because it is the
subject's self that is projected."

The descriptive use of the term *projection* is not interchangeable
with the metapsychological; Freud gave it a specific meaning, certain
aspects of which have been retained in spite of subsequent variations.
One uses projection to rid the ego of anxiety associated with unac
ceptable or incompatible instinctual wishes by *exteriorizing* them or
*relocating* them in an object. In true projection, however, the hitherto
exteriorized wish now delegated to an external object boomerangs as
a threat, apparently coming from outside against the subject's own
self. Freud's early descriptions of projection in paranoia, phobic
constructions, and jealousy indicate this. Here, when a mother projected
her aggressive wishes onto her baby, she was unconsciously manipu-
lating the return of the delegated aggression. She often then misper-
ceived its behavior and conflict was compounded; negotiations between
mother and child were tense, conflictual and anxiety-laden. Externalization, seen as linear and lacking the boomerang effect of true
projection, is used to avoid blame and attack on self-esteem or to

counter fear from the external world. Projection, on the other hand, relieves the ego of instinctual or superego anxiety.

## PROJECTIVE IDENTIFICATION AND MATERNAL MISPERCEPTION

Nover and her collaborators (1985) observed that mothers were less socially interactive with their babies and less emotionally available when (1) they had a distorted perception of them, and (2) when they thought their behavior abnormal. The babies' sleep disturbance was associated with maternal perceptions and interactive behavior; infants of unresponsive mothers tended to sleep less than others. Mothers who scored high on overall anxiety scored lower on contingent responsiveness, and higher on frequency of misperception and on some selected distortion items.

When maternal distortions became pathological, Nover and her collaborators asked whether the difference between maternal misperception in normalcy as opposed to pathology was a difference between preconscious awareness of misperception and unconscious projective identification. Their study noted the extent, frequency, and direction of maternal misperception. To answer the question about preconscious awareness and projective identification they would have had to study the content of the distortions and their qualitative changes over time. One might consider projective identification the primary content of maternal misperceptions, and expect intervention to change these misperceptions from being defensive or destructive to being empathic and exploratory, promoting adaptive interaction and the child's development and reducing the mother's conflictual sense of self. Since childbearing greatly alters the mother's internal world, it seems better to consider the risk to her or her child rather than to try to identify its pathology.

Bell (1982) notes that

> the concept of risk implies the ability to identify groups of individuals who, on the average, do not show a disorder, or only show components of the disorder, but who have a statistically significant likelihood of showing the disorder in full form at a later time, in comparison with a non-risk group (p. 46).

Such a concept of risk applies to such a wide range of pathological conditions such as schizophrenia, learning disabilities, delinquency, addictions, and child abuse. But Bell goes on to say, if "we see risk as a transaction between the individual and the environment, rather than as a property of the individual, it should not be surprising that individuals move in and out of risk status" (p. 53). Bell advocates assessing risk to determine the need of intervention to prevent behavioral disorder; the risk should outweigh developmental and situational changes. One should also consider age-specific manifestations and ultimate outcome, distinguishing them from the fundamental basis for risk to allow for anomalies. Such distinctions make it possible to accommodate a child's moving in and out of risk as far as age-specific manifestations are concerned, although without necessarily changing the basis for defining risk. Knowledge of a woman's development or life history, the basis for risk, and age-specific manifestations points to the best time and mode of her intervention. I find Bell's observations about risk status particularly helpful in offering psychological support to expectant mothers.

Raphael-Leff (1982), reporting on the psychotherapeutic needs of expectant mothers, systematizes "Personal Risk Factors":

1. *Over-valued pregnancies*: repeated miscarriage, sterility, previous stillbirth, prenatal death, or pseudocyesis;
2. *Ambivalent pregnancies*: those unwanted or occurring in adolescence or for the first time after 35; feminine revolt; lack of support;
3. *Life events*: accidents, serious family illness, bereavement, divorce, eviction, redundancy, emigration;
4. *Historical sensitization*: mother's death in childbirth, sibling's abnormality or stillbirth, subject's having been adopted or born posthumously, eating disturbances (p. 13).

## REASONS FOR PSYCHOTHERAPY IN PREGNANCY

Many contradictions and paradoxes are involved in giving psychological support to the pregnant woman. Although a crisis, pregnancy is not an illness; and although it gives the woman a chance to progress developmentally, she is likely to regress. Also, the act of delivering a baby may be a psychological way of delivering its mother from her own mother. Having treated pregnant women in individual and group psychotherapy, and following their cases for an average of four years, I am impressed with the complexities of providing what is now called *pregnancy psychotherapy.*

Like Benedek (1977) I see motherhood as a developmental stage in which the girl becomes like her mother but fulfills her early yearnings to be free of her. Although a young woman feels reborn in her child, her delight in it is marred by the persistent hatred of her mother. The "happiness of motherhood" is often an illusion, and pregnancy is a period of crisis that brings fears about the body and possible damage to it. It does not dispel old conflicts. An awareness of being competent wars with an unacknowledged failure to keep worries about being "a bad mother" repressed, and depression results. The young woman's anxiety about being ugly, unwanted, and unlovable threatens her relationship with her infant. Urged to breast-feed but reluctant to do so, the new mother may use a bottle to avoid close partnership with the baby, and feel guilty. The helplessness and passivity with which she may try to avoid blame do not promote competent nurturing. Having a baby may indeed threaten the very survival of a psychotic woman.

Childbearing necessitates mourning for the loss of one's ideal self. Some women adopt a child to avoid labor, which represents not only a threat of bodily harm but conscious and unconscious fears of bodily incompetence. Adoption may be a way to avoid blame by being passive. Some women feel an unconscious need to be punished in retaliation for what their mothers suffered in bringing them into the world; and many who are pregnant feel guilt at having conceived. ("If I told my mother I am pregnant, it would kill her.") Some dread the idea of losing control and "making a mess" when delivering.

The prospect of having a baby evokes the conscious idealization of the mother as a complete woman, worthy of emulation, that the now-pregnant girl had entertained as a child. She unconsciously wants to have all her badness and failures expunged, phantasying the need to be a good little girl in her mother's eyes. This is like the fear of midwives whose perceived competence is a standard against which the younger mother feels like an imposter. She is afraid of being unable to live up to what will be expected of her; the psychotic, potentially suicidal woman in this situation may fear her child's outstripping her. We know from visits in the home that when relatives tell a depressed new mother to let someone else wash the diapers, she is likely to feel herself a failure. A Caesarian section, which lets a woman avoid affirmation of mature female competence, may affect the woman's subsequent sexual life. The persistent unconscious desire to be a little girl and the fear that the responsibility of child care is incompatible with this may make a new mother aggressive toward her child. Since she expects to be capable in an adult way but feels like a little girl, she considers herself an imposter, not a real mother. This makes her afraid that physical examination will disclose a lack of maturity—or make her phantasy of being still a child untenable.

To be a successful mother a woman must be able to regress appropriately for childish play with her baby; and she must forgive the child whose sex is a disappointment. One young mother felt that she had lost a little girl when she gave birth to a boy and had to mourn her "loss."

In analytic work one can soften the primitive superego and mobilize loving feelings to compensate for any belief that the self or internal objects have been hurt. In the absence of such treatment it is well for the new mother's mother to help care for the baby, so that the new mother can incidentally get some mothering herself, placate her mother by following in her footsteps, and gain approval for her own motherhood. The baby's father should encourage the new mother to feel still lovable, sexual, and intact, lest distress threaten maltreatment of the child or its surrender to an adoptive or foster home. The therapist should be alert to the absence of such support and realize in any case that the young mother may feel like a child waiting to be told what to do. In coping with the mother who must regress in play with her child but maintain a well-functioning ego, the therapist is likely to be tempted to take command.

Otherwise humane and loving women are sometimes unsettled by the psychological pain of childbearing. Winnicott (1947/1975) noted that hatred often appears in the mother-child relationship:

> The baby is not her own mental conception. . . . It is a danger to her body in pregnancy, and at birth, and interferes with her private life. . . . It has been produced to placate the new mother's mother . . . its nursing is painful, and it is ruthless, treating her like a slave. . . . She has to love him, secretions and all . . . till he has doubts about himself. . . . When he gets what he wants, he forgets her. . . . She must not

be anxious about holding him. . . . He does not appreciate what she does and sacrifices for him. . . . He makes no allowances for her hate, is suspicious, refuses her good food, but eats well with his aunt, making her doubt herself. . . . After she has had an awful morning with him, he will smile at a stranger, who exclaims, "Isn't he sweet!" . . . If she fails him now he will get even later. . . . He excites but frustrates her. . . . She mustn't eat him or trade in sex with him (p. 201).

The new mother marshals a whole army of defenses to protect herself from such hateful feelings, perhaps using reaction formation to overcompensate, to be as loving as possible. She may displace her hateful feelings onto someone else, or project then onto the child, only to be victimized all over again by fantasying that the child is an aggressor. She may try to avoid blame by externalizing unacceptable feelings, or may adopt some defense to transform them into affects acceptable to society or to her ego.

It is surprising that the crucial issue of projective identification has had so little attention in pregnancy psychotherapy. The Bibring studies (1959, 1962) on psychological processes in pregnancy and defenses used in early mother-child relating do not consider it. Anna Freud (1967) saw its role in loss but made only casual reference: "We take it for granted that we feel unhappy and miserable after losing one of our possessions, even if these moods are hardly justified by the circumstances" (p. 308). She wrote of the sense of deprivation over the lost object's subjective value and of guilt over the possibility that it was lost intentionally.

We notice, first, that the loser seems to ascribe some independent action to the lost object. He can be heard to say, "I have lost something, mislaid it, forgotten where I put it, etc.," but equally often: "It got lost," or "It has come back" (pp. 3–9).

In a footnote Anna Freud (1967) refers to "projective identification, a concept introduced by Melanie Klein in 1932." Klein described a process related to the importance of the concept of projective identification and hence evoked by loss and intolerance of separation. A threat or dread of loss often appears in pregnancy, especially when the woman has had a previous miscarriage or an abnormal child. Accident, divorce, bereavement, stillbirth—and the possibility of having been adopted—seem to threaten.

## CLINICAL LANDMARKS IN THE UTILIZATION OF PROJECTIVE IDENTIFICATION

The defense mechanism of projective identification is currently central to psychoanalysis, psychoanalytical psychotherapy, and dynamic psychiatry, but it is particularly stressed by the Kleinian school, perhaps because of its work with psychotic or near-psychotic patients. Kleinians often induce deep therapeutic regression that reveals a primitive defensive form of projective identification, and they have reported psychotic manifestations in neurotic patients.

This study is new in taking projective identification out of the consulting room and observing it empirically among 48 childbearing women in the course of research on clinical intervention. Recordings of interviews based on structured and semistructured questions showed changes in its quality as the program unfolded. A sequence was apparent: (1) *the gathering of projective identifications*: prenatal observations disclosed much about their nature and motivation; (2) *the emergence of components of projective identification*: after the birth the components of projective identification, including projection, displacement, identification, and other forms of delegation, began to emerge; (3) *the return/retrieval/reowning of projective identifications*: when her child was about a year old, the typical mother began *retrieving* delegations hitherto exteriorized and located in the child; and (4) *the emergence of empathic projective identification*: with intervention the mothers began to transform massive, intrusive, or destructive projective identification into an empathic form useful for exploring and serving their children's developmental needs.

The four phases were phenomenologically consistent with some physical changes. During the third trimester the physical symbiosis of the mother and fetus paralleled the emotional identification of mother and child; this in turn paralleled emotional symbiosis with the new mother's own mother. This three-way interaction between the phantasied infant, the new mother, and her mother, along with physical stress, brings considerable regression, and even in clinical intervention research, treatment promotes more therapeutic regression. The patient then tends to use primitive defenses, including projective identification, to deal with separation anxiety. The physical separation of the postpartum period reduces projective identification, and this evokes component defenses.

When a child begins moving away from its mother, its drive needs such as hunger cannot be defensively wished away by the mother, who must meet its needs with realistic planning. When her parenting strategies prove successful, she feels a mature sense of herself as a mother and cannot connect the original projective identification with mature, realistic nurturing techniques that serve her child's developmental needs. Psychotherapy for expectant mothers should thus focus on preventing pathogenesis or on the removal of such risk factors as ambivalence and overvaluation of pregnancy due to maternal misperception.

## AUDIOTAPED RECORDINGS AS DATA BASE

A related systematic study of socio-affective development in disturbed mothers' perceptions of and interactions with their infants was reported by Hoffheimer and Apprey (1989). I base my limited inquiry here on audiotaped recordings of what mothers said about themselves and their interaction with their babies. The chapter appendix includes the Caretaker Perception Profile (CCP) used to elicit verbal responses from mothers in clinical interviews.

Caretaker Perceptual Profiles (Liebermann et al. 1977) of 48 mothers and clinical descriptions of their preconscious utterances were studied for the manifest and latent content of projective identification. Structured and semistructured questions were asked about the subject's unconscious phantasies about her baby before and after its delivery— in the third trimester; three days after delivery; at four, eight, and twelve months; at two and three years; and, in some cases, four years after delivery. The CPP was one of the assessment tools of a National Institute of Mental Health (NIMH) infant research project (Hoffheimer and Apprey 1989).

Content of the CPP was analyzed retrospectively. Subjects were initially divided into groups A, B, and C. Group A had only assessment, but group B subjects were referred to community agencies and were assessed by our clinical research team from NIMH, which gave group C both intervention and assessments. There was a significant policy change after 15 were assigned to each group; some group A subjects had serious breakdowns and one was taken over by a court's protective service; and a few members of group A and group B had to be transferred for intervention and assessment to group C. Then

all were put in group C to minimize the hazards of absent or failed
intervention. Although all the subjects were at risk, some came from
general hospitals or pediatric outpatient clinics and some were self-
referred. Five years after the project started, the 48 in group C had
been given comprehensive assessment that included periodic interviews, home observation, psychological tests, Brazelton Neonatal
Behavioral Assessment, pediatric examinations, the Caretaker Perceptual Profile and other protocols. Individual and group psychotherapy, toddler groups, work with families and liaison-consultation work
with pediatricians were made available. Transcribed interviews were
studied for content to determine the clinical landmarks in the use of
projective identification by all subjects.

It should be stated that all the subjects had had a first or second
baby before entering the study. I am not able at this point to verify
empirically that there is a drastic difference in maternal misperception
when a mother is a first-time mother from when she is an experienced
mother, as it were. I can only state that, from my preliminary research
experience and from clinical observations, there is little or no difference. Each baby is indeed a suitable target for some kind of parental
project. For constitutional and other reasons which I cannot go into
in this limited study, some children succeed in rejecting the delegated
attribution and others fail to do so.

The clinical descriptions of five mothers below will give further
examples of utterances with reference to time. The emphasis on the
utterances above is simply on the emotional shifts in the emotional
world of the mother. In the throes of regression disturbed mothers
are at the mercy of conscious, preconscious, or unconscious impulses.
Intervention, which in the Clinical Infant Development Program
included individual and group therapies, home visits, infant assessments and feedback sessions, and consult-liaison services with pediatric
units, made it possible to reduce the emotional pain they experienced.
In the experimental group destructive projective modes were reversed
after several months of intervention. Similar changes in the control-
group were less systematic, but an occasional control-group patient
was psychologically minded enough to use the feedback from assessments as if they had been actual psychotherapeutic interventions.
Although more research is needed to confirm these preliminary findings,
we can see in the following clinical descriptions how mother and
infant affect each other, and how intervention leads to progressive

steps that help the infants remain on course in psychic and physical maturation.

## CLINICAL DESCRIPTIONS

The clinical descriptions were obtained from responses to structured and semistructured questions in the Caretaker Perception Profile administered from the third trimester to toddlerhood (see chapter appendix). The time frames were not all synchronous, for in intervention research, conflict, transference, and other technical issues can interfere with data collection. Nonetheless, we had a unique situation in which mothers themselves spoke about their inner world and its influence on their caregiving.

Observations acquired from retrospective inspection of our data from mother-infant intervention research will enable us to intervene proactively on much firmer ground. We will be more sensitive to the points of tension in the mother-infant interaction, beginning with the prenatal period, and will be able not only to further anticipate and recognize the nature of anxiety-laden conflicts in mothers and how they are transmitted to the child, but to know with greater assurance what intervention methods are appropriate and effective. Below are five mothers addressing some of their hopes, fears and anxieties, conflicts, and other concerns, however irrational some may be. The mothers' pain and eventual joy are the central focus of this inquiry.

## [*Case 1*]

**Prenatally.** This mother's "feelings run in so many different directions concerning the birth of this baby and the pregnancy itself. I guess a lot of fears and a lot of anticipation on its arrival and what it will be like." But because she herself feels "different," she expects that the child will be different, too. She is upset that "everyone is already labeling it a certain way" because "it has really been a very strainful pregnancy." These concerns come after a question about how close the mother feels she will be to her baby. It seems she herself fears that what mother is, so her child will be; if mother is troubled, she will have a troubled baby—hence her attributive projection that other people are "predestining what the baby is going to be." In the midst of this turmoil she is anxious that other people's "remarks toward

that baby . . . really shape how the baby will be as a person." She
herself clearly wants good things for her child, who is to have "big
eyelashes, lots of curly hair, a nice big smile." After her protest that
negative identification can be forced upon a child, and after wishing
for good things for the child, she realizes there is something incongru-
ous about her protests and wishes: "It just sounds funny to be saying
things like that. It's like you are making little orders or something"
(laughter). It is as if *wishes* amounted to *"little orders."* Nevertheless,
for this mother, what others label, predestine, or wish upon the baby
could materialize. What she herself wants for her baby could materialize, too, but she has greater trust in the actualization of what she
perceives others to be wishing for it.

**4 months.** The mother is noticeably relieved that her projections did
not materialize. She has given birth to twins. Her children "don't have
any particular type of illness or development problem or anything like
that. They have all their limbs. They can see and hear. They seem
to be growing fine." As a result she feels particularly close to them.
"They are happy personalities" and "they make me feel like a mother."
The disorganization of this mother is noticeably absent during this
period. She exhibits relative psychic equilibrium and can now enjoy
her babies and the emergent harmony in herself.

**12 months.** At 12 months the mother discovers to her surprise that
babies are delightful not only when small, dependent, and frail, she
can enjoy them when they are "semitoddlers." She enjoys the pleasant
mutuality and reciprocity inherent in mothering: "I give to them, they
give to me." With this in mind she can foster both children's need
for closeness and separateness.

**2 years.** This mother's development as a mother continues. She used
to enjoy babies only when they were small and dependent, but she
now sees their merits when they are older. Their autonomy can bring
rewards even when they seem stubborn. She says quite aptly of one
child: *"She is growing older and she is growing away.* I mean, she
is *growing up now*, and she is *not a little baby* any more, and you
kind of look back but, you know, it's all for the better." She can allow
her child to be different, free from her projects, projections, and so
on. Asked how child K. is different from her, she replies:

> Oh! K. is different from me when, uh, well, as I say, she's very mis-
> chievous, and she's very adventurous. *She had more opportunity in her*

*stage of development* from infant to toddler than I have had because when I grew up, *there were problems in my development that my mother might have been aware of,* but that she really couldn't do anything about because she didn't have the *resources to deal with me in a more understanding way.* So I feel that in terms of development and in terms of environment, K. has a much better start, and she has had much more advantages than I had, and I can really, you know, give thanks to God for that. ...

What tremendous shifts! Even better than her understanding of her construction of her own genetic developmental issues is this mother's ability to put her understanding into an *empathic* mode of parental intervention when her child needs correcting:

I just have to explain things to her in a way that she can understand, and I think it helps when you take time to talk to them, instead of just shifting them off to a room or something: you just tell them to be quiet because a lot of times people don't realize that although children are children, that they have minds of their own, *they have their own thoughts and their feelings,* and a lot of times when it comes to correcting them, people seem to forget that.

## [*Case 2*]

**Prenatally.** This mother uses projective modes to deal with her intolerance of separation. It is as if she were saying, "If I have a boy, then I can have Mike, Sr. If I can keep Mike, Jr., I can hang on to my man": "If I have a boy, I will have a little man, a big boy. If I have a beautiful child, then I am attractive, too." Mother's preconscious attributions center around the child being beautiful to reverse ugliness and damage. She is anxious about aggression ("I'll never kill a baby if I didn't have to"). For this mother the hands can damage and distort. The child will make her feel complete. She will have narcissistic completion and through the little child—miniature Mike— she can hang on to her man.

**4 months.** Physical separation has now been forced on the mother by the delivery. To spare her ambivalence toward the child and to reverse the fear of killing or losing the child, or the fear of being controlled by it, she resorts to defensive maneuvres to gain homeostasis: *reaction formation* and the conversion of sadistic wishes into a passive experience of being the *victim of her child's demands.* Instead of expressing fear of her child's being little, she speaks of its as big:

instead of hearing of her aggression, we hear about her child's being asleep. Instead of facing the fact that he is not perfect, she claims perfection for him; instead of deprecating his appearance, she declares he is gorgeous. Another defensive component of projective identification is *undoing*, as when the mother undoes her sadism by making a joke of it. When she feels controlled, she controls. This mechanism *turns passive into active*.

**12 months.** Why does this mother take back her attributions? The reality of her child's needs, behavior, and drive demands dawns on her. His maturation forces her to face his separateness. Such defenses as splitting do not work; she has to acknowledge her female children's aggression, which she had hitherto delegated to the boy child. Soon the delegation has to be dismantled as well but only to a point—when similarity between her and the girls provides a point of reference. Differences between him and her disorganize her so she beat submission into her son through discipline and punishment to meet her unconscious desire that he will be unlike his father.

**2 years.** This mother's son must not be aggressive like his father, and not even male. She prefers to sit him on a pot or dress him up as a girl, and so on. He must be like her: loving, caring, feminine, compassionate. Her disorganization defends against her savage response to her child's maleness, which she denies when she pries him away from his tractor, and sees him at the tender age of two as a man of God—frocked as a minister. The price she pays for her unconscious and preconscious attribution is that she falls apart; the psychotic picture is a defense against the greater catastrophe of a murderous rage.

**3 years.** In the CPP three years after her child's birth this mother turns sadism into caring, showing shifts even in a single interview. The child now resists his mother's projection but submits from time to time. His insistence on playing with his tractor is the first evidence of his refusing his mother's intrusion by being objectionable when she wants to be always in control. At these times his mother refers to his behavior as his "two-year-old attitude," deprecating his emerging phallicism. However, *to ward off his fear of being abandoned if he doesn't oblige his mother, the child submits to mother's effort to force him to be like her.* The mother's rage at her son's failure to be submissive comes out when she blames him even when it is his sisters who are misbehaving. She would prefer his being a dancer to being a pilot. But towards the end of the three-year interview there is some promise of her relinquishing her hold on him, partly because of his own steps toward autonomy and partly because of clinical intervention. *Now she has resigned herself to taking care of nursery school children, rather than seeing little Mike as big Mike; there is a dawning awareness that she is going to lose him as infant. It is inevitable. He has to grow away.*

## [*Case 3*]

**Prenatally.** In the third trimester the expectant mother states, "I've never not felt close to my babies." She expects to be close to her child after birth. She says she likes infants who are small and dependent and can feel close to them. She expects this child to be born with dark hair and blue eyes. She does not expect to be nervous about it at birth. There is a relative absence of projections and destructive attributions on to this child.

**12 months.** This mother reports that she loves her child "so much." Except "there is only one thing about her that does get on my nerves in the way she screams, but she is learning now, I'm telling her, 'no, no.' She screams sometimes real loud, it's just a piercing scream. . . ." The mother feels "a little too close" to the child and is hardly ever separated from her: "the child is always in our bedroom," although the parents discuss whether she should not "sleep somewhere else." As in the prenatal interview this mother's use of double negatives, such as "I don't usually hardly ever have any negative feelings," is provocative, and may indicate her ambivalent cathexis of the child. Nevertheless, the loving feelings towards her child are greater than the occasional outbursts of negative feelings: "I enjoy her lovableness . . . I think I have a real, uh, wonderful personality baby." The relative absence of projections and destructive attributions upon the child continues.

**2 years.** The predominance of this mother's positive feelings towards her child continue to generate good feelings from the child. The child's objections, such as "no, Mommy, no" when she does not want to eat any more or do something else after she had been satisfied, are accepted by the mother and understood in the right context. The mother understands the child's yearnings to be autonomous, and we discover why she is able to free this child from her projections or destructive attributions: "Since I was a twin, there is a lot of ways I had to [be different] I feel I was repressed in a lot of my things that I could have been, and I think I am trying in a way to help her, and she is also being able to let herself be herself as an individual, which I couldn't do." We see now why this child is not a suitable target for her mother's projections and externalizations.

## [*Case 4*]

**Prenatally.** The mother states that she is "tired of carrying the baby." The baby is in her way, she insists, and for that reason she does not "want to talk about the baby." Nonetheless, she adds some comments that reveal her inner thoughts and expectations: "I think I am going to have a baby boy ... a strong baby boy, a bouncing baby boy." He is going to be "mean, because I am." The mother will not like his crying, which will make her feel negative about him.

**4 months.** This mother thought she would have a baby boy but has a girl instead. But the girl "is a good baby, she doesn't cry much, she is fun and delightful, she likes people, and likes to talk and play with other people and herself." In addition, "I can see her learning and growing." Seeing her daughter as delightful, the mother recognizes that she feels "differently about her now" than she did before "when you asked me these questions. But now I feel more together about her, and I feel closer to her in a better, very sure, and understanding way." Notice that in the four-month interview this mother has begun to institute reaction formations and repressions to deal with the hostility toward the infant in the prenatal interview: "I don't even get made if she pees on me or has a bowel movement, even when I have just changed her. It doesn't bother me. I don't know what I told you before, it doesn't matter, but now she is great. I do like her. I'm crazy about her." However, there is a limit to how much reaction formation can overcompensate negative feelings about the baby, and how effective repression can be in keeping down unacceptable thoughts of the mother. This mother likes her child because she is good, "pretty, just like me," is "very soft and has a soft complexion." But she still wishes she had a boy child to fit her original projective identification;

having a girl has forced her to drop most of the original attributions, although some remain. "She looks like a boy, still." In spite of some of these uncertainties, her sense of self as a mother has begun to emerge. Asked what makes her feel like a mother, she says that responsibilities make her feel like one. In addition, "I am hooked on the fact of the word 'Mommy.' I feel more mature now. I am not pregnant now. The babies are older. I can move around more." Mobility is important to this woman; in the prenatal interview she focused on the relative immobility of pregnancy to articulate her hostility towards the child. Four months after delivery she is using her sense of greater mobility to articulate her relative sense of freedom from her destructive feelings towards the child and her emergent sense of self as a mother.

**8 months.** Eight months after her child's birth it seems that this mother is going to maintain the gains of the previous interview in which she began to acknowledge her child's relative independence: "She's not like the other kids." Also, in the previous interview she said of her expected child: "I can see her learning and growing. . . ." Now her attribution to the child's relative understanding is articulated in this way: "Well, Mom, you've got things to do, and I see how busy you are, and I'll be cool and play by myself." While this mother is trading her articulation of her understanding of her child with her child's understanding of her as mother, she begins to disorganize: "What did you ask me?" The disorganization was evident in the rest of the eight-month interview. To the question "when do you feel close to your baby," she responds.

> I forget about her sometimes when, not really forget about her, I know she is mine and I got her and all, but when I am not there, say when I am working or if I am away, you know when I'm so busy or something. I have to keep my mind on what it's on. Even so, I think about my other kids like my oldest daughter and all. With her, I feel closer to her. You know, when I'm right there I can see her and I know she's there in the house.

And to the question "what makes you feel like a mother?":

> I just have to feel, I mean, you know, I live with it. I am a mother. I beared the pain and, you know, the experience and the time. Everything I do, really, I do things for myself, I sometimes wonder. I question the fact about me being that individual but, you know, not to the extent

to where I did before because I can find myself sometimes, but other
than that, I'm Mom all the time. I don't know if that is good or not.

The dysfluency and disorganization in this otherwise articulate
woman are startling. Conflict about the child's growing independence,
and anxiety about the mother's own instinctual trends, such as her
previously warded-off hostility towards her child have resurfaced, and
by their disruption of her psychic equilibrium, have contaminated her
verbal utterances.

**12 months.** At twelve months the mother has recovered from her
regressed state. She sees that her child is still happy, very active, with
a good appetite, sleeps well, plays well with people, is cute when
she is by herself, and so on, but "I don't feel negative about this baby
any more." In the past the mother feared that the child's crying would
antagonize her, but now she interprets her child's cries as messages:
"She cries for me. . . ." But the disorganization has not altogether
disappeared; it threatens to reappear towards the end of the interview:
"She looks like her Mom and, um, 'cause she's a small baby she
concentrates and studies."

**18 months.** There is a great improvement in the mother's psychological functioning as a mother, her articulation of her sense of self
as a mother and of the work of mothering. She sees her child as a
"very smart" infant, who plays well by herself, is strong, and whose
"legs stretch so far I think she is double-jointed." Still the child is
"very lovable" and will be "very intelligent." "I think she is like my
brother . . . I feel it's this instant attraction when I think of both of
them."

**2 years.** The improvement is maintained, and the mother is once
again coherent and articulate: "I feel good about being a mother. I
felt there was a big chance with the last baby. I really feel fantastic
about it. I grew with them. . . ."

## [*Case 5*]

**Prenatally.** This mother wants to be a better mother to the expected
child than she had been to her first. She wants a boy child this time;
he could protect his sister when he is older and she gets into trouble.
She herself now has a new boyfriend, who treats her better than her
first boyfriend. Things will be different because, in the mother's view,

when her first boyfriend beat her up, she in turn beat up her daughter: "I think that some of what he did to me rubbed off on me hitting her." This mother is in conflict. It looks as if she thinks the second boyfriend will look after her better. Yet she misses the first one, who used to cook for her but disappeared after the child was born. The second boyfriend does not cook for her but treats her nicely. However, he, too, could disappear after the baby is born, especially if he gets to watch the delivery. As if the men are afraid of seeing blood during delivery, she herself soon confesses: "I'm not going to touch it right then. I am going to wait until they clean it up, you know." Why would blood frighten men? The first boyfriend was violent anyway, so seeing blood did not make any difference. But the second boyfriend who is gentle, could sicken, and this would in turn cause her to be violent. Frightened by the aggressive impulses of her men, she is equally frightened about sexual impulses in girls. This mother is going to ensure that she raises her daughter, her first child, with respect so that when the daughter turns 12, she won't start flirting with men and scorning her mother. She does not like sex mixed with aggression, so she is relieved that her second boyfriend is different from the first, who used to beat her and make up with love-making. She can talk with her second boyfriend. The new baby is going to be "tall, slim, and handsome," if it is a girl, it will be "cute."

**4 months.** This mother has a girl, not a boy, and she now describes her child as "fussy, grouchy, wanting to have her own way," like her first boyfriend. But the baby is also like her when she whines or cries, and she is smart and looks like her. The four-month profile gives little more information as to how much change has occurred in the mother's perception of her child or of herself as a mother.

**12 months.** This profile is even sketchier, but we get some idea of what makes the mother feel like a mother. She likes to help her daughters and comfort and nurse them when they are sick. She also likes to play with them.

DISCUSSION

These descriptions indicate how, with appropriate intervention and improved tools for clinical observation, we can be more precise about the inner and outer world of the regressed mother. In all these observations one principle holds: the ego, once at the mercy of instinctual trends, can become much stronger in dealing at a later stage with intrapsychic and extrapsychic impingements when under pressure from a primitive superego and in an external world not in tune with the needs of the regressed mother. Intervention can help regressed mothers become very capable observers of their own symbolic and nonsymbolic network with their children. Intervention can also help the observing ego of such regressed mothers join forces with other integrative ego functions so that the mothers become able in time to lend strength to their children.

We see in these five cases the many intrapsychic tasks confronting the expectant mother. Gordon (1978) aptly wrote:

> We still tend to think that pregnancy should be a state of bliss, and of childbirth as a time of fulfillment and harmony, free from stresses and inner conflicts. For incalculable number of women reality falls short of expectations. They discover that pregnancy and childbirth are times of crisis, of unexplained fears and forebodings, of self-doubt, disappointment and depression. The expected blissful moment when the mother holds her baby for the first time is often overshadowed by anxiety and feelings of emptiness, inadequacy, even hostility (p. 201).

In this crisis the mother is not helped by her tendency to treat inner excitations as though they were external. At the same time she selectively determines what kinds of behavior she will accept from her child, what kinds she will encourage, and what hopes she will foster in her child. It is hoped that this study will prompt further research into the mechanisms involved; how the mother encompasses her child in her symbolic world, how the child accepts or refuses its mother's unconscious messages and, finally, how these interchanges affect development of the mother as a person in her own right. In such research I believe that the vicissitudes of projective identification will remain central.

# Caretaker Perception Profile

I. Before delivery
  A. Free association
     Mothers usually have ideas about their babies even before they are born. What are your ideas of feelings about this baby?
  B. Structured questions
     1. All women when they are pregnant wonder how they will feel about their babies. Will you feel close to the baby, or will you often feel that you don't understand him/her?
        *a).* What about the baby will make you feel close to him/her?
        *b).* What about the baby will make you feel not so close to him/her?
     2. What will make you feel that this baby is really yours?
     3. When do you think this will happen? (that you will feel that the baby is really yours?)
     4. What about your baby will you enjoy the most?
     5. Sometimes mothers feel negative about their babies, for example, because they cry a lot or are spoiled. What will make you feel negative about your baby?
     6. How would you describe the kind of baby you'll have? Then add, as appropriate: Physically? In term of personality?

II After delivery
  A. Free association
  I have been asking you many questions about the delivery and the way things have been for you and your baby. Please tell me now as much as you can about your baby. What is he/she like?
  B. Structured questions

1. All mothers have different kinds of feelings about their babies. Do you feel close to the baby, or do you feel you don't understand him/her?
2. When do you feel close to your baby?
3. When do you feel not close to your baby?
4. What makes you feel that this if really your baby?
5. What do you enjoy most about your baby?
6. Sometimes mothers feel negative about their babies, for example, because they cry a lot or are spoiled. What makes you feel negative about your baby?
7. How would you describe the kind of baby you have? Then add, as appropriate: Physically? In terms of personality?
8. What makes you really feel like a mother?

## CAREGIVER PERCEPTION PROFILE—FORM FOR PARENTS OF TODDLERS

**Note:** A parent's initial response when asked just to talk about his/her baby is the most critical one for the CPP. If he/she does not say much, first try to encourage him/her further to tell you a little more before proceeding with the questions. If a parent spontaneously answers one of the specific questions before being asked, it is not necessary to ask it again.

Babies grow a lot during their first years, and mothers feel different things as they grow older and change. Please tell me as much as you can about your baby. What is she/he like? And what are your experiences or feelings about being a mother (father) now?

I would like to ask you a few questions about your baby. Some of these you have heard already and some of these are new.

1. How would you describe your baby now? What is he/she like physically? What about his/her personality?
2. How is it different for you being the mother (father) of a toddler, compared to being the mother (father) of a little infant?
3. All mothers (fathers) have different kinds of feelings about their babies. What feelings do you have? Sometimes they feel closer or warmer, sometimes angry or distant. When do you have such feelings?
4. What do you enjoy most about your baby now? Enjoy least?

5. How is your baby like you? How is your baby different than you? Is he/she like anyone else?
6. All babies at times get very angry or very loving. When does your baby get this way, and how do you deal with it?
7. All babies at times feel like they want everything done for them and are very passive, while at other times take charge and want to control everything. When does your baby get this way and how do you deal with it?
8. What do you think your baby *will be like* when he/she grows up? What will make him/her that way?
9. There are different ways women (men) really feel like mothers (fathers). When do you *really* feel *most* like a mother (father)?

# 3/ Dreams of Urgent/Voluntary Errands and Transgenerational Haunting in Transsexualism

*Maurice Apprey*

In a note on transgenerational haunting, Nicholas Abraham (1988) observed that all civilizations hold as a tenet or as a marginal conviction that the spirits of the dead are capable of returning to haunt the living. In his elaboration (p. 75), Abraham explains: "More often than not, the dead do not return to reunite the living with their loved ones but rather to lead them into some dreadful snare, entrapping them with disastrous consequences. To be sure all the departed may return, but some are predestined to haunt." Which of the departed are predestined to haunt? Those "dead who have been shamed during their lifetime or those who took unspeakable secrets to the grave." Abraham stresses that the phantom is an invention of the living and the purpose of such an invention is to objectify "the gap that the concealment of some part of a loved one's life produced in us. The phantom is, therefore, also a metapsychological fact. Consequently what haunts are not the dead, but the gaps left within us by the secrets of others." Abraham grants that his theory of transgenerational haunting is in a very preliminary state and for that reason his grand thesis will have to follow. *How* the transmission of transgenerational haunting occurs has yet to be determined. Below, I shall attempt to make a contribution towards this determination.

Within the same horizon of transgenerational haunting, Dennis Donovan (1989) asked what anorexia nervosa, gender identity disorder, night terrors, and telepathy had in common. He posited the notion of the "paraconscious," as opposed to the "dynamic unconscious," to describe prelinguistic and pansensorially encoded cognitive activity in prenatal and neonatal periods that impacts adversely on the conditions in question. Donovan wished to push back the attachment continuum to the prenatal period, when mothers were shaping attitudes to their children and basing their interactions on those preconscious thoughts. Because he wanted to emphasize pansensorially encoded cognitive activity in the prenatal and perinatal periods, the issue of transgenerational haunting remained implicit, and not explicit, although Donovan provided generous clinical material that points to infanticidal and related unconscious matter.

In this chapter I shall attempt to do three interrelated things: (1) to reconsider Abraham's notion of transgenerational haunting in a way that points to the nature of transmission; (2) describe a specific form of dreaming that I have called dreams of urgent/voluntary errands; and (3) answer Donovan's question as to what anorexia nervosa, transsexualism, night terrors, and telepathy have in common.

To answer this question in a clinical context I shall draw on findings from previous studies (Apprey 1991; Volkan and Bhatti 1973; Volkan 1980; Stoller 1968, 1973). In a recent study (Apprey 1991), where I used a phenomenological praxis based on Husserlian thought (Giorgi, 1985, 1979; see also chapter appendix) to collect data and subsequently used psychoanalytic thought to determine and articulate my findings, I concluded that transgenerational issues are critical to determining the intersubjective constitution of mother-daughter perceptions and relations in anorexia nervosa. I observed, inter alia, that mother and daughter perceive and relate to each other as though each were the face of the other and that the face of one reflects the other. Furthermore, grandmother, mother, and anorexic daughter have a relationship whose borders exist both in contemporary relations and across generations. Across generations, there are unfinished projects that each generation must embrace as if the projects were its own. Each project is simultaneously feared and appropriated but it never comes to be identified for what it is. It thus appears to be some nameless dread that can only be articulated through concrete events. A mother of an anorexic is not only a mother but also a daughter who capitulates, willingly or unwillingly, to the mission of the other. As to the anorexic daughter, her world is but a dead-end (*aporia*), where a compromise is made. In other words, she carries out the mission by flirting with death, appropriating the lethal project, and at the same time striving to protest that mission. The result for her is a living death through the pathological formation of anorexia nervosa or bulimia nervosa as its counterpart.

While I struggled with the problematic distinctions of subject-object, subjective-objective, and linear causality, I came across the work of Charles Scott, a philosopher of continental thought who had already written *Boundaries in Mind* (1982) and who had introduced the notion of "suffusions" to describe what I have called "plural and appositive relations between transgenerational subjects" in anorexia nervosa. From a Heideggerian tradition, and attempting to overturn and/or expand the relative simplicity of the I—Thou relation, Scott (1982) defined "suffusions" as follows:

> By "suffusions" I mean the ways that different dimensions of events or of an event are simultaneously present with each other. Suffusions are types of immediate awareness in the sense that it is an alertness composed of the immediate adjacency of regions. The border, however, is pervasive presence in the region and composes a special kind of immediacy. Or it can be the enmeshing of various, nameable elements in the composition of an aware event" (p. 101).

Scott's description of "immediate adjacency of regions" is horizonal with my notion of subjects in apposition across generations. Situated in these imprecise border regions are welcome and unwelcome tasks to be negotiated by blood relations who are invested in continuing or discontinuing the generations. It is my view, as stated above, that *anorexics and their maternal lineage are invested in both continuity and discontinuity in the adjacent border regions of the mind.*

Clinical investigations by Volkan and Bhatti (Volkan 1980, 1989; Volkan and Bhatti 1973) and Stoller (1968) present clinical material about diagnostic and treatment considerations on transsexual patients and their parents. In their respective accounts dreams of transsexuals and their parents are generously provided. I shall turn to these dreams below to show that plural intersubjectivity exists in the immediate adjacency of regions transgenerationally in transsexualism and in much the same way as it occurs in anorexia nervosa. Before exploring those similarities, let me first recount in brief one account of the transsexual phenomenon by Volkan and Bhatti (1973) and another by Stoller (1968).

## A MOTHER AND HER SON/DAUGHTER, MAY: VOLKAN AND BHATTI'S ACCOUNT

The mother in question had lost her own mother. In a state of pathological grief she hoped that she would give birth to a child who would continue to provide her with mothering. She hoped that this new child would be a girl who would develop large breasts and be pretty. The baby girl, however, did not come, but a boy did in her place. Housed in this boy was now the mother's representation and the mental picture of the dead grandmother, thus continuing a relationship with the deceased through the boy child. In Volkan and Bhatti's (1973) words:

> The mother saw the infant as a female, and was able after 23 years to describe in vivid detail how she and her neighbors had accepted the new baby as a "pretty girl." When the patient, by now an adult, acquired breasts through surgery, the mother's earliest perceptions of the child were rekindled; she was carried away by admiration of her bosom and his generally female appearance (p. 272).

We can see from this account how Volkan and Bhatti would describe the boy, now a young woman, as a "linking object" who connects an otherwise suicidal and depressed mother with her mother whose death has not been mourned.

May, the male transsexual, never owned his given masculine name as a child. For him *that boy* was dead. To develop his sense of self as a girl he had to diet to control his obesity and see his phallus as belonging to *another* man. After surgery he dreamed one set of dreams in which he was a girl with male organs and in another in which he was a natural-looking girl.

Volkan and Bhatti (1973) report three dreams of May's before his surgical operations. First, May dreams of seeing *the death of a brother*, which saddens and depresses him, having in reality no brother. In another dream, May dreams of standing outdoors with a movie actor, Kirk Douglas. *Douglas is dressed in a manly cowboy costume and is wearing a cowboy hat.* He invites Douglas to accompany him somewhere. Douglas refuses. *Douglas is bitter about something* and will not accompany him. May starts to walk away but turns to find

Douglas hitching a ride on a truck. When the truck starts off, *Douglas loses his balance and sinks into a puddle* a few feet in front of May. May tries to rescue Douglas, but fails. Volkan and Bhatti report that after this dream May goes to watch a real Douglas movie, only to find that he has lost his ticket. And after seeing the Douglas movie "At the End of the Rainbow," May dreams that he is in a theater as both male and female, conflicted between the two roles, and further, preoccupied and uncertain about the exits in the theater.

After the surgical operations, May, now externally and bodily transformed, dreams that she is a woman who is both flying a plane and helping the actress Debbie Reynolds pilot it. They land the plane in John F. Kennedy Airport in New York, where the patient makes her debut as a singer under Debbie Reynolds's auspices. In May's debut she plays the organ. When the scene shifts into a high school scene she/he is playing a piano but is uncertain as to what gender he/she is.

While the story of the mother and her son and their dreams as told by Volkan and Bhatti (1973) gives us a window into the experiential realm of transsexualism, the authors summarize their findings in psychoanalytic terms:

1. The male transsexual is partly fixated or symbiotic at separation and early separation-individuation levels.
2. A fused identification with his mother remains as a strong core within the male child. Later internalized object- and self-representations do not modify this core and are not integrated in it . . . .
3. The male transsexual feels himself to be at the mercy of untamed aggression should he progress from the symbiosis with the mother within this core. To follow the opposite route leading to total identification with her seems less dangerous . . . .
4. While the core of undifferentiated self-object representations . . . persists, the patient also retains the objects in the external world through a splitting mechanism, and his more undifferentiated segment goes through the genital development . . . winding up by charging the penis with value (p. 271).

Volkan and Bhatti contrast their view of transsexualism to that of Newman and Stoller (1971), who suggest that "a profound identification with the mother precludes investing the penis with psychic energy so that patients having this identification desire rather than fear castration" (Volkan and Bhatti 1973, 271).

The views of Volkan and Bhatti (1973) are clear and firmly grounded in mainstream psychoanalytic thought. But an independent phenomenological analysis of the same dreams in that paper reveals additional findings which supplement their psychoanalytic understanding.

Phenomenologically, the dreams of Volkan and Bhatti's male transsexual patient, May, and of their female transsexual patient, Dominic, who has not been mentioned above, reveal the following:

1. *There are ambitendent or Janusian tendencies in the dreams and fantasies of transsexuals and their mothers. These ambitendent reveries, that is, both dreams and fantasies, point to the separation of life and death; a separation which is personified by two people.* For example, May is both herself and Kirk Douglas, or, as in another dream, herself and a brother. Dominic *dies by entering water and lives in another form after the submergence in the water. One dies, another lives. Water sustains death, water sustains life.*

Echoes of Bachelard (1942/1983): "Water, the sustenance of life, is also the sustenance of death for ambivalent reverie"; and of Jung (1927): the desire of a person "is that the somber waters of death may become the waters of life, that death and its cold embrace may be the maternal bosom, just as the sea, which, although it swallows up the sun, gives new birth in its depths ... Life has never been able to believe in Death!" (as quoted in Bachelard 1942/1983, 73)

2. *In these ambitendent reveries there are not only two messengers but also an implied third. One summons or calls upon another to do something; to go somewhere to carry out yet another task.* The second person refuses as does Kirk Douglas, who pays a price, death.

3. The use of such concepts as "splitting" and "dissociation" to describe the attempted solution of the psychological task at hand captures what we can know about anxiety and defense organization mostly in psychoanalytic terms. However, to unpack those same manifestations from the standpoint of the phenomenal field of the patient reveals ways in which the patient has appropriated a mission from the external world and is attempting to resolve *contrary life goals*, so that a human being may be, not immune to influences, but at least not destroyed by them.

## A MOTHER AND HER SON: SOLLER'S ACCOUNT FROM THE ANALYSIS OF A MOTHER

Stoller (1968) provided an eye-opening account of a mother's role in the creation of her son's transsexualism, and I shall only briefly recount the mother's story as told by her analyst. A mother in her forties reluctantly agreed to analysis in order to understand more about her son's desire to be surgically transformed into a girl. She was reluctant because she considered herself "nothing," a "cipher," even a "mirage." Her son had been wearing female clothes since 11 months of age. According to Stoller, "neither the patient nor her husband had considered this odd until a few months before she was first seen, when the patient was scolded by a neighbor for allowing the boy to walk about in his sister's clothes" (p. 109).

The mother in question came from a family of "prize-winning" lace makers. Both her maternal grandmother and great-grandmother were lace makers. She herself was a creative dressmaker and designer. In her first dream in analysis, there were echoes of designs and designations through the generations.

> There were two of me—an amazing, unpleasant feeling. *One was standing facing one way, the other another way—backward.* The latter was holding a lot of cloth and *moving backward toward something dark.* It was like a study in *perspective* in painting, like a *dark tunnel.* I felt myself to be the one who was looking at myself—the other one, going backwards. *The look on the other's face—the one going backwards—was sly.* She had taken the cloth (p. 110; emphasis added).

Stoller tells us that his patient, deriving pleasure from clothing, had "a sensual pleasure approaching voluptuousness in the feel of cloth" (p. 110) and throughout her childhood, she had wished to be a nun. Stoller links the patient's wish to be a nun to being "nothing" a "cipher", a "mirage," indeed, "none."

Describing the patient's and her son's easy access to each other, Stoller gives a flavor of how mother and son were without boundaries. The mother spoke of her son as follows: "This morning I was in the bathroom undressed. He came in while I was facing backward and didn't know he was there and slapped me on the fanny and said with a laugh, 'What a lovely butt.' I laughed and told him how cute he was" (p. 111).

In another description of this patient's imprecise boundaries with her son, Stoller gives us an opening into the world of this mother and son. In the words of the mother: "Last night I was looking at a photograph of when I was twelve. I looked just like a boy. Here's a dream I had last night. *I am radioactive.* At that point I was awakened because Lance [her son] was shaking me. In my first waking moment I thought: 'He mustn't touch me; now he is contaminated too' " (p. 112, emphasis added). Stoller adds that as mother and son became more separate, the son, who had hitherto been fearless, became *phobic*.

We learn also from Stoller's account that the mother's bisexuality showed itself both in how boyishly she dressed and also in her dreams. Accompanying her bisexuality was a sense of emptiness which the mother reportedly shared with her mother. Stoller speaks of the transmission of this experience of emptiness and supplies a most compelling dream from the mother's childhood: *"I had died and was now dead. But my mother kept sending me to the store on errands because she hadn't even paid enough attention to know it"* (p. 113; emphasis added). In the same vein, we get another opening into the mother's empty world; a world that borders on sterility through this dream account: "I was in a room trying to reach some *wooden milk bottles*—like children's toys—on a shelf" (p. 115; emphasis added). Stoller interprets her emptiness variously as identification with her mother, who was unable to lend femininity to her; as both the expression and denial of her disappointment and rage in her mother; as "a camouflage that permitted her bisexuality to persist"; and as a screen for her "object-hunger" (p. 115).

Finally, we are told that, earlier in her analysis, the mother had spoken of her younger brother as though it was her mother who had made him cross-dress. Later in the analysis Stoller learned two things: first, the brother's name was Lance; and second the mother had herself raised the brother and in her role of mother substitute had frequently dressed him up as a girl. Toward understanding of the mother who wished to transform a boy into a girl, Stoller states:

> A bisexual mother with severe envy of, and anger toward, males promotes an excessive symbiosis, producing a pathological identification between herself and her son (phallus) by means of unlimited physical contact and other intimacy in the first months of life. The main purpose of her identification with her son . . . is her need for him to "cure" her of the emptiness she received from her own mother. It is this need

which lies behind the bisexuality and the penis envy which so dominated her life . . . When the boy's father does not put an end to this process of two people of opposite sexes devouring each other's gender, the boy who feels he is a girl may be produced (p. 125).

While these findings are cosistent with mainstream psychoanalytic thinking, phenomenological analysis reveals the following: *a mother intuits that she is non existent, dead-in-life, and imbued in contrariness.* In that state she perceives herself to be subject to sly and ominous forces. At the same time she is, herself, *equally dangerous in her imposition on her son.* Just as she can be captured by antecedent (m)others, just so she can ("radioactively") kill her son. In her world everyone is on a mission, hers *to die and carry out yet another deathly errand.* This errand constitutes *killing her son in one form, and resurrecting him in another form, as a girl; a constructed girl without reproductive capacities; a dead-end.*

## MAKING THE TRANSCENDENTAL TURN: A HUMAN IMPERATIVE TO MAKE URGENT/VOLUNTARY ERRANDS

We have seen how *the anorexic must live but as though she were on the brink of death* (Apprey 1991). We have seen how *the transsexual must die in one form but survive in yet another, sacrificing his or her reproductive capacities in the process, indeed bringing his or her lineage to a dead-end, an* aporia.

To answer Donovan's question as to what anorexia nervosa, transsexualism, night terrors, and telepathy have in common, it would be reasonable to say provisionally that *anorexics and transsexuals carry out an urgent/voluntary errand, where a death occurs in fact or fantasy and a concurrent transformation follows.* In this vein of thought, night terrors are another version of this life-and-death struggle. *One dies at night and lives by day,* as it were. *Telepathy may indeed be one version of how humans intuit their urgent/voluntary errands: to discontinue their lineage and/or continue it in yet another form; a tragic drama of a peculiar kind and yet one that humans have known throughout history in art form, but dare not fully own in any other way.* It is a though we need to *stay in the dark* to live out these urgent/voluntary errands. Bennet Simon (1987), a psychoanalyst, defines tragic drama "as the study of how *the family can both wish to propagate itself and its values and simultaneously act* in such a way as *to foreclose that possibility.* Ancient, Shakespearian and modern tragic dramas deal in characteristic ways with these issues" (p. 152; emphasis added).

And in accord with our findings on anorexia nervosa and transsexualism, although in the context of tragic dramas, Simon goes on to say: "The very conflicts which threaten the continuation of the lineage, the proper sequence of generations, seem to undermine the conditions that make story-telling possible, namely a new generation that is able and willing to hear the tales of the previous generations" (p. 152).

Subjects suffering from primary anorexia nervosa and core gender identity disorder do indeed have a story to tell. That story is a haunting one, and with treatment it can be adequately told, provided we think of subjects as serially positioned, rather than in terms of subject-object relation.

From a phenomenological standpoint, Abraham's notion of transgenerational haunting can show itself in a specific form of dreaming and acting out, that is, remembering in action, where two sides of ambivalence present themselves in variations and/or derivatives of killing and sustaining. In addition, the pathological formations that Donovan discusses are subserved by highly structured forms of transgenerationally delegated infanticidal projects.

## DISCUSSION

If constructive and destructive impulses can be bound by the ego through its synthetic function; if life and death instincts, in their most dynamic forms can be compromised by the ego in anorexia nervosa and transsexualism in the form of urgent/voluntary errands, how does the ego effect these changes through the generations? I suggest that a return to early Wilhelm Reich, Hartmann, and Anna Freud could yield fruitful results. They implicitly or explicitly use the concepts, "change of function" and "secondary autonomy."

### Change of Function and Secondary Autonomy

Anna Freud (1936/1966) considered the ego's defensive operations as an object of analysis. In so doing, she wrote about defense against instinct that shows itself as resistance, defense against painful affects, and the manifestation of the ego's defensive operations in *permanent defense phenomena*. In the last of these three operations, she recognized the contribution of Wilhelm Reich (1933/1945) to our understanding of the "armorplating of character."

Hartmann (1958) refined Reich's and his own observations about the change of function of the instinct that can defensively and permanently come to have a life of its own. He recognized that "a behavioral-form which originated in a certain realm of life may, in the course of development, appear in an entirely different realm and role" (p. 25). To this point:

> An attitude which arose originally in the service of defense against an instinctual drive may, in the course of time, become an *independent structure*, in which case the instinctual drive merely triggers this automatized apparatus . . . but, as long as the automatization is not controverted, does not determine the details of its action. Such an apparatus may, as a relatively independent structure, come to serve other function (adaptation, synthesis, etc.); *it may also . . . through a change of function turn from a means into a goal in its own right* (p. 26; emphasis added).

In other words, those structures born of conflict may with their new and relative autonomy become apparatuses of secondary autonomy. They are secondary because they come out of an original situation of conflict, as opposed to innate structures of primary autonomy that are their own origins such as locomotion and speech.

In a conversation with Anna Freud, Sandler (Sandler and A. Freud 1985) noted that:

> when Heinz Hartmann developed his idea of secondary autonomy and change of function in relation to such things as skills (he spoke of "apparatuses"), he did not take the step of speaking of the secondary autonomy of symptoms and of character traits. We know that there are symptoms which are not necessarily solutions of conflict at the moment, but have crystallized, just as Reich's character traits have become "fixed." I suppose that one could speak of a *secondary autonomy both of symptoms and of character traits*, and in analysis we would have to look at symptoms of this sort differently from the way in which we look at *recent symptoms* or those which develop during the analysis, which may be compromises of a neurotic sort (p. 86, emphasis added).

The opening here is that we could isolate symptoms and character traits that have acquired secondary autonomy, recognizing that "processes of adaptation are influenced both by constitution and external environment, and more directly determined by the ontogenic phase of the organism" (Hartmann 1958, 30). Hartmann (1958) spelled out his view of "the historical-developmental factor" (p. 30) as follows:

> Man does not come to terms with his environment anew in every generation; his relation to the environment is guaranteed by — besides the factors of heredity—an evolution peculiar to man, namely, the influence of tradition and the survival of works of man. We take over from others (prototypes, tradition) a great many of our methods for solving problems . . . The works of man objectify the methods he has discovered for solving problems and thereby become factors of continuity, so that man lives, so to speak, in past generations as well as in his own (p. 30).

In Hartmann's view, therefore, this appropriation from past generations subserves "a network of identifications and ideal-formations which is of great significance for the forms and ways of adaptation" (p. 30). These networks of identifications and ideal formations operate between families, races, institutions, and perpetuate or transform themselves in peculiar ways. They are usually adopted and maintained for psychological reasons so that "inasmuch as certain social phenomena which originated as expressions of definite psychological tendencies can become the expressions of different tendencies during their historical development" (Hartmann 1964, 33), *psychological trends of antecedent generations show themselves and impose themselves on individuals in consequent generations as realities*. It is Hartmann's view that frequently, but not always, the psychological trends of antecedent generations "continue to satisfy along broad lines the same psychological needs to which they originally owed their creation" (p. 33). In this instance, dread of and an impulse toward infanticide can linger in a lineage as diffuse or circumscribed anxiety or as a misread danger, or the same impulse may persist through the defense against the anxiety in ways that allow the defense organization to develop a life of its own. Through a change of function, this new and resulting defensive organization can become stable or irreversible. This development, now stable or irreversible, can serve autonomous functions in a secondary way (as opposed to primary autonomy which is "originary" or is its own origins).

*Conclusion: Generating a Posterior Hypothesis*

If through a change of function a defensive organization becomes stable, as in anorexia nervosa, or irreversible, as in transsexualism, what is the critical mechanism utilized by the mother and supported by the father that facilitates the injection of the deathly project of the anterior (m)other(s)? My conjecture is that projective identification (Klein 1946) is a defense mechanism frequently utilized by the mother of the anorexic and transsexual-to-be. I want to suggest further that when the defense mechanism undergoes transformation and becomes irreversible, as in transsexualism, the change of function that allows the expectant new life of another gender develops secondary autonomy. In this state annihilation, separation, castration anxiety, or any combination thereof, and the defenses that guard against anxiety become so thoroughly concealed that it is understandable for a clinician to posit that castration anxiety, for example, is nonexistent, although I believe that there is enough compelling intrapsychic material, as in dreams, to suggest that castration and annihilation anxiety exist.

Let us now explore my hypothesis that projective identification and change of function leading to secondary autonomy dovetail to create the transsexual phenomenon. In a study of maternal misperception (Apprey 1987) I investigated in disturbed mothers the state of projective identification that distorted the development of their children. Thus in that study I reversed the study of projective identification of the child towards the mother so that we now had a window into the mother's use of projective identification with her child and examined its transformation from destructive to nondestructive, empathic forms. There, and following Rosenfeld (1987), I stated as follows:

> We may now define projective identification as an unconscious defensive process which exteriorizes an incompatible aspect of one's self organization into a representation of an object in ways which permit an unburdening of an unacceptable attribute or a preservation of an aspect of one's self away from hostile primary process presences. In the process of actualizing the delegated self organization one maintains a fantasied picture of control and oneness with the object. The result is that there is a change in the subject's own self representation as well as a change in the perception of the object (p. 5).

Here there is splitting of two images of the self, a translocation of one part of the self into an object who is a custodian, so to speak, of the exteriorized self or image, there is a *coercive closeness* with that custodian, and three is a coercive transformation of the custodian, who must now do the subject's bidding.

Nowhere in the literature on transsexualism is the use of projective identification more clearly described than in Volkan's (1980a) case of a nine-year-old transsexual boy. A 46-year-old mother who already had a 21-year-old son gave birth to a new son after a series of *miscarriages*. In her childhood she saw herself as a *tomboy* who often dreamed she was *turning into a boy*. As tomboy, she never learned how to dress or walk like a lady. When she became pregnant with this second child, who was to become transsexual, she felt there was "something special" inside her body; *something that she feared would not grow*. When the child was born she thought of him as an "angel"; a thought that alternated with fear of aggression toward this baby. She was convinced that this *child would die*. This child in turn feared his mother and he showed this fear by his *refusal to drink milk*. In Volkan's words, "the 'closeness' between them was accompanied by a dread of being close to one another, and the image each had of the other was contaminated with fearful aggression" (p. 210).

The circumstances surrounding the conception of this boy are equally striking. At 45 the mother decided to have an affair with her supervisor at work. He was 65. She lived a *double life* and claimed to have a "split personality." She was a lover at work and a serious mother and wife at home after five o'clock in the afternoon. When she became pregnant, she was uncertain to which man her child belonged. Nevertheless, she gave the child a name that was almost her lover's. Only one letter differed. Subsequent to her giving birth, she insisted that her son was "two people." When her husband was away, she treated her son as a *lover and mother*, thinking of him as a girl in the process. Volkan concludes as follows:

> It is clear that the mother's experience with "multiple mothers" was transferred to her having "multiple husbands," and accordingly "multiple children" in her son. The father's experience with "multiple parents" furthered this split. The mother related alternately with libido and aggression to the two images of her son. He, in turn, could not integrate corresponding self-images, but had an image of himself as "two persons" (p. 212).

In this story, we see a tomboy who does not know how to be a lady create a boy who wishes and learns to be a lady *for* his/her mother. As custodian of his/her mother's design, he houses two people, a lover and a mother *for the mother herself*, and the mother creates peculiar domestic and living arrangements that can only coercively control and continue this relationship. Father goes to bed at 8:30 P.M., leaving them to stay alone and later to sleep together. Subsequently, special child in her, that child who during pregnancy *might not grow*, becomes transsexual. Surgery would permanently transform this boy into the concrete reification of the mother's wishes for her son to become a lover and mother for her. He/she dies, so to speak, as boy and lives in another form as *mother's consort. The projective identification is sealed in a change of function.* What was once a defense will now develop a life of its own and will remain *irreversible* over time.

In another compelling story in that same paper, Volkan tells the story of a a male-to-female transsexual who returned to him for "consultation"/and helped the author to learn the following: her soap phobia had persisted after the surgical operation; she had a boyfriend and would feel complete if she could conceive a child; and while she was outwardly pleased with the alteration by day, at night she was terrified by dreams, night terrors, and other oneiric presentations of a midget. A midget showed himself at night between midnight and two o'clock in the morning. He sought union with her *through the ribs*. "Sometimes, the midget, as a spirit, succeeded in entering her body, whereupon she would break out in a cold sweat and feel *half dead*" (p. 221). She then became interested in knowing through visits to some hypnotist what lives she might have lived in those previous incarnations. She reported to Volkan that she was always a woman and in a recent hypnosis session "she had been an Indian maiden who had been given a golden stallion which she grasped with her thighs as she rode" (p. 221). Volkan saw the phallus as externalized as a weapon of aggression. Externalized, the phallus as midget haunted the new woman by night. However, the golden stallion is represented the good phallus, thus preserving a split between one form of aggression and another.

In contrast to a psychoanalytic reading for the two stories above, a phenomenological reading, concretely formulated, would take into account the destruction of reproductive capacities, the spirit that entered the body by night, causing the new woman to have night terrors, and the golden stallion she had to travel on, inter alia. Again, not to discount the psychoanalytic reading as inadequate but rather to see it as proximal, concrete psychology (Politzer 1973, 1976), one can see that a heinous event was taking place between the adjacent borders of the mind, that those borders were imprecise, that in their imprecision, a deathly design had to be accomplished through a messenger spirit and by the hand of another. *Somebody must die.* That is the urgent/voluntary errand. This errand, however, has traveled *through the lineage amongst subjects who are situated in apposition and who lure each succeeding generation into appropriating the heinous errand.* It is *urgent* because of the spirited, coercive form the statement of the errand takes. It is *voluntary* because the individual appropriates with recalcitrant resignation the task at hand and with his or her own embroidery. In short, and returning to psychoanalytic thought, *projective identification is the means by which a dynamic communication of death is given to the subject and the seed for the act is planted.* Upon its hardening into a *stable or irreversible organization,* the individual must decide *through a change of function* what tragic drama must occur: *a total death, living but on the brink of death, dying in one gender but living in another. Invariantly,* to be sure, *no new creation occurs.* It behooves us, therefore, to explore the continuity of projective identification, change of function, and secondary autonomy. By this orientation we would be closer to determining which syndromes are so adapted in such an ossified manner that analysability is precluded. I am referring here to pathological formations like anorexia nervosa, transsexualism, primary autism, multiple personality disorder. Of course applications and modifications of psychoanalysis, psychoanalytic psychotherapy, and psychoanalytic management will have a place in the treatment of these hard-to-reach patients. Further study and clarification will be needed to increase our scope of interventional possibilities.

# Phenomenological Method Demonstrated

In his preface of *Phenomenology of Perception* (1945/1962), Maurice Merleau-Ponty explained that

> phenomenology is the study of essences, and according to it, all problems amount to us finding definitions of essences: the essence of perception, or the essence of consciousness, for example. But phenomenology is also a philosophy which puts essences back into existence, and does not expect to arrive at an understanding of man and the world from any starting point other than that of their "facticity" (p. vii).

Giorgi (1979, 1985) grounded this philosophy into a psychological research praxis. In 1979, he described the phenomenological praxis in the following way:

1. The researcher reads the entire description . . . straight through to get a sense of the whole.

2. Next, the researcher reads the same description more slowly and delineates each time that a transition in meaning is perceived with respect to the [phenomenologically] intentional discovering [of the experience].

3. The researcher then eliminates redundancies and clarifies or elaborates to himself the meaning of the units just constituted by relating them to each other and to the sense of the whole.

4. The researcher reflects on the given units, still expressed essentially in the concrete language of the subject, and comes up with the essence of that situation for the subject with respect to the phenomena [under consideration]. Each unit is systematically interrogated for what it reveals about the [phenomena] for that subject. The researcher transforms each unit, when relevant, into the language of psychological silence.

5. The researcher synthesizes and integrates the insights achieved into a consistent description of the structure of [the phenomena] (p. 211).

I shall now illustrate how Giorgi's phenomenological praxis works by using the case of the renowned ophthalmologist, Dr. Renée Richards, a male-to-female transsexual.

By 1985 Giorgi had simplified his phenomenological praxis into four steps. Step 1 requires that the researcher collect the data from which new discoveries are to be made by using a transcribed audiotaped text acquired by means of an interview. Or, as in the case of Dr. Renée Richards, the subject of this study, we will use his own words from his autobiography *Second Serve*, written in 1983. In the interest of efficiency and brevity, I shall use only the first four chapters of Richards's autobiography, where he tells us about the first ten years of his life. In step 1, then, the researcher reads the text to get the sense of the whole.

In step 2 we read the very same description more slowly. Each time there is a change of thought, meaning, or idea, we draw a slash. By the end of the second reading we would now have separated the text into several meaning units which would become the object of analysis in Step 3. Each meaning unit is numbered.

In step 3 each meaning unit is individually interrogated and unpacked, so that we can arrive at a deeper meaning for the subject in very concretely expressed terms. In this step each meaning, when relevant, may be expressed in both concrete terms and in a psychologically meaningful language.

In the final step, step 4, all the separate meanings and essences are collapsed into a total structure of experience for the subject. We enter into the phenomenal world of the subject to see how he or she situates himself or herself in the world.

The structures, then, are the results of the study which must now be considered in a dialogue with the scientific literature to explicate specific knowledge or further our fund of knowledge with new discoveries. It is crucial to bear in mind that in a phenomenological study we do not, as in natural science verification-oriented studies, make a reduction toward closure of the phenomenon under the study into a narrowly conceived hypothesis. Rather, we proceed with the open and discovery-oriented position that we want to know more about some phenomenon. We proceed with the study until we have arrived at consistent descriptions of the structure of the phenomenon in ways that synthesize and integrate the essences in the motivational and phenomenal world of the subject. For detailed descriptions of Giorgi's method, one should consult his 1979 and 1985 publications.

Briefly, then, to arrive at the structure of experience of the subject, I considered each of the first four chapters of Richards's (1983) autobiography as a separate text. Then I decided that each chapter constituted a sufficiently circumscribed experience to warrant a particular structure of experience. In chapter 3, however, there were two sets of circumscribed structures of experience and for that reason, the chapter will have two structures of experience, one based on meaning units 57–70, and the other based on meaning units 71–104.

Because of copyright restrictions I cannot reproduce the chapters that constitute the naive descriptions of step 1. However, I shall provide a few passages from the book (Richards 1983) that will show the relative coherence of the meaning units that make up step 2. I shall follow up each meaning unit with an example of the transformation that would occur in step 3.

Meaning unit 1:

> My mother was a headstrong woman. On the day of my birth she suffered a massive hemorrhage. Her reaction to this was to get into a 1934 coupe and, bleeding profusely, drive the rutted roads from Queens all the way to Manhattan. Apparently, it didn't occur to her to have someone else drive the car or even try to reach a closer hospital. The important thing was that she give birth in the right place and with the right person in attendance (p. 1).

Step 3: Transformation into psychologically meaningful language:

> Subject perceives his mother as a *headstrong woman* with a particular set of urgent dictates that she must follow so that, even when the pregnant woman is *on the verge of delivering* her baby, she feels driven to get to a *particular hospital* and to a *particular obstetrician*. In a sense, there is a *design to be independently followed at any cost* to her health or to her baby's.

Meaning unit 10:

> Dr. Bishop [subject's mother] was examined by Dr. McLoughlin and informed that she had placenta previa . . . There were two possible remedies. The first was a maceration maneuver. This is a violent process wherein the baby's head is crushed and the uterine contents are pulled out through the vaginal canal. The child is killed for the sake of the

mother's safety. The second possibility was Caesarean section. Unfortunately, much blood had been shed during the long ride to the hospital. My mother was weak; a section could kill her. Then again, my head was in the birth canal making extraction difficult and, so, doubly dangerous (p. 2).

Step 3: Transformation into psychologically meaningful language:

Subject ponders what choices her mother had to make concerning the possibility of his birth after the profusely bleeding expectant mother had arrive at her female obstetrician's hospital. As a result of the *dangerous ride* to the preplanned destination, she faces two possibilities: *she might die to allow the baby to be born, or she might have to have the child killed inside her and abstracted to allow herself to live.*

Meaning unit 11:

Dr. McLoughlin emphasized in great detail the risks involved in a section. Though she left the decision to my mother, her recommendation was clear. I should die (p. 2).

Step 3: Transformation into psychologically meaningful language:

Subject recalls that his mother risked her life to give him life when she decided to go against her doctor's recommendation to have him killed to save herself.

Meaning unit 13:

It was the morning of August 19, 1934. I was named Richard Henry Raskind after King Richard the Lion-Hearted, though it was my mother who had shown the courage (p. 3).

Step 3: Transformation into psychologically meaningful language:

Subject senses that *it was her mother who had shown courage in possibly risking death to give him life*, thus reversing the fact that her heroism in choosing life for him made her the courageous one. Subject, however, pushes the memory of the mother's choice to drive a long way to the hospital, which in the first instance could have killed him, into oblivion and thus does not recognize that he indeed survived a long and dangerous ride.

Meaning unit 14:

Perhaps I've been running to catch up ever since (p. 3).

Step 3: Transformation into psychologically meaningful language:

Subject surmises that it is *his* appropriated goal to show courage, *to live in the face of death*, to meet an ideal standard of existence.

## STEP 4: STRUCTURES

*Structure of Experience 1 (Chapter 1, meaning units 1–8)*

In this subject's world, a matriarch of a mother sheds massive amounts of blood on her way to where she could be among women and be delivered by a woman obstetrician in a birth emergency that ironically seems preplanned but set up to be potentially problematic. Such a matriarch mother could hold her own in a contest of wills in the outside world of professional life dominated by male physicians. As Dr. Muriel Sadie Bishop in the public professional world, she must carry out a mission, that of representing female strength. As mother, in a private and personal world, this matriarch must fashion a child's life with every calculation and precision. As though she were always in control, such a matriarch must will her first born child to be a boy and when the child comes out a girl, she must still be raised as a boy. By the same token, when the child is born a boy, the mother can choose to raise him as though he were a girl.

In this world of reversals, mother may still choose to represent the world to herself and to her children as more categorical than it is. Nevertheless, confusion plagues this world that the son shares with his mother: faced with the possibility of mother choosing to die so that her son could be born alive, or with the possibility that she could live and the child die, she risks a Caesarean section, which means she could bleed to death in her particular medical condition. When the mother survives, she reverses reality once more by calling her son the survivor, one who must be named Richard, after King Richard the Lion-Hearted.

*Structure of Experience 2 (chapter 2, meaning units 9–26)*

When subject tries to understand how he became troubled, he finds it both embarrassing and incredible because he feels so remote from that little boy of long ago who experienced "the anguishes of identity." Now the "anguishes of identity" seem to constitute for him a provocation and most compelling set of circumstances for creating "an imaginary transsexual" (p. 5). Subject would, however, like to believe that his condition is due to some biochemical factor.

The set of circumstances that constitutes subject's imaginary transsexual includes the following: (1) a house full of women where father's presence is nominal and leaves the boy child defenseless in the hands of a dictatorial mother and her ally, a terrorizing but warm sister; (2) a situation where an impotent father, who is always on the verge of success, never becomes the outstanding surgeon he could have been; and (3) a situation where subject has direct access to mother's soft and fragranced body every morning, when for years he would cuddle up in bed with her and later watch her ritually dress her body and glorify her sensuality before putting on her cold and severe exterior clothes, no makeup, and rolling "her abundant hair tightly over a 'rat,' a sausage-like piece of felt, then [tying] it in a severe bun at the back of her neck" (p. 10). When the attention of the matriarch turns to her son, she insists that he dress himself in male clothes of twenty years before, clothes that are vestiges of an earlier generation and long ago discarded by all. Subject includes in the constitution of his imaginary transsexual a set of legacies that traverses three generations. A maternal grandfather, a drunk wastrel and womanizer the first half of his life, turns ascetic the second half of his life when, as a recluse, he withdraws from the family to read his Talmud; in one phase a licentious lecher, "a maniac", whose pictures showed a "Rasputin" character, and yet in another phase of his life the "scoundrel" turned ascetic, who "demanded that his daughters be absolutely virtuous" (p. 10). Subject's mother, then must become the responsible, dubiously rewarded, and guilt-ridden "son" of the family upon whose shoulder stood the well-being of the family and the dubious honor of concealing the seamy errand.

*Structure of Experience 3 (chapter 3, meaning units 27–56)*

For subject, a mother who fails to save her father's life may resolve to be perfect thenceforth, never to make any mistakes, but like a cannoneer, aim to make her cannons shoot targets with greater precision. When a mother is shaped to be the "man" in the house by a father who wanted a son, she, too, can shape her daughter into a "man" of the house with responsibility, privilege, and the burden of guilt over unreachable goals. As designs can be implemented by one generation, so a succeeding generation can follow through.

In this sense, when mother's father lives one half of his life as womanizer with every excess, and the other half as a ascetic recluse, the concealed and apparently given up urges may be picked up by the next generation of offspring. Thus, a daughter of a sexually driven man who turns ascetic may treat her body with utmost sensuality but conceal it with a cold professional exterior. In the same fashion, mother's first child, a girl, can be flagrantly masculine and infuse her femininity into her brother.

A sister, named Mike after the womanizing/ascetic grandfather, may now carry out her errand with every precision and she must do so in a variety of ways. She must kill her two-year-old brother with random blows to the back of his head, unannounced and unexplained. Failing to kill him with blows, she must strangle him. Failing that, she must shock him to death with the idea that a bear will come and eat him up. Failing that, she must kill his masculinity by dressing him up as a girl, she must make his penis disappear, then turn it into a game of a penis that appears and disappears and gets bigger upon its return. Failing to make his penis disappear, she must teach him how to be a better athlete than his peers, especially one who can hold his breath underwater longer than most: a double-edged sword of a lesson that teaches athletic competence, but risks killing a six-year-old child by making him swim a mile.

In subject's world, then, the push to nearly have him killed must be explained away. He sees that, even his matriarch of a mother must live in a world where there is a sense of "inevitability" and *immovability*, so that the same mother who can fight her way among male professionals and successfully treat her patients with a successful "cannoneer's hit" can be overcome by and infused with dictates "learned largely form her mixed up father." The injunction is to be a man, the best man, even if born a girl, but the mother must despise or kill manhood and its connotation in others. According to this injunction, *what killing cannot or may not be done by one's hand may be put in the hands of another, but the transgression must be supervised so that it must nearly kill to elicit subservience in a man.*

## Structure of Experience 4 (chapter 3, meaning units 57–70)

In subject's world, where questionable legacies such as the injunction to kill or nearly kill can be handed down, good things can happen, too. Perceived as impotent in the face of terror by women upon himself and upon his son, father can still teach his son to become attached to tennis and give his son a male voice, speaking of a physical attribute. According to subject's calculation, athleticism and a male voice can hide his secret of *privately* cross-dressing at home, so that his peers *outside* will not suspect him of having a perversion. However, the strength of the appropriation of an injunction to rid himself of his life and/or his masculinity is so deep and so pervasive that he must now yield. More than yielding to the transgressions by mother and sister, subject must now "go solo," as if he were in control of his life and his choices. Cross-dressing—and his guilt about it and what it stands for—is his act alone, his alone to enact with relaxation and for relaxation, his alone to enact with trepidation, lest he be found out. *What starts off as a transgression by the hand of others can become the pleasure or mixed pleasure of yet another's, even if the injunction to transgress is three generations removed.*

Subject's experience of his sister's hostility, which stopped when he was seven years of age, gave way to his own self-adornment, which now increased with greater frequency. Sister Mike did not have to oppress him with deadly games; rather, he would now assume a girl's persona with even more frequency. He had to adorn himself in multiple female guises so that he could make himself turn into a little girl. Like Narcissus he "pined" (p. 27). Subject notes that when he stole many "movements of doing dull things in dresses" (p. 27), he realized he was hooked like an addict. Now he had to be seen outside (dressed as a girl) and for him outside meant freedom from a tense family situation. With increasing urge to become a girl and increasing need to define this girl, his feminine side had to have a name, Renée. The name Renée, for subject, also meant containing his "nerve-racking impulses" (p. 30). He construed this naming as embodying a material change into an ordinary little girl, who in fantasy could be a number of things: a little boy who could replace the little girl when she could not perform on a trapeze because of injury; an ice-skating partner of a boy schoolmate while subject wore skating skirt and impressed the crowd; a look-alike of the child Chopin, who would wear a long, flowing nightgown.

Subject's experience of women like his mother and sister terrorizing him now gives way to Renée asserting herself and desiring to exist. Like "a soft enemy" she must return periodically to overtake his masculine side, named Dick. Like a multiple personality he can now accommodate two people, Renée and Dick. However, while Renée can terrorize Dick, Dick can at least exist intact, cloistered in Renée, even if subject were subservient. As if to affirm subject's increasing role as a girl, subject recalls his sister, now a friend, asking mother, "What do you do with men who want to be women?" Mother answered,

"You send them to Scandinavia." In jest or in earnest, subject recognizes the mild misgiving of the women (who once dressed him)
as affirmation that indeed he can become a woman. However, the two
sides exist side by side in daydreams.

If he should remain Dick in his daydream, he would want to marry
a very feminine homemaker who would raise children better than his
mother did. If he should become Renée, he would become a happily
married woman with a family. He prayed to become Renée, and began
to feel erotic sensations as Renée. In subject's own words, "Renée,
like a siren, beckoned him into softer realms, into the gentle rustle
of fabric, into the disturbing harmony of aloneness, into the smooth
but impossible night" (p. 39). *The Bar Mitzvah proclamation of* "I
am a man" *could not save him from Renée*, "the soft enemy" *who
must exist in place of Dick, and in replacing Dick, Renée embodies
a precarious and ironic sense of freedom from Dick's demise. Richard
must die*, by injunction, but *if he must exist, he must be cloistered
in Renée.*

## TOWARD AN INTERSUBJECTIVE CONSTITUTION OF
## TRANSSEXUALISM

Having determined the subject's structures of experience, let us
foreground the prevailing intuitions of the subject that compelled
themselves into presence in a rather pervasive way. These intuitions
show themselves as a series of paradoxes:

1.  Subject intuits that his mother wanted him born "without the aid
    of Men" (p. 1). He must be delivered by a woman in a women's
    hospital. Such a wish, by itself, is not uncommon, but subject's
    intuition carries with it a related intuition, that for his mother, birth
    by women would diminish the role of a man.

2.  After narrating the dangerous circumstances of his birth, subject
    tells us that he was named Richard Henry Raskind, after King Richard
    the Lion-Hearted. He intuits that it was rather his mother who had
    shown courage, and undeserving of this name, he has been "running
    to catch up" (p. 3) with the expectations of that name, ever since.
    Here, mother as survivor is pitched against child as survivor. One
    side of the story shows mother as survivor when she decides against
    her obstetrician's suggestion that the child should be killed and
    extracted form her womb to ensure survival. Another side of the
    story shows mother as endangering herself and/or the birth of the
    child when she chooses to drive to a very distant hospital with a
    massive hemorrhage.

3. Subject wonders how his father could be large, handsome, somewhat gruff, possibly intimidating, seemingly strong, and yet prove himself weak and passive. Here, subject's wish to be defended by his father is opposed to the reality of his defenseless condition in the face of a strong mother and sister.

4. Subject contrasts his mother's elaborate efforts to treat herself with gentle and considerable self-indulgence when she dressed in the morning with the cold severe exterior of a professional look with no facial makeup. Here, soft sensuality is opposed to the severe posture that reflects mother's need to do battle against male physicians at work.

5. Subject contrasts grandfather's lecherous behavior with his sudden transformation into an ascetic recluse. Here, lechery and asceticism clash, and yet by subject's reference to him as a scoundrel, he reveals the continuity between the lechery and asceticism, as opposed to a manifest contrast between them. Subject shows further the untransformed nature of his grandfather's excesses when he speaks of him in this way: "Like all scoundrels, he demanded that his daughters be absolutely virtuous" (p. 10).

6. "My sister Michael" indicates a rather loaded opposition. Subject experiences oppression of colossal proportions when he faces his sister's masculinity and femininity. The same sister that was dressed boyishly was forced to have long hair. The same sister that nearly killed subject would shower affection on him after dressing him up as a girl. In subject's own words: "These moments of strangulation brought on some of the warmest moments between us" (p. 12).

7. Subject is ordered by his mother and sister to attend a Halloween Party as "a normal little girl" (p. 14), but is a normal little boy. Subject's intuition is that his mother wants to be subtle in contrast to other Halloween disguises. In reality, he stands out "like *Alice in Wonderland*, a perfectly groomed little girl surrounded by animals, knights, and cartoon characters" (p. 15).

8. Subject opposes his being dressed up privately at home by his mother and sister to showing up dressed in public: he sees the former as an inevitable terror imposed on him by a mother-sister team and the latter as perverse. It is as though the moments of *private* pleasure were too perverse to be perceived as such. It is as though it is perverse only when an *outsider* sees him cross-dressed. In this last instance, to be seen threatens to reveal the possibility that he has moments of enjoyment or relaxation, and therefore complicity when he is exposed.

9. Subject opposes Renée to Dick and intuits that "this split" is "similar to the rare cases of multiple personalities" (p. 30), but is confused that, in his case, the split is between two sexes. However, he sees a connection between them. Renée could read and do homework

for Dick and the two personalities are conscious of each other. Seeing the connection between them, in spite of the clear demarcation between the sexes, allows him to say, "Renée is coming back" and so "Dick [can] remain intact even if subservient" (p. 30). *We have the suggestion for the first time that Renée's presence both ousts and conceals Dick's presence.* Renée's presence is therefore not a complete annihilation of Dick. Dick is absent but cloistered and subservient.

The paradoxes are pervasive. Subject makes a summary statement about them when he says: "Every significant person in the house was a paradox. My father was so big and gruff and strong, yet so prone to crumble under pressure. My mother was so soft and yielding in her womanly guise, so cold and intellectual as a professional, yet so ready to enter into a screaming argument at home" (p. 13). Subject notes that his sister's obvious femininity contrasted sharply with her efforts to become a boy. Overpowered by these paradoxical figures, subject watched the rest of the family "move[d] about the house as if it were perfectly normal, and I looked on wondering why I could not adjust" (p. 13). Subject wonders further that if the family had been completely insane, perhaps, he might have fared better. However, "my mother seemed always able to cover the craziness with a patina of rationality" (p. 3).

We can now collapse the structures of experience and their essential paradoxes into the following intersubjective constitution of transsexualism: *Somebody must die. Somebody must obey this injunction and design its completion.* It is a dubious honor that must be carried out by one's hand or delegated to yet another. Accordingly, what killing cannot or may not be performed by one must be put in the hands of a trustworthy other. *The transgression must be supervised so that it must occur or nearly kill to elicit subservience.* The injunction to kill is *deep and abiding, with possible roots in three previous generations.* Thus, ritual proclamations like, "I am a man" or conscious pleas could not save the chosen sacrificial one. *The enemy is soft but formidable,* and in working between the interstices of sexual differentiation, *one gender can conceal the other.* Absence of one gender spells both its demise and its sequestration; a death and yet rebirth. A transsexual, then, is reborn (Renée) after his or her demise.

PART TWO

# PROJECTIVE IDENTIFICATION AND INTRAPSYCHIC STORIES OF PARENTAL PROJECTS

# 4/ A Prefatory Note on Motives and Projective Identification

*Maurice Apprey*

It has often been said by critics of Melanie Klein and her followers that (1) Klein's clinical observations are clinically useful but not well conceptualized; (2) Kleinians are phenomenologists and, as such, fail to communicate with their conceptualist counterparts; and (3) Kleinians have failed to describe adequately the impact of external reality.

Nancy Mann Kulish (1985) joins these critics by pointing out some of these weaknesses. In the process, however, she herself falls prey to the limits of her understanding of some basic tenets in Kleinian metapsychology. These have, after all, been insufficiently understood by classical analysts. Kulish raises three objections: (1) Klein's confusion over whether the object of a *projective identification* is an internal object or representation or a real external object; (2) Klein's failure to "belabor the distinction" between "fantasy and structure"; (3) Klein's assumption of ego capacities at birth, which allowed her to infer the use by 3- or 4-month-old infants of projective identification as a mechanism. Given the conceptual problems rooted in these three objections, Kulish "would limit the term *projective identification* to a specific fantasy content and would isolate for further study the concomitant attempts to actualize the fantasy." For Kulish, the rubric of projective identification has been overburdened to encompass an ego defense mechanism, an object relationship, "a fantasy," and a mode of communication.

Although it is true that the term *projective identification* has been extended in those numerous ways, I wonder whether the solution to the conceptual problems she has cited is to provide another "conceptual phenomenology" or descriptive articulation of projective identification. I strongly suspect that we would be on more solid ground if we examined contextually the use of projective identification in clinical material in a way that allows us to observe more fully the motives for its use. If projective identification as "fantasy" is in evidence, what is the motive for its use? If it is used to describe a particular form of object relationship, why is this mode chosen? If it is a form of communication, how does one account for this method of communicating? Donald Meltzer (1967) referred to the motives underlying the use of projective identification: "intolerance of separation; omnipotent control; envy; jealousy; deficiency of trust; excessive persecutory anxiety" (p. 14). Although the list of motives may not be exhaustive, a study of the context often reveals that a common thread in regard to the use of projective identification is the obliteration of differences between self and other. At the root of projection lies an exteriorization onto an external object of an incompatible instinctual wish or superego anxiety that recoils to haunt the subject in a way which distorts the original source of the wish. It is as if the wish or anxiety originally came from without, as in the case of phobia. An underlying motive for using externalization may be to shore up self-esteem by externalizing (without the boomerang effect in projection) the unacceptable impulse in the subject. An examination of motives helps us capture more clearly what is accomplished when projective identification is used and how it is accomplished. Kulish, like other classical Freudian analysts, makes an apparently simple but confounding error when she uses interchangeably "fantasy" and "phantasy." Kleinians, especially since Isaacs's (1952) exposition on unconscious phantasy, restrict "fantasy," as Freud did, to conscious fantasy as in fiction, daydreams, and the like. In contrast, they use "phantasy" when referring to dynamic unconscious phantasies, which are psychic representatives of instinctual drives. Although classical analysts, such as Kulish, have not adopted this topographical distinction, I believe they share with the Kleinians a common enemy in the conceptualist who fails to specify the topographical level of the unconscious phantasy under discussion, thereby failing to distinguish between merely descriptively unconscious material, which would include the preconscious, and phantasies that belong to the dynamic unconscious (see Freud 1923/1961). "Phantasy in the Kleinian view is primitive, dynamic, and constantly active, coloring external reality and constantly interplaying with it" (Segal 1981, 5).

With this classification, we can return to the specific questions that Kulish raises. Her first objection is that Klein does not specify whether the object of a projective identification is internal or external. And yet for Klein there is a constant psychic interplay between the internal object and the external object, the images of the internal mother and the perception of the external mother. To make her point that the ego's method for dealing with anxieties pertaining to the internal mother and the external mother are interrelated, Klein (1975) writes:

> In the baby's mind, the "internal" mother is bound up with the external one, of whom she is a "double," though one which undergoes altera- tions in the mind through the very process of internalization; that is to say, her image is influenced by his phantasies, and by internal stimuli and internal experiences of all kinds. When external situations which he lives through become internalized . . . they follow the same pattern: they also become "doubles" of real situations, and are again altered for the same reasons (p. 346).

Klein's followers, notably Bion and Meltzer, contributed to our understanding of "objects." Meltzer and his colleagues (1982) sug- gested that for conceptual clarity the term *claustrum* be used for the object of unconscious phantasy, whereas the term *container* should be reserved for the more abstract, symbolic, or mythic level of dis- course. In an ordering scheme such as the one Meltzer and other post- Kleinian analysts outlined, the premise is that the infant experiences his or her body in spatial terms. The infant child is and has a body. Other people are and do have bodies. Superimposed on this premise of the infant's body-self as space, thanks to the expansion of sec- ondary process thinking and the continued use of word presentations to define one's needs, is the additional attribution of a metaphorical inner space. The result is that when there is *formal regression*, that is, regression from secondary to primary process thinking, as in schizophrenia, the "object" is seen in more concrete and actual terms. Nunberg (1948, 31) used the term *transitivism* to demonstrate shifts in cathexis from objects as actual persons to objects as perceptions, as in transference, to objects as overdetermined representations. In a brief discussion it is impossible to offer the detailed examination that this subject merits. Suffice it to say that our most effective means of observation of "deep" or "early" material in analysis is a genuine therapeutic regression. Without the therapeutic regression and the appropriate therapeutic stories with their recurrent unconscious phantasies, we are more apt to speculate. In a therapeutic regression we can observe better what constitutes the body-self as space, what part of it is delegated to an object, how aggressively the inner assignment is carried out, what phantasied retaliation takes place, and so on.

Whether we are referring to a claustrum (that is, by Meltzer's definition, the inside of the object penetrated by intrusive identification) or to the container (the inside of the object receptive of projective identification), internal *shadows still graduate into external objects* in the Kleinian scheme. These shadows are based on the child's memories and phantasies. In this context, images and phantasies are continuous and have a common origin, as Marjorie Brierley (1944) would put it. Images and memory images are reactivated from past experience. In a footnote to her useful paper on the nature and function of phantasy, Isaacs (1952) quotes from Brierley (1944):

> It was suggested that, artificially simplified, the concept of an "internalized good object" is the concept of an unconscious phantasy gratifying the wish for the constant presence of the mother in the form of a belief that she is literally inside the child. (Isaacs 1952, 121).

One function of this concretized unconscious phantasy is to allow a child the sustained illusion that its mother is still present. More importantly, it preserves gratifying sensations during a short-lived absence. But as Brierley pointed out, a 2-year-old child's memory images of its mother constitute a complex system, as a result of two years with the mother. Thus, what the 2-year-old retains in consciousness is a residue of an extensive dynamic unconscious mother-system that is rooted in earliest infancy.

When we focus on motives and functions, we are able to put theoretical constructs in their true perspectives. We can then see that even a concretely sounding concept like Bion's (1962) "container" is an abstraction that, as Meltzer and his colleagues (1982) put it, fits "the chamber maiden thought of projective identification" (p. 200). As such, the container in projective identification has boundaries. It must be perceived as private and exclusive, as "a place of comfort, sheltered from irrelevant stimulation coming from the interior of the body . . . the modulator of pain, the "toilet breast" (p. 201).

The direct answer to Kulish's question of whether the object of a projective identification is internal or external is that internal objects provide associative links to external objects. There is an "identity of perception" (Freud 1900/1953) between the internal shadows and the external objects with which those unconscious phantasy shadows are continuous.

This question of the nature of internal and external objects leads naturally into Kulish's next concern, Klein's leap from "fantasy" to "structure." For Klein and her students, phantasy and personality structure are connected. The structure within the ego is the product of complex unconscious phantasies. There are way stations, as it were, from unconscious phantasy to structure. First, the child exteriorizes his or her own aggressive phantasies or libidinized aggression onto the parent. The child then incorporates in phantasy the same parental figure whom he or she has externalized or projected, repeating the process until the parental figure has acquired a presence. This presence is now fertile soil for attributions that reflect various attitudes and functions.

For Klein, the superego was indeed such an introject. However, she also underscored more instinctualized introjects which were endowed with primary process presences. Some of these primary process presences are tempered or altered by reality testing, whereas others remain split off and shape the invariant unconscious phantasies, personal myths, and idiosyncratic and ideographic perceptions of the analysand's world. If we let these "phantastic" ideographic perceptions acquire a degree of coherence in the analysis, that is, if we do not tamper with their emergence, we will have access and insight into the analysand's abiding unconscious phantasies. When we have access to them, we can mobilize them and facilitate their entry into the transference, and thereby effect structural change.

Following the usual classical objections, Kulish questions what kind of ego functioning a 3-month-old child is capable of. Kleinian metapsychology is, first and foremost, a preoedipal psychology. As such, the ego in Kleinian metapsychology is an instinctual ego. Again, when we attend to functions and motives in the clinical situation or even in direct observation, we are able to infer that the early ego is an "affective summoner." When it projects and exteriorizes instinctual wishes, the early ego also summons succor by translocating the mother and assigns qualities to the world on the basis of projection, but when it uses projective identification, it obliterates separateness. The instinctual early ego is, from the onset, an urgent omnipotent ego. It is this instinctual urgency that distorts perception when the early ego observes the world and assigns qualities through projection.

To conclude, I think we miss the point when we linger over descriptive and definitional issues related to theoretical constructs, and move from there to clinical data. I believe greater understanding is reached when we use motives and/or functions as the starting point of our inquiry. Until we do that, we shall run the risk of replacing one conceptual difficulty with another, which may prove to be equally problematic. Even though the notion of projective identification appears to be "overburdened" by multiple meanings, the phenomena it denotes nonetheless obey the principle of multiple function. For instance, when projective identification is used as a defense, we do indeed observe an attempt to mitigate anxiety. When projective identification appears as phantasy, we have an opportunity to observe both a defense against the impact of reality and a psychic representation of instinctual drives which become manifest as wishes. When projective identification is used as a mode of communication, we discern an urgency and an omnipotence behind the analysand's wishes. And insofar as it describes first and foremost a primitive wish, we can see how aggressively projective identification obliterates differences and, in phantasy, aborts separateness. In fact, the opportunity to observe a multiplicity of unconscious behaviors through projective identification makes the concept more useful than otherwise. It embodies an elaborate mode of functioning that is unique in its capacity to connect instincts, unconscious phantasy, and defense.

# 5/ "When One Dies Another One Lives"

## The Invariant Unconscious Phantasy in Response to a Destructive Maternal Projective Identification

*Maurice Apprey*

Pregnancy and childbirth are frequently associated with fulfillment of motherhood, a fulfillment of yearnings of an earlier or later period in a person's development. However, for a countless number of women the joys of motherhood are an illusion, where conscious feelings of competence and fulfillment are undermined by hostile internal maternal presences. Conscious feelings of helplessness may mask an infantile wish to be exonerated from blame. The conscious ideal of completeness may be equally matched by an unconscious wish to undo one's badness and failures. Many other anxieties exist that clearly need to be studied and restudied, and common features must continue to be documented.

The analytic case material in this chapter illustrates how each pregnancy has a story of its own to tell. One intrapsychic story, as it were, is told in some detail to enable the reader to participate in the inquiry; one woman's resolution of problems posed by her invariant unconscious fantasy: "When one dies, another survives." In the process we learn how the analysand, who had hitherto met her mother's disguised infanticidal wishes by the mechanism of identification with the aggressor, emancipated herself psychically. We learn how she

137

became a woman in her own right, free from the destructive projective delegations from her mother, delegations for which the analysand had been a suitable carrier. The unconscious strategy used by the mother to transmit her own incompatible destructive impulses, fantasies, and wishes was projective identification. The mother of the analysand, in a state of projective identification,

(1) *split* off her own infanticidal and destructive wishes;
(2) *imparted* these destructive wishes and impulses to her daughter who wove them into her pathogenic fantasy that one should live whenever another being dies; and,
(3) having thus exerted her *control and influence* over her daughter through the injection of her murderous fantasies, induced rage, fury, murderous impulses in her daughter at will, as when she told her daughter: "You should not give birth to a girl; girls are difficult to raise."

Analysis focused on tearing the analysand away from her mother's destructive projective identification, which was mixed with a transparent reaction formation against infanticidal wishes such as sitting by the analysand's bedside to prevent crib death.

## FOSTERING THE THERAPEUTIC STORY IN PREGNANCY ANALYSIS

There is very little published material on how to analyze expectant mothers so that they can become aware of the meaning of their pregnancy. Deutsch (1945), Bibring (1959), Lomas (1960), Pines (1978), Kestenberg (1976), Benedek (1959), and Raphael-Leff (1982) give us a firm beginning. These authors have dealt with such issues as pregnancy as a period of psychical reorganization and reconciliation, and motherhood as another developmental phase. Although this does not diminish the value of their work, they have not dealt with the theory of technique in the analysis of expectant women. It is here assumed, rightly or wrongly, that going from clinical matter to theory or to theory of technique would provide the wealth of data needed to make strides in the analyses of expectant women. I wish to use the case below to document in some detail the analysis of an expectant mother. It is a case that could easily have focused on the interplay of mourning and pregnancy, aggression, and pregnancy, inter alia, and ended up with a crisp coherent paper. However, I have chosen to present the process of the analysis. This report covers the first two years of a successful four-year analysis. I have chosen to use the term intrapsychic story to describe the unfolding of the analysand's intrapsychic issues and her invariant fantasy.

In the report that follows, my overriding concern will be how an analyst knows what he knows and what it is that he knows. Melanie Klein (1945) acknowledged this difficulty in the struggle to articulate the nature of the inner world to incredulous colleagues:

> The fact that by being internalized, people, things, situations and happenings—the whole inner world which is being built up—becomes inaccessible to the child's accurate observation and judgment, and cannot be verified by means of perception which are available in connection with the tangible and palpable object-world, has an important bearing on the phantastic nature of this inner world (p. 346).

This phantastic nature of the inner world presents problems for analyst and analysand alike, thanks to repression and the immaturity of the early ego, whose experiences are the platform for later idiosyncratic view of one's self and the world at large. In a sense this paper can be said to be about footprints of the unconscious—word and deed, icon and gesture are all metaphors of unconscious ways of knowing through the use of affects, defenses, compromises, indices of instinctual trends. These methods by which the ego negotiates ways of knowing all play a part in the way they reveal through derivatives hitherto hidden unconscious material.

The latent meaning of transference, extratransference, and extratherapeutic material, dreamwork, and the analysand's associations provide the ground and platform for the intrapsychic story. The analyst can nurture the derivatives expressed in the analysand's preconscious stream of thought with sufficiently correct interpretations and with adequate distance from the patient's id, ego, and superego discouraging any premature or inappropriate interpretations. By not tampering with the analysand's material, the analyst can foster the sequential collection of derivatives into the intrapsychic story. The analysand's psychic reality then takes primacy over historic reality.

## NARRATIVE AND DRAMATIC STATUS OF THE INTRAPSYCHIC STORY

According to Robert Scholes (1980), when we speak of a narrative,

> we are usually speaking of story, though story is clearly a higher (because rule-governed) category. The object of a story is the sequence of events to which it refers; the sign of a story is the text in which it is told . . . ; and the interpretent is the diegesis or constructed sequence of events generated by a reading of the text. . . . Narrative is always presented as if the events came first, the text second, and the interpretation third, so that the interpretation, by striving towards a recreation of the events, in effect completes a semiotic circle. And in this process events themselves have become humanized—saturated with meaning and value— at the stage of contextualization and again at the stage of interpretation (p. 210).

Likewise, the intrapsychic story has a *sequence*; it is the relatively *coherent* sum total of drive-derivatives; its content is repetitive and so verifies the relative correctness of the unconscious wishes and fantasies that strive to surface; it is told to someone, especially in the context of transference material. There is a sense of time, so that in a temporal regression, for instance, the analysand can tell the analyst that what she says to him or her is what she thought for a moment she was saying to, let us say, her dead husband. The richness of the intrapsychic story is that it is both a narrative and a drama. As narrative, it speaks of *events*. But it goes further, and through transference we see a new edition in the here and now of past events. As drama, the intrapsychic story is a *series of enactments*. At its best it is unique, idiosyncratic to the analysand, and psychoanalysis emerges as a very human experience in which the analyst and analysand renegotiate intrapsychic tasks that hitherto have had only maladaptive or symptomatic solutions.

## EPISODE AND CONFIGURATION

Paul Ricoeur (1980) suggests that

> every narrative combines two dimensions in various proportions, one chronological and the other nonchronological. The first may be called

the episodic dimension which characterizes the story as made out of events. The second is the *configurational dimension, according to which the plot construes significant wholes out of scattered events* (p. 178; emphasis added).

The episodic dimension is comprised of the singular events in the analysand's enactments or transactions outside analysis that are suitable targets for the expression of unconscious issues. These are analogous to the scattered events that lend themselves to the configurational dimension. In the intrapsychic story the "configurational act" (Mink 1972) that pulls together the scattered events, derivatives, and so on, progresses into a verifiable and more convincing narrative as we hear several different versions of the pathogenic fantasy which, in the course of the analytic inquiry, takes an invariant form. *It is the task of the analysis to enable the analysand to triumph over the otherwise invariant pathogenic fantasy.*

## PATIENT'S HISTORY: INITIAL FORMULATION

Robin was the second of three children, with a sister two years her senior and one a year younger than herself. Their father had longed for a son, and Robin's birth had disappointed him on that account. She had reportedly been told as a small child that she had been born on a stormy night and that the conditions of her delivery had been such that the obstetrician in attendance had been faced with choosing between saving the mother or saving the baby. As it happened, both survived, but the aunt who had resuscitated the frail baby ultimately became a suicide.

When Robin underwent the usual childhood illnesses, her mother cared for her well, but Robin's relationship with her younger sister was always tempestuous and rivalrous, and she felt hostile toward her mother, who seemed to her to dislike her because she was unlike her sisters. The mother was a teacher. The father, a businessman, taught Robin to hunt and to play baseball. She went to college to become an emergency medical technician, changed her goal to become a nurse in community psychiatry, and later qualified as a clinical psychologist.

She sought analysis in her mid-thirties, five years after the death of her first husband, Hector, in a racing car accident. She had undergone grief therapy and had remarried. She had been married to Bert for a year before seeking treatment.

Robin was agitated at her first visit, asking many questions. Would I scorn her interest in Eastern religions? Would I think that her desire to have a baby was acting out? Her urgency required intervention, so I said, "The way you ask about birth and the completion of your work of mourning suggests that you link the two issues and have much work to do." She burst into tears, but sat back in a way that suggested that she felt I understood her. After a brief interview she wanted to go home to decide whether to return to the analyst who had referred her because he had no opening, or whether to start analysis with me on the basis of four sessions a week. I told her I would have a vacancy within two months, and she called back promptly, saying she had decided to start her analysis, and I was able to accommodate her.

After taking her history, I wondered how, as a year-old child, Robin had been able to process the withdrawal of her mother's attention because of the demands of a still-younger baby. I surmised that the mother's perceived withdrawal would have created problems, given the relative immaturity of the child's ego. The mother must have been unable to gratify Robin's drives and bodily needs, and have experienced them as dangerous in view of the mother's ignorance of how to organize and process new experiences. I surmised also that Robin's intense hatred of her mother would interfere with Robin's conception of herself as a woman. The deficit in her sense of self as desirable could not be corrected by her father's psychological investment in her since he regarded her as the boy he had wanted. How could she have the body of a beloved female and become a mother enjoying the body of her child? It was also necessary to consider what Robin's understanding of having been born dying would do to her narcissistic libidinal investment in her body self. Would she unconsciously assume that her baby would threaten her life, as she was said to have threatened her mother's? I noted also that her first husband had died a violent death, and wondered how that event might condense with early preoedipal material from a time when the ego was unready to process correctly her experiences of the world. Might not death be unconsciously seen as representing her aggression toward her siblings, her parents, and her first husband's "other women"? If so, how was Robin going to deal with her unconscious triumph over her foes? Finally,

I considered how Robin was ever going to separate intrapsychically from her mother while gripped by intense hatred toward her; in the unformed mind of a child, to separate is to lacerate the self or the one from whom one separates. In order to separate, and hence be psychologically born, Robin would have to shed blood. To become her own person she would have to mourn the loss of her mother. Robin's desire for a baby might contribute to the process of intrapsychic separation, but the problem was that birth and death had been processed intrapsychically as hazards. Therefore, I thought we would have to reexperience her history in the transference to grasp the meaning of Robin's life, and her needs.

This chapter is divided into three parts, the first covering the analyst's attempt to piece together the many derivative versions of Robin's intrapsychic issues and pathogenic fantasies that had culminated in an invariant unconscious fantasy. The second part deals with the analyst's work in enabling her to triumph over this fantasy; and the third represents the work of pregnancy as a further attempt on her part to become a woman in her own right, intrapsychically separate from her mother and capable of letting her child be a separate person also.

## TREATMENT

In her very first session Robin said that if she ever saw or heard of my being with another woman, she would leave analysis. She said that a friend had seen me at a cocktail party without my wife. She was serious, but could see how irrational she was being, and added, "I don't even know whether you are married." In the transference she was seeing me as her dead husband, who had had many affairs, and who had died while on a "business/pleasure" trip. I was soon to realize that other women competing for her husband's attention were like sibling rivals, who must be eliminated.

## PHASE 1: Anxious Hatred of Children as Siblings and Fantasies of Destructive Aggression toward Siblings

Robin's associations at the start of her analysis showed much diffuse aggression. Her material was full of feelings of being persecuted by her internal objects; her own aggression; a perception of herself as deformed; and her fantasies of destructive aggression, like those directed toward her siblings, which led to her concern about bodily damage. Besides anxiety over aggression, there was her anxious hatred of children as siblings. Could Robin give a girl child total attention, especially when the child could easily become a competitor? In view of the extent of Robin's diffuse anxiety and fantasies of destruction, I thought she probably could, but that her transition from being her mother's daughter to being a mother herself would require support from treatment. Robin spoke of planning to have a baby the following year. She wanted to see if this met my approval; if not, she would fight me. She admitted that this plan put her under pressure, but she wanted to be ready for it. Now she felt anxious, knowing that she would resent having a baby and caring for it. She would hate having her child refuse food and hurt her pride. She associated children with fighting; would she fight her child as though it were an older sibling? Once, as a child, Robin had assaulted her sister and been so severely punished by her father that she could not go to school. Aggression must be met by aggression according to talion law. Robin thought herself so "obnoxious" that she laughed at those who thought of her as "a nice person." She believed that aggressive thoughts toward others must lead to her own victimization, but now, although she had conscious fantasies of aggression toward her friends she was not punished, and they liked her.

She wondered when children begin to have an idea of death. Her sense of vulnerability arising from her fantasies of aggression from within and from without was clearly exposed, and I began hearing of her husband's death and its effect on her. *She feared she would die if I left her during a break, and she could not continue working with me were I to have an affair.* In either case, I would be running away from her love, betraying her, and investing love and attention in another woman, who would be a competitor, like a sibling, and this behavior would surely damage someone. At best, one of us would be lacerated.

Robin dreamt of refusing to have a mastectomy while I was on vacation. In her associations to this dream, she said that women like her younger sister are always the cause of her being deserted by the objects of love. "*Even when my mother left me for my younger sister, it was a woman involved.*" Her first husband had encouraged her to be friendly toward his mistress, but she had felt very hostile toward her. *"It comes back to this: you either kill them or join them."* There were siblings everywhere.

She asked if on my forthcoming vacation I were going to "some meeting on 'The Therapist's Pregnancy,'" but said she knew I would not reply. Her associations to where I was going recalled her own abortion years earlier, in which she had been greatly humiliated by the impersonal treatment. "They didn't even say if it was a boy or girl; they just took it away. It was the first time I have even been anesthetized . . . I had a cervical tear. It was awful. I met Hector soon afterward. Surprisingly, he was very understanding, but then he died. Although I have Bert now, I still miss Hector. I feel that crying is not accepting his death." In retrospect I note that here, too, a therapist's pregnancy is juxtaposed with her abortion and Hector's death, which came soon thereafter.

In this early period of her analysis Robin had concerns about bodily damage, and fantasies of destruction. On my return from my vacation she reported having had a dream.

> I was in a house. My older sister was there, too. A simulated murder took place in a pretend kitchen. My sister had pricked her finger, and we smeared blood all over the place. Someone called the police, and I started to make popcorn for everybody. When the police came, the kitchen caught fire. I looked into all the cupboards for a fire extinguisher, but every time I pulled open a cupboard door, there was the face of a policeman.

Her associations pointed to anger at me for going away. Robin saw the policeman as representing me, policing her impulses in analysis. She said, "When I think of your going away, my feelings are primitive; but when I think of your return, I get myself together and can put my feelings into words." Her untamed aggression had been evident when I was about to depart; her modified aggression, when I returned. When I spoke of this, she said, "You don't know what I have to go through to come here." Robin reported a dream to confirm the toil involved in her analysis. In it she was riding a bicycle uphill to her session, and when she arrived she was surprised to find me with others, and to see that I was white. In associating to this dream, she spoke of how my teaching activities reduced my investment in her: I was not giving her my total attention, and thus betraying her. I assume that my transformation in the dream to someone of another race spared me from her aggression, and I interpreted this.

As if to confirm my assumption that she needed to protect me from her aggression, she dreamt that I was an infant. To her that meant that she herself felt like a child, and how she felt too much like a child herself to have one. She was also afraid that if she regressed much more in her analysis she might be unable to get herself back again. She returned to the wish to be pregnant. A novel she was reading made her wonder if she would enjoy being pregnant, except for disliking having her body swell. She began to weave the novel— Heinlein's *I Will Fear No Evil* (1967), a book of science fiction— into her therapeutic story. "That book is getting crazier and crazier," she reported. "Now the hero is pregnant!" She related the plot, which deals with a rich and obnoxious old man who wanted to avoid death by getting into the body of someone young, but did not stipulate the race or sex. He ends up inhabiting the body of his own attractive young secretary. (My white patient did not know that I knew the book, and that Heinlein had stated that the secretary was black.) He then inhabits this body in such a way that there is an ongoing dialogue between the cantankerous old man and the young woman. When the protagonist gets pregnant, she and her husband plan to go into space. *She does not survive the trip, but the baby does.*:

> A baby cried, a world began.
> "Heart action dropping!"
> (Jake? Eunice) (Here, Boss! Grab on. We've got you!)
> (Is this a boy or a girl?) Who cares, Johana—it's a baby!
> One for all, and all for one!
> An old world vanished and now there was none.
> (p. 512)

When asked to treat this story as if it were a dream, Robin went back to one dying, while another survives, recalling the story of her delivery, during which the doctor reportedly had told her mother that either she or her child would survive, but that one would die. She recalled also the later suicide of the aunt who had resuscitated her when no hope was held out for her. Robin had many fantasies about death during childbirth, but by the end of this phase of her analysis I realized that the one that dominated in her intrapsychic world was the belief that *when one lives, the other dies*: that one woman must conquer another for possession of her husband; that Robin should beat to death the younger sister who was her mother's favorite, that either

Robin or her mother should have died in childbirth; and, with reference to the story, that the rich old man made a woman must die if his/her child is to be born.

What does a child do when she learns she was born dying? Robin seems to have woven the external reality into her symbolic network, and many derivatives of her unconscious pathogenic fantasy coalesced into an invariant personal myth. When, after six months of treatment, I interpreted for the first time the possibility of this invariant fantasy, she lay silent for a long time, seeming to nod assent without speech.

She then told me that while I was away her mother had given her an antique silver service from which a few pieces were missing, and that her grandmother had disapproved. I saw something uncanny in her being given an *incomplete* antique silver service, especially when the gift was made when the two older women were at odds with one another. I found it interesting, too, that the gift was not to be shared with Robin's siblings, or even shown to them.

Robin commented that when, as a child, she had received a gift, she was hurt soon afterward. After being given a ball for her birthday once, she had almost lost an eye; and a pogo stick, also a birthday gift, had caused her severe injury. At the time of her second marriage, she had discouraged gifts. I completed her remark, saying, "Because, for you, gifts are Trojan horses." I surprised myself with that analogy, at which she laughed, but I saw it was apt, encapsulating a whole chain of issues Robin was negotiating in analysis. Instruments and agents of destruction had emerged from the belly of the Trojan horse, a gift, and this notion was in accord with her fear of danger from the baby that would emerge from her belly. Could she transform the fantasy that the womb is a dangerous place into one that could liberate her?

Her fear that her baby would endanger her as she had endangered her mother made for intrapsychic warfare between her baby, herself, and her mother. I conveyed my thought, also, that the gift of the silver service under the special circumstances surrounding it made me wonder if her mother were not indicating who should have the phallus in this family, or which of her three daughters should be the carrier of the family aggression.

Aggression and the anxiety it brought appeared in Robin's fear of childbirth. It was clear now that she had unconsciously sought analysis because of fear that she or her baby might not survive gestation and delivery. She did not want to die in pregnancy, and to be saved she must be transformed by both pregnancy and her analysis. Would fantasies of transformation by pregnancy amount to her mourning the loss of her infantile ideal self in order to make room for a new integrated self? Must she expel something in order to make room for a child? Must someone die for another to live? How was she to triumph over the compelling unconscious fantasy?

I had begun to understand that the two-sided structure of Robin's invariant unconscious fantasy (birth on one side and death on the other) represented a two-sided motivation (having pleasure and avoiding pain). Nevertheless, the unconscious outcome, was the removal of siblings to enable her to live without fear of retribution:

## PHASE 2: Fantasies of Transformation by Pregnancy

Fantasies of Robin's being transformed began to emerge; her defective body self should be changed. She should expel representations of her mother to make room for a child, who had the burden of transforming her into a fertile, gentler woman amongst women— a child who would also be a complex reincarnation of her two husbands as well as of her own transformed self.

It was time for her annual gynecological checkup, and she pondered whether to tell me about it or about an enraged patient she had seen; her mind wandered into a story her husband had read to her about a spiritual leader from India who had many allergies. It seemed inappropriate and ironic to Robin that this Enlightened One should be vulnerable. Was he preparing for his own death? I observed that she was still pondering about the sense of danger she connected with transformation, and noted that one can be made vulnerable to a second coming, enlightenment, being born again. Laughing, she said she wished her gynecologist had not explained amniocentesis, since knowledge and birth can be dangerous. She was frightened, wondering what she would do if the amniocentesis findings were bad.

Robin came to her next session very uncomfortably swaddled; she had been ill and had a bad cold. She had lost her prescription for birth-control pills, and was terrified that pregnancy would transform her into "a very demanding person." She spoke of helping to transform a friend's little girl; she was giving the girl a cedar box filled with trinkets from Robin's own childhood which the little girl could use to pretend to be grown up. Robin's dreams recalled a memory of playing with a Madame Alexander doll and being relatively happy with her family. She made a point of telling me that the doll came from her godmother, rather than her mother.

It was hard for Robin to resolve fantasies of transformation because she had competitive feelings; her closest friend had become pregnant before she had. She had met a woman with three children, who was pregnant with another she did not want. Robin's transformation fantasies were complicated by anxiety over the thought of siblings merging; this mimicked homosexual feelings toward a woman friend. A women's group of which Robin was a member had recently broken up because of differences about inviting a poetess friend of a famous homosexual female golfer. Did Robin have the ego autonomy to have a sibling relationship with her woman friend, or would she merge with her? Or did Robin simply want to be a woman among women? These and other questions went through my mind as I noted her associations about womanhood and femininity appear and reappear, cloaked in ambivalence.

Robin's therapeutic regression deepened; she would say, "When I lie down here, I feel like a child, small and vulnerable." She was anxious about losing control if she became pregnant, and talked about accidents. She recalled her "brush with death" at the time of birth, and spoke of a friend's automobile accident that she thought might have been a suicide attempt, and that it had been followed by an abortion.

Terribly frightened by the thought of losing control if Robin became pregnant, Robin spoke of how greatly she would dislike being dependent on others. "*It's never appropriate to be dependent!*" she snapped. "*It never is!*" It was now hard for her to think of pregnancy as transformation in view of her fears. She became concerned with the thought that she must give up something to gain something; she was ready to bargain to become pregnant (and get the phallus). She felt that she would have to deprive herself of something. She had given up smoking on her birthday, but she recalled that her first husband had done the same and had worked hard for fitness, only to die.

In what follows Robin seemed to equate giving up tobacco with shedding the image of her first husband, and creating a child with giving him a decent burial. She said she had neglected to tell me this before.

Robin's doctor had told her to stop smoking in preparation for the conception of a baby, but, to her disgust, she had taken a cigarette and had thrown the rest of the pack into the fire. Then she went to her jewelry box (a symbol of femininity), which was filled with treasures (a womb with a child), and got a bone from Hector's ashes and threw that into the fire also. She said she had been dazed; she thought this behavior "weird," but by throwing the bone into the fire she had destroyed one external link to her dead husband; she was giving him a decent burial to ready herself for childbearing. She cried out, "Everything boils down to grieving, but never ever completing one step!"

Robin wore black to her next session in order to be ready to go to her grandmother's funeral. The issue now was chaotic: "to smoke or not to smoke—no, that's not it—it's leaving or not leaving." She was reading Kubler-Ross's book on death and dying as a stage of growth. She noted that if she were unsuccessful in giving up cigarettes she might turn to a pipe, which did not require inhaling. She thought of trying cigarette candy, and said, "It's altogether in the mind, a feeling of wanting something you can't have, something you'll never have again."

While in this mood, and grieving in order to allow herself to get pregnant, another concern arose: was she a girl or a woman? Man or woman? These largely intrapsychic issues surfaced. Robin recalled bathing with a girlfriend when she was at puberty and discovering that she had pubic hair, but her friend did not. She had shaved it off. Still another set of associations centered around her reading about transsexuals; she had been startled by accounts of amputating a penis. Still another set of associations centered on the silver service her mother had given her. Behind these issues lay the question asked before more urgently: who should have the penis? Robin was dominated sometimes by images of completeness, then those of deformity, mutilation, and castration. She saw the film *The Texas Chain Saw Massacre*, and reported that it was "horrible, the ultimate of massacres." Castration was the ultimate of massacres, and that brought to mind the graphic pictures of transsexual surgery she had seen in a magazine and thought disgusting.

Robin came quickly out of this fog of delirium in which she saw images of death, castration, and other mutilation. She now reduced her image of death to a personification: she thought of an author of a book on after-life experience as "thin, gaunt, and aggressive," like death itself. She thought of "roundedness" (like pregnancy) as a characteristic of gentle people. She was intrigued that she still liked to swear, more than her second husband, who had served in the Navy.

"The way I was treated as a child makes me think I should have been a boy," Robin said. It had been her father, not her mother, who told her about wearing pads when she began to menstruate; he had explained that men wear protection when engaging in sports. "It didn't make sense," she said. "But he was serious. He didn't know anything about cramps." Our relationship was different, she flirted, "It's different here—intimate. It's funny—I write your name M.A. as if to point out to myself that you are my mother."

I intervened for the first time in months, saying: "You have many questions such as 'Am I going to get pregnant?' 'Am I going to become a woman?' 'Who will take care of me?' You had to cling to your fantasied deformity or kill someone—someone had to be deformed, someone had to die. Miraculously, *physical birth took its course, but psychological birth was incomplete.*"

Robin reported a "weird" dream in her next session. In it, her gray-striped cat had a yellow kitten. She instantly linked the yellow kitten to the yellow couch, but no sooner had she made that connection than more thoughts about surviving a pregnancy came through. Would she survive? If so, would it be a humiliation? Would she feel demeaned by the shaving of her pubic hair?

It occurred to Robin that she did not know what I thought about all this. "I still don't know whether you think it's all right for me to have a baby; I want you to tell me!" She felt special urgency because I was about to take a break. She asked if I were going to Ghana; she would like to be an invisible observer if so. "It would be less intimate; I could observe without reacting to people in your family."

When I returned, Robin reported dreaming about an argument with her second husband, Bert. His face had turned into mine as they argued, and she smashed my head against the wall. She was perplexed on awakening because she had decided not to worry about my absence, and making this kind of decision was her idea of being in control. That reminded her that, although she had felt confident about being able to conceive at will, her period had come again. "I get so angry when I can't will something to happen," she said. "I can't wait when I want something." She returned to dreaming of smashing my head, and told me that she had been upset that I was away. "I was also upset that I had my period." She had bled so profusely that her mattress was badly stained, and she reported that on the previous day, when coming to her sessions, she had had to allow time enough to go to the toilet lest she stain my couch. She mentioned an aunt who had a fibroid tumor. I made the interpretation that Robin was telling me of her anger at my absence and her guilt at smashing my head. I said I felt her accusation: "Look what you have done to me! I turned into a bleeding female with inner damage." In response she said, "Maybe the bad things you do come back to haunt you: *I hated my sister so much*; *I hated my first husband for his affair with Miss Sweden*; *I hated my mother*. I left you out of it except for dreaming that I was shaking you. But I can't imagine your being more important than my husband, though I tell you things I can't tell him. If you were, I would feel bad, but it would be different."

I made the interpretation that Robin was wordlessly saying, "*A man will die. All the people close to me that I am angry with will die. Who am I going to kill or save*? If you are important to me, then you, too, will be in danger. I will kill you, too!" Closeness awakened her rage, and established targets for her aggression. She agreed with this assessment, and indicated that all this aggression she was dealing with was distorting her perception of the world. She had been in some professional committee and had been disagreeable and complaining, but in spite of that "they had good things to say about me," she reported.

It troubled Robin to observe that her desire to be pregnant was "becoming an obsession," and she felt she should do something about it. She wondered if she could magically make herself ovulate; she had read somewhere something about focusing different lights and colors on the pelvis. "But what if I pick the wrong color? Can I imagine myself with my pelvis wrapped in lavender, declaring that I must ovulate?" She wondered whether the intensity of yearning for an outcome would prejudice its attainment.

Robin recalled that soon she would have been in analysis for a year, and wanted to mark the anniversary with a gift for me. She considered giving me an "angel wing" plant because "it is almost indestructible and hard to kill—if you want it to die you have to work at it. Its colors are intense, and it's available all year around." I told her she was talking about her wish to have me all year around, indestructible and safe from her aggression. She said she was actually thinking about reincarnation, referring to the notion that a spiritual being taking on a physical body is attached as an angel to the cell where it divides first. To her, I was one of those particular angels given to someone to work on her problems, and that is why she was referred to me.

Robin finally was able to announce: *"Good news! The rabbit died !"* She said she was thrilled and that everybody was happy for her except her mother. Reportedly angry at her mother's lack of enthusiasm, Bert had said, "I used to think you exaggerated when you talked about your mother. Don't you see that's her problem?" To which Robin replied, "It's how I react to it." We were back to the invariant fantasy:

> The rabbit died, she conceived a child.
> *Where one survives, another dies;*
> *Indeed, where the rabbit dies, another being survives.*

## PHASE 3: Vicissitudes of the Intrapsychic Story throughout Pregnancy

To utilize the intrapsychic story as a guide to the patient's invariant fantasy, the analyst refrains from tampering with the patient's material early in analysis, even when he is confident of his understanding. He gives no premature, incomplete interpretations but waits until enough derivatives have been collected to reveal a relatively coherent intrapsychic story that culminates in transference neurosis.

Barbara Johnson described the outcome of good deconstruction in Lardner 1983, G10:

> Suppose you were in therapy and you came to the point where you realized, "Aha, this is the contradiction I have been struggling to repress. This is what has been structuring my behavior. . . . What good deconstruction does is to say, "Here is the conflict, or here is the contradiction, or here is the aporia, which drives the work. And it can't be reduced further."

Ricouer, writing on "Narrative Time" in *Critical Injury* (1980, vol. 7, 190) asks some pertinent questions about the fit of invariant fantasy in the intrapsychic story:

> Must not something or someone die if we are to have a memory of it of him or her? Is not the otherness of the past fundamentally to be

seen in death. And is not repetition itself a kind of resurrection of the dead, as any reader of Michelet will recognize?

Psychoanalytic observation of the analysand's pregnancy helps the analyst understand the impact of her invariant fantasy on her overall functioning and on her development as a mother in her own right.

**First Trimester.** Robin's joy over being pregnant was modified by anxiety over what her mother might say or do to her. She had come to town for a postmastectomy follow-up. About this time Robin became a mediator between the two sons of her dead husband; they were at odds over a girl, and her present husband talked to them about falling in love and other concerns. This brought home to Robin how much they missed their father.

A visit from a small niece led to Robin's expectation of having to contend with the fussy, messy, and aggressive ways of a small child when she became a mother. She confessed wanting "to strangle the kid a couple of times," but thought through her feelings, surmising that her intolerance came from her mother. She wondered if she would treat her child as her mother had treated her. Robin had not been allowed to be fussy, messy, or aggressive; she felt her mother disliked her independence. She noted that both she and her mother were Aquarians, but although she thought of her mother as an atypical Aquarian, Robin had begun to wonder how many of her mother's characteristics she had herself, and to disavow any they might share.

Her mother hoped Robin's child would be a boy, saying, *"Girls are so much trouble; you have to worry about them more than boys. Your sister's child is in love, and that is a worry. When you were little and sick, I had to sit by your bed to see that nothing happened."* Robin wondered what sitting with a sick child had to do with its gender. "I kept your bed next to ours for the first three months," her mother went on. *"Crib deaths . . . I don't think you should keep the baby in a separate room"* Robin thought this advice "crazy," and said, "What bothered me most was that she wished I were a boy or that *she hadn't had me.* I was surprised she could be so insensitive, and Bert was shocked." Robin would not let her mother stay with her after the baby came.

> She stayed with my sisters. There's no way Bert or I would tolerate her, especially if it's a girl after what she said about girls. The way she was so watchful over me must have *seemed to be aggressive. Her*

*going overboard to see that nothing bad happened. She must have wanted us to die—the first three months with each of us she hardly slept. That's extreme.* That's how she must have taught all of us—*to communicate the opposite of all aggressive feelings.* The funny thing is that I don't think I felt it much as conflict until Hector died violently, and it all got stirred up in me. When I first chose to be a nurse, and got married, I wasn't aware that my *helping career* must have come from her communicating that I should be *overly caring.* It was fun to take care of people. Intense feelings about *dying*, and the way it happened to me for real, so suddenly and violently, woke me up to those feelings all at once. At times I was angry at Hector's seeing other women, and wished he were dead, feeling that I didn't know him. I think I must have felt that way about my parents when I thought I was trying to mediate their fights and take care of things.

Robin now saw how she had internalized her mother's feelings, turning them around, like her mother, *overcompensating death wishes by sustaining life in the emergency room, reversing boyness and girlness*, and so on. Although the source of Robin's reaction formations was clear, she soon reported how drive activity periodically undermined them.

When Bert's sister and brother-in-law came to visit, Bert suggested they be given the master bedroom, but Robin objected that his hospitality was excessive, feeling selfish in so expressing herself. She likened the situation to her treatment, saying, "You are my therapist and *this is my space.* But that's ridiculous! This is not my space; it's given to me (although I pay for it), but that doesn't make it all mine." I spoke of the squabble over the silver service, which I now understood must have contaminated almost every family interaction. Robin recalled how she had *nearly killed her younger sister when they were children:*

When I was sharing a room with her, she took my jewelry and we had a big fight. I beat her up, wanted to kill her. She shouldn't have my things! It seems dumb, but it was very important at the time. I didn't have any identity at all. *We wore the same clothes then—everything was duplicated.* It gave me empathy for twins; we didn't even look alike. It's crazy; I can't believe my parents did that to me.

She remembered one thing of her own, a little rocking chair her grandfather made for her when she was little. "When I grew older, I put it by the window to rock in and sing—songs from *The Wizard of Oz*, and militant hymns like 'Onward Christian Soldiers.' I must have been a depressed kid!" So much for the drive activity that threatened to undermine her reaction formations.

Robin began to think that her pregnancy made her feel more unsafe. (Pregnancy, with its accompanying regression as well as the regression of her analysis, released further drive activity that made her feel greatly endangered.) She wanted amniocentesis, but was afraid I might be on vacation when she had it. "I'm afraid something bad will happen," she said. "I'd be so nervous about it that it will be hard for the doctor. I'm like a little girl wanting her mother to come with her." Seeming to disapprove of her being dependent, she added, "That's not like me; I like to do things myself. *When my mother did things for me, she seemed to be suffering. I feel she intentionally made herself emotionally unavailable. With you, it's different. I'd be disappointed if you weren't here, but that's different."

Robin dreamt that someone killed her mother and tried to kill her. "I tried to talk him out of it. We had been watching a TV show in which a young man killed his father and his siblings, and would have killed his mother had she been there. The show was about the insanity plea, and dealt mostly with the man's relationship with his family and his psychiatrist. He was only partly responsible." Her dream had a faceless male figure. "I made somebody else responsible," she explained. *If I wanted my mother to disappear sometimes I would try to be more accepting or forgiving, but it's hard to forget she wanted a boy and wished she hadn't had me.* Sometimes I still resent having been left out of things because I'm a girl, like when cigars were for men at the seminar. Or when we were kids and wanted to get on the football team."

Robin still longed for her mother, in spite of being angry:

> There is still part of me that wishes she would change and be more fun to have visit. I'm losing my voice. It may have something to do with you, too. I think that although I have concerns about your being away a whole month, they don't seem as intense as when you went away at Christmas. Also, I looked at the calendar and saw that you would be back before my amniocentesis, so I could talk to you about it. But I still wonder where you're going, maybe all the way to Ghana. Maybe that's why you'll be gone so long—or you are taking a luxurious vacation, by the sea, relaxing and doing nothing. Or going to London. That would be nice; it's a nice city; it's foreign but you can speak

the language. I don't visit my old school, but I can imagine your going to Hampstead. I suddenly feel there's nothing to talk about. . . . I just had this weird thought: it's long to wait till February. I'm ready to get it over now. It seems strange to take a long time to decide to do something, and then to get it over with quickly. Another thing—if I knew where you are going, I'd feel I would *reach you—touch you.*

Robin felt not only emotional but also physical stress at this time, "a little bit tired," "on the edge of being sick," "out of sorts," and so on. "To feel that way day after day is weird," she said, "even though I know there's nothing wrong. When I was playing tennis yesterday, I got belly cramps like something was pulling in my side. Maybe I was doing something wrong that would hurt." Like a boomerang, aggressive impulses which originated in her returned as if she were now the object of aggression from some external source. She reported a dream: "I was pregnant. Only it was bizarre. I could feel my uterus. It was a weird shape—long and narrow." She explained, "When I woke up I was afraid I would have an abnormal child." She compared her fetus to "E.T." and "some sort of amphibious-looking creature" in the film *Alien*. Her aggression made her wonder if there was something evil about her that made "bad things happen to her." Robin consulted a Tibetan monk, a physician who made diagnoses by taking the pulse.

He felt my pulse and said I had a healthy son. It felt like divination. He said there are three basic constitutional pulses: male—stronger, firmer and rougher; female—quick, gentle, and subtle; and neuter—long, peaceful, and soft. Maybe that's why I have all these troubles about masculine and feminine. He said that a female with a male pulse will have long life, wealth, happiness, and a lot of children. If I had another child, it would be female. I'll have no problems carrying the child. . . . Since he is a monk, he is serene and confident. That in itself is healing. It was fun. I could see you more like him than Dr. Black— both foreign. Not the medical model. I see you as fairly peaceful and serene, introspective, and sensitive in that way.

Robin made preconscious associations about wanting a girl during her first trimester. She wanted to show her mother that girls are not such a bother, that "it's not so terrible to be a girl." If she had a daughter, she would "raise her to know she is as capable and powerful as a male." Although she said that would be fun, she added, "males are neat, too." She dreamt of being with her whole childhood family:

> We had two different houses, my big sister and my mother and me
> in one. We were waiting for my father and *littlest sister*, but he came
> *without her*. I got really upset, and cursed: "That's fucking ridiculous
> to leave a strange woman with her—a crazy woman." We quarreled.
> I wanted him to go back to get her.

Robin asked what was the word I had used in the previous session
about her not wanting me to leave. She recalled the word and went
on:

> "Protest!" About your being gone. It was like that, telling my father
> he should take better care of my little sister, not to leave her. That's
> the child part of me not wanting to be left. The crazy woman—maybe
> my mother. In the dream she might have hurt or kidnapped my sister.
> I could get sick while you are gone. I wouldn't have you here to talk
> to. I had a particularly strong reaction to the terrorist bombing in London.
> I have a feeling you're going there. It's really horrendous—you'd better
> not be gone in February!

My anticipated vacation brought up Robin's fear of being left alone
to die, and memories of her father's death. She was frustrated that
she could have done nothing to save him; and there was nothing she
would do to keep me from going on vacation. Her fantasy that only
one of two people could survive persisted, and her identification with
the baby during her first trimester activated childhood memories.
Further regression in analysis let us study her aggression and other
drive activity. The combination of unconscious but willfully effected
reaction formations was clear, an overcompensation that lent itself
to such sublimations as her career choice. Her use of reaction for
mation was in some respects vulnerable to drive activity. The
boomerang effect of her projected aggression was the greatest threat
to her ego. When aggressive in reality or in fantasy she would in
the end fear attack from something fantasied. Her mother was always
a suitable target for her externalizations and projections. In the
transference I was like her first husband, who ran away from her love
by dying. I was like her father, whose death she could not prevent
and who left her alone in danger—in the hands of some "crazy woman"
to die. I was like the sensitive Tibetan monk-physician who would
relieve her anxiety over the possibility of having a deformed baby,
a phallus—like lizard, or a girl. A girl would be defective in her
mother's eyes and in her own as well.

**Second Trimester.** In this period there emerged a preverbal myth that Robin killed her mother, and the omnipotent belief of infantile sadism that she could control life-and-death situations by magic. Her intrapsychic story at this time showed aggression encompassing the object configuration of her mother, me, and her mother's mother. The content and means of transaction within this configuration were death, devastation, and rebirth, and these rekindled the myth about birth and death. Mother devastates child; child devastates mother. This resulted in the analysand's being confused as to which is the mother and which is the child—who kills whom—and who survives. But subject must honor her superego. Her aggressive wishes concerning her mother were so strong that she could not even telephone her, lest the contact kill her.

Robin's pregnancy fed and exaggerated these intrapsychic issues. She asked what she was to do, feeling guilty over the desire to create something as well as fear that someone would die. Much of the manifest content in the second trimester concerned the anger her mother and mother-in-law would feel toward her if she bore a daughter. The proposition was. Mother is going to kill me for bearing a girl; whom will I kill? The ego responds to instinctual trends by eliciting constraint from the superego.

These intrapsychic issues manifested themselves in analysis: "I am tired . . . I have a headache . . . I feel irritable . . . There are these vascular throbbings in my head . . . I am getting used to feeling rather than using words . . . Tennis and exercise make me feel better." "My sister-in-law's pregnant, but they kept it from us," Robin complained. "Her due date is three days after me; they didn't tell us because they didn't want me to feel bad—*as if I couldn't cope with us both getting pregnant at the same time.* They treated me like a child. Maybe I was angry, too, because I felt displaced." She went on: "It just popped into my head that while you were not seeing me, you met a friend of mine. I was pissed—envious. I wasn't having my sessions, but he was seeing you."

Arrangements were made for the amniocentesis. Robin was "real excited." She had heard the child's heartbeat for the first time. But she reported some anxiety, soon overshadowed by physical discomfort. She felt "weak, tired of being tired, naggy," and with too little energy for sex, which she wanted. She spoke of a friend who recovered miraculously from paralysis from the neck down, of the trauma of delivery, and her abhorrence of home delivery related to her narrow escape at birth when there was nothing really wrong. She had missed all the bonding of very early life; she had been kept in the hospital after her mother's discharge. She recalled her frequent childhood illnesses.

The trauma of Hector's death came up in Robin's associations, followed by reference to her father's. But her father's long, drawn-out denial of his state, and her inability to help him had been the most traumatic, leading Robin to conclude that "*there is nothing in this world I can depend on.*" Although she said that this had "for a long time flipped me out," she conceded that it now made sense to her.

Robin felt betrayed, being unable to depend on one who would rather see her friend than her. She felt unable to handle the dependency of her own child. She dreamt of her delivery:

> It was frustrating and unpleasant. I had already delivered, and was at home. I asked my husband to tell me what happened during the delivery, and what the experience was. And! It was not an infant but a two- or three-year-old girl with blonde hair. I was so disappointed! I kept trying to get someone to explain, but they thought I was the one who was strange. Soon the child was almost a teenager. No matter how hard I tried, I couldn't remember [the delivery and the child's early infancy].

In her associations Robin noted how long it took her to have a dream about having a child, and her terror over the delivery. Pre-occupied with accidents, she hoped none would befall her. An in-law had fallen in her eighth month, so she thought of practicing falling backwards to protect her child. She reported that the baby had begun to "poke and punch, bouncing around." She had seen its motions on the sonogram. "Whenever I think of strangling, I think of my mother," she said. She gave an article about Grimms' fairy tales to her sister-in-law, who disliked having her son show aggression. He had pushed and hit his sister and bitten his peers, but Robin noticed that when she played "love taps with him," his behavior was dramatically improved. She recognized herself in him, saying, "I must have been a real terror."

The amniocentesis disclosed a normal baby girl. Surprised, Robin said her work was now cut out for her; it might be harder to raise a girl, but it would be fun. In spite of her protests, she echoed her mother, but a dream shed light on how she dealt with this inwardly: it was "a weird story with no heavy emotion."

> I was at grandmother's house; she was there. There was a big oak tree. It caught fire. I was trying to decide whether to call the fire department or try to put the fire out myself. The tree still stood, with its outside burnt over. A fireman said it really hadn't been a fire, that if we would make a donation, that would be fine. So who was going to pay the fireman, my grandmother or myself? I woke up.

Robin associated to this by recalling scarred, burnt stumps left after "big trees like redwoods thousands of years old were devastated. One planted new trees. I felt sad thinking what terrible destructive things are being done to the land." A friend wanted to cut down a tree in her backyard for firewood, and then to plant three dogwoods as a present for the expected baby.

Robin thought of the possibility that something might be wrong with her baby. "When I think of being castrated," she went on, "I think of a pregnant friend whose husband took pictures of her. One was so phallic! With her dark dress and against a white background you could see her abdomen in profile. Such a funny picture! It reminded me of small boys competing to see which can pee the farthest, standing in this pose with her stomachs sticking out."

She could not escape the question as to the nature of a female; was a female a burnt tree stump? An object of aggression? Had she acquired these internalized perceptions of females from the mother who reportedly despised the female child?

Robin finally told her mother-in-law that the baby was a girl, and of course heard that "boys are so much easier . . . it's nice to have someone strong around the house to lift and make things, and understand how things work." Her mother-in-law had "appreciated having two boys at home when her husband died." Her own mother responded to the news with the remark, "Well, that's all right. Just as long as it's healthy." Robin's comments on her child's gender conveyed much information about herself:

> Wouldn't it be nice to dress a boy in lace a hundred year old? It would *seem funny to turn the tables.* Like I was supposed to be a boy. I guess sometimes I liked it, and sometimes I didn't. I guess part of what I would not like is how amusing it would be to dress a little boy in lace.

> I felt I was a girl made to be a boy. My father showed me how to
> hunt. It was scary. I wasn't sure I liked it, but now I'm glad I learned;
> he wanted me to be a son to him.

She reported a dream concerned with femininity, castration, and
aggression:

> I was going to a woman to have my hair cut [my real hairdresser is
> a man]. I was pregnant. We were sitting talking about cutting my hair.
> She let out this aggressive, assaultive scream and ripped my blouse
> and ripped my shirt off and started sucking at my breast. I started to
> push her away.

Her associations amplified that she wanted the hairdresser to do
something for her, "but she attacked and fed from me." Robin spoke
of feeling humiliated when her mother cut her hair against her will,
and of deciding to be more concerned with her mother's postoperative
treatment. Robin felt that she should be mature enough to provide
more for her mother, who, if left alone, would slowly yield to strokes,
metastases, and other deterioration. One could envision a continuing
three-way struggle involving her with her baby and her mother. But
Robin had to pay for her aggression by having a haircut, and, as
though this were inadequate ransom, she saw herself changing places
with her mother. As long as her aggressive wishes dominated, food
could be obtained only by aggression and attack.

> Robin reported a dream that seemed to confirm my construction:
> I was watching this bird, a *robin*, build a nest. Half the nest was built
> on a porch. I pointed out to my husband how strange it was. And then
> this bird brought this make-believe creature, something nondescript like
> a rabbit, a fox, or a raccoon—four-legged and furry. It was much larger
> than the bird, but the bird was going to eat it anyway. When I went
> back, *everything was gone but a bloody spot.* It felt strange in the
> dream.

Robin's associations made clear how vulnerable she felt:

> "Maybe my mother is the make-believe creature." "I'm not sure which
> one devoured the other. Maybe the bird didn't devour the furry creature.
> The nest was unprotected there on the porch. Sometimes I feel
> unprotected or lacking privacy. My mother is coming next week. I'm
> concerned that something might happen to me or the baby. I've thought
> about who hurts whom in a pregnancy. I keep getting dizzy, I wonder

if something is wrong with my diet. So much stress on my body! I am either hurting the baby or it's hurting me. I think of my mother again, but I usually think she's hurting me instead of my hurting her.

It began to appear from her story in the second trimester that *the girl was the end result of the damage by aggression*. Her body-damage concerns were condensed with penis damage.

**Third Trimester.** This trimester was no less stormy. There was still a great deal of instinctual turmoil.

Robin reported a dream:

> We were walking toward the parking lot. You were leaving to speak to someone else, driving a huge Mercedes. You hit my car and dented it. It was strange that you didn't stop. When I pushed the dent out it was okay. No more dent—it was magical! I drove off.

Her associations began with the waking residue of the previous day; she thought she saw me leaving the car park in a new car with a woman: "Seeing you leave with that woman is what I can't believe or let myself see. I guess I have an image of you as being unmarried, alone, and not having any woman in your life. I don't know why I make myself have that image. I guess *I feel left out*. My worst fear came out—that like Hector you would go off with another woman." The feeling of being left out was intolerable, and Robin delegated it to her husband. Will he feel left out because she has two male doctors? "He might be concerned, or might not want Dr. A or Dr. B to be the most important person." It was almost as though there could not be two men with her at labor.

Robin was helping her mother schedule an operation about the time of her delivery. Was this another way of ensuring one birth and one death at the same time? The answer came with the death of her grandmother. "*I wonder if my mother will be different now her mother is dead*. Would I be different if my mother died?" I wondered to myself whose delivery it would be when Robin came to term, because she would then free herself from her mother. I surmised that the physical delivery of her child would be psychical delivery from her mother.

Although she had little energy, Robin protested against the dependence of pregnancy. She hated being helped to drive up her steep driveway in bad weather, but she also hated having to bring in the firewood by herself. She began to consider the possibility of staying home with her baby. I asked if she still feared that she might be unable to keep herself from destructive behavior. And did her sense of destruction link with fantasizing delivery as dangerous?

She said, jokingly, "If Bert won't go to the delivery room, I won't go." I made the interpretation that she needed him to mediate the destruction, and thus to reassure her that she was unharmed, intact, and still lovable and attractive to him. "I hadn't thought about it that way," she said. "Thinking about birth reminds me of birthdays; this Thanksgiving would have been Hector's."

Robin returned to battling with her mother; it now occurred to her that she had won the silver after a fight between her mother and her younger sister, whose child had injured her eyes while her mother was babysitting. After that quarrel, her mother had stopped baby-sitting. It occurred to Robin that her maternal grandmother had suggested the silver be divided among the three sisters, but their mother had had other ideas.

The next day Robin reported a dream:

> You and I were seeing a patient together, both talking to this patient at the same time. When the session was over and we were leaving, you put your arms around me and kissed me on the neck. It was like I knew that was the relationship. One time in the session, you were talking more than I. When the patient said something, you seemed confused, so I said something to fit things together and your face told me that was the right thing to say.

In Robin's associations, the patient was hers but the analyst made interpretations. "The romantic part of it makes me think of the sessions as a peaceful, quiet time. X saw me yesterday in this building and was surprised; I felt like I was doing something *clandestine*." Here were two perceptions: her analyst approved of her; and she was anxious about doing something "clandestine." Robin's association with the latter unleashed a series of like thoughts. She recalled the complicity of Gary Gilmore's wife in a joint suicide pact; the wife was said to have carried a drug for suicide in her vagina when she visited him in prison. Robin recalled how a friend had hidden marijuana in his rectum to take to a prison, and she recalled having seen her ex-lover's estranged wife. She expressed anxiety lest her analyst think her "too wacky or something."

The next day Robin said that a friend had delivered. She was envious, but as though consoling herself or pleading, she said, "This will be one birthday I won't have trouble remembering." Her dead husband's birthday was also the birthday of her friend's child. There was no escape from her invariant fantasy of one birth, one death. Nevertheless, it seemed as though she were pushing out one introject to make room for another; replacing the memory of her dead husband with attention to an infant's birthday.

Still anxious about the outcome of her pregnancy, Robin considered asking an astrologer the accurate birthdate to gain more control. When she partially came down to earth, she considered whether to buy a child seat with the color of a *silver cloud*, or one the color of champagne. It was still hard for her to come down to earth; she still had memories of Hector, his affairs, and even his reincarnation through her dreams and fantasies. She thought the full moon would bring her delivery, and wondered if she could depend on Bert when the time came. She felt "magic all over the place." There was anxiety in all her associations. Her overdetermined question was: What is going to happen? Who is going to be born? Hector? Or Ben (a colleague who wanted her to deliver on his birthday)? Will it be Bert or herself? Who? Who will survive? She did not consider the possibility that the infant might arrive in its own time. Her mind was fixed on a particular date that suited her work schedule.

Three weeks before Robin was due she called to say she had delivered on the previous day a healthy girl with a 10, 10 on the Apgar scale. She asked for an appointment for the day after she left the hospital. She rejoiced in the baby's ten toes, and when asked what she had expected, replied she had thought there might be something else. She explained that an in-law had webbed toes. Her concern over unseparated toes was interpreted as indicating preoccupation over oneness with and separation from her child and her mother.

Robin negotiated the question of whose delivery it had been, and began to appreciate what was unique about this child, and empathized with her mother. Surprised by her mother's positive attitude, she gratefully found their relationship improving. There had been a difference of opinion with her doctor in which Robin stood her ground and was "*constructively aggressive*." "Bert was pretty impressed," she said. "*All this work really paid off*. It's amazing. Everything went very smoothly. All the doctor did was catch her. Well, he did do an

episiotomy and then sewed me up. He saw some things I hadn't
expected. A bump where he did the episiotomy—he had to remove
a precancerous lesion. I should have regular Pap smears."

After two months, the nature of Robin's analytic material changed.
The interpretation was made that she regarded her getting through
her delivery as the passing of a mystical test. Nobody had died, and
her triumph was such that she felt her analytic work had been accomplished, but although her goal had been met on the physical level,
there was much psychical material left to deal with. She agreed after
a brief silence, saying, "I must have seen it that way. Sure, I didn't
die, and the baby is all right. Last night, while I was working on
bills, Bert said, 'That's a lot of money; when is it going to end?' I
thought 'I feel okay. What next?' When I was with a group of women and we were talking about death and birth and how you think
about your *immortality* when someone dies, I wanted to say *mortality*."

The analysis went on for another two years, although it went flat
after the delivery. For a good six weeks following her delivery Robin
offered few associations, and the interpretation was made that her flat
state of mind indicated that the heavy burden of expecting danger
in childbirth had been laid aside: nobody died, and everyone survived.
Robin was angry at first because this interpretation had not been made
earlier, but the course of the analysis then altered, becoming more
like a classical analysis of a neurotic patient. It was interesting that
Robin's dreams had portrayed her as an infant at first, then a three-
year-old, a menstruating pubertal girl with her mother, and finally as
a young woman receiving instruction from an older one. This provided an intrapsychic chart of her rebirth, which had been forestalled
by her failure to repress her dislike of her hostile representation of
her mother. In the external world Robin recovered her poise, and
became sophisticated in employing appropriate nondestructive aggression in dealing with peers.

## CONCLUSION

When aggressive phantasies are involved in the experience of
pregnancy, the preparation for motherhood can be torturous. Pregnancy can be cathected with transformation fantasies wherein she
may feel herself reborn, but the hope of pleasurable feelings fails
because the mother is still hated. The conscious feeling for the mother

as competent, versus the failure to keep negative feelings repressed about the "bad" mother, contributes to a depressive affect. The feeling of being ugly, unwanted, and unlovable hides and contains the fear of destroying the new relationship. A mother who cathects her baby as a failure consciously or otherwise may fear that she might damage her body in the process. Even in favorable circumstances there is a need to mourn the loss of the ideal self during the process of carrying the baby. However, if, as in Robin's case, the death of a loved one has to be mourned as well, the situation is more complicated. How does Robin mourn the loss of her ideal self when her dead husband has run away with part of her? Furthermore, how does she mourn the loss of her ideal self when part of her self representation is intimately involved with the hatred of her mother? It was Robin's good fortune that she had tremendous capacities to use analysis to shed the hated and intrusive internal object. Furthermore, she had a supportive second husband to help her go through the process of treatment, one who was capable of making her feel lovable in spite of the overwhelming internal feeling that she was destructively aggressive.

Each pregnancy has a story of its own to tell. A story such as Robin's can be heartrending to hear. Fortunately, the resolution of her story can provide heuristic clues to some problems of technique in pregnancy analysis and psychotherapy. A little girl grew up with an invariant pathogenic fantasy that when one dies, another should live. Robin grew in analysis to withstand the pain associated with the acting out, the remembering in action, as it were, of the fantasy. She grew furthermore to anticipate where she had to be intelligent, that is, when she had to use the invariant fantasy as a signal for danger. In the end, we have a detoxified Janus-faced myth of birth and death that incorporated a powerful reaction formation. Infanticidal fantasies of the mother's conveyed through projective identification, but cloaked in reaction formation, were internalized by the child through the mechanism of identification with the aggressor. Analysis freed Robin from possible untoward dangers and threats accruing from identification with hostile internal presences.

An analysis of this kind provides an opportunity to do some integrative thinking about theory and practice. Three key technical and related issues coalesce in order to promote optimal effectiveness in pregnancy analysis. First, the fostering of the intrapsychic story in a way that leads to the discovery and confirmation of the unconscious invariant pathogenic fantasy is primary to analytic work with expectant mothers. The controlled regression that results from both the analysis and the physiology of pregnancy provides a fertile ground for discovery. Second, Melanie Klein's (1945) view that the child's infantile depressive feelings, which are a consequence of aggression and feelings of hatred and are an important part of the child's object relations from the very beginning, is crucial to our discussion. The aggression and hatred experienced by the instinctual ego provide a primitive and subjective experiential world that lacks definition and refinement. Brierley (1951) is apt in her formulation of this issue:

> It remains desirable to insist that the earliest subjective animistic ex-periences almost certainly lack the detailed definition and the emotional refinement which are imparted to them when they are reanimated by regression from a later phase of development in which self-object relationships have been more highly elaborated (p. 84).

The uncovering and processing of these early subjective and animistic experiences while the patient is in the throes of a therapeutic regression account in part for the vivid and sometimes exaggerated infantile responses in the analysis. And third, therapeutic regression and reanimation of core depressive affects experienced by the primitive ego together activate a whole range of hitherto repressed aggressive impulses and feelings of hatred, requiring the analyst to perform a superego analysis that is essentially an analysis of aggression or in the case of Robin, the detoxification of destructive aggression. Put another way, superego analysis concentrates the transmutation of destructive aggression into constructive aggression in ways that give the individual aim and direction.

This tripartite theory of technique, which includes the fostering of the intrapsychic story, the management of a controlled therapeutic regression that reanimates core depressive affects, and a superego analysis that is essentially an analysis of aggression, requires a paper of its own. It is briefly sketched here to show the way to further integration in the area of theory of technique.

# 6/ Ambivalence, Rigidity and Chaos
Integrating Individual and Family Therapy in the Treatment of Chemically Dependent Adolescents

*John Ehrmantraut and Maurice Apprey*

The integration of individual and family approaches in psychotherapeutic treatment has been a topic that has generated much excitement and enthusiasm in recent years. This chapter examines an approach that integrates individual and family approaches in the treatment of four adolescents with major chemical dependency problems. In the cases under consideration a dominant theme was the profound *ambivalence* with which the members of the families dealt with themselves, with each other, and with the issues of chemical dependency. *Ambivalence* is here defined as having "two alternate images of the same object without making any effort to connect them or notice in reality that they relate to the same object and the same person" (Merleau-Ponty 1964, 103). Freud's discovery of the centrality of ambivalence in psychopathology may have been his most important and original contribution. Similarly Mahler's (Mahler, Pine, and Bergman 1975) conceptualization of the role of coming to terms with ambivalence and splitting in the development of the sense of the self may have been her most important contribution. Here we examine four families with chemically dependent adolescents and the role of resolution of ambivalence in their recovery.

Four treatment cases are examined in this study: the patients were Jan Hull, a 15-year-old female; Rob Schaffer, a 17-year-old male; Jim Kirby, a 15-year-old male; and Sean Shotruff, a 15-year-old male. Each had at least three previous psychiatric hospitalizations; each had a history of substance abuse and the failure to respond to earlier outpatient and inpatient treatments. The greatest differences were at the overt level of family structure: two were from very traditional, almost compulsively rigid family structures, and two were from chaotic family structures. Rigid here means that the families had established a very structured and organized existence in which there was a "mask" that everything was in order, under control, and there was no doubt as to what right and proper behavior was. Further, there was little psychological mindedness or tolerance of emotional ambiguity (Frenkel-Brunswick, cited in Merleau-Ponty 1964). The other two families were chaotic: chaotic in the sense that disorder, domestic violence, neglect of emotional and sometimes physical needs, and lack of protection from negative adult behaviors prevailed.

Based upon our previous work with chemically dependent adolescents and their families, we chose these families to study the onset of severe chemical dependency in the context of a developmental breakdown (Laufer and Laufer 1984), where the family system could not provide the structure the developing adolescent needed (Minuchin and Fishman 1981; Scharff and Scharff, 1987; and Stierlin 1981). We expected that the onset of major chemical dependency had occurred in situations where the family system either provided implicit permission for it or where the family system was unable to provide norms, structure, and guidance which would help the adolescent function in the out-of-family world of young adolescents. The therapeutic intervention was then structured to stop the developmental derailment, help the family again be able to provide the "holding environment" (Scharff and Scharff 1981) the developing adolescent needs and to decrease the barriers to the adolescent's internalizing the Alcoholics Anonymous/Narcotics Anonymous (AA/NA) 12-Step Program. "Holding environment" is here used in the sense that the family should be able to be a "container" that can tolerate the developing child's distress, pain, hostility in such a way that the child can then reclaim those parts of him- or herself and reintegrate them back into the totality of the self (Sandler 1987).

## INITIAL PHASE OF THERAPY

Therapy focused initially on developing that "holding environment" and on developing a working alliance with both the adolescent and family. Initially, this tended to be something of a mirroring transference (Kohut 1971), although it was based more on Aichhorn (1983) and Nosphitz (1990). In essence each of these severely disturbed adolescents was approached from the viewpoint of a cultural anthropologist who wanted to understand their inner world and the world in which they lived. The material was dealt with in an accepting manner. It was important for the therapist not to move into being an external superego or to split off projection, but rather to be a "container" (Bion 1967) for this material. "Container" in this sense refers to the therapist's ability to tolerate the patient's hostility, negativity, concreteness, ambivalence, denial, distress, and other feelings, and the therapist's capacity to process those feelings without being overwhelmed and then "return" those feelings to the patient in such a way that the patient can accept them as a part of him- or herself (Sandler 1987). Levin (1987) has stressed the importance of a nonjudgmental approach in the initial phase of treatment.

### Initial Sessions with the Adolescents

The interview technique of the naive observer demands that the therapist approach the material without preconception, without theoretical bias or prejudgment (Heidegger 1968; Merleau-Ponty 1964), so each of these severely disturbed adolescents was approached in that manner. After a brief period of resistance, each settled well into individual therapy. It needs, to be emphasized, however, that the settling into therapy did not translate into the rest of their lives. There were fights, running away, putting in demands for discharge against medical advice, and other major resistances for several months for each of these patients.

Jan was admitted after a major suicide attempt. This was her fifth psychiatric hospitalization. She had used every drug except heroin. Her chemical dependence had developed very quickly after onset in middle school. Up to that point in her life she had been quite a model child, but quite enmeshed with her mother. When Jan entered middle school in a suburb of Washington, D.C., her mother was still fixing her hair, telling her how to dress, and giving her "nutritious" lunches to carry to school. That and her Texas accent alienated Jan from her peers who turned on her with the ferocity that young adolescents can show on a child still enmeshed with the family. Alienated from peers, rejected and lonely, she found a group, the "druggies," who "accepted" her, and within a fairly short period of time she had accepted their drugs, their values, and their images. Indeed, it was apparent that she remade herself in their image, almost in the same way that she had been an image of her mother's wishes before. In this remaking of herself Jan denied almost all of herself that had existed before the onset of substance abuse, insisting that she just could not remember any of it.

Bob Schaffer had four previous hospitalizations. He had used almost all drugs, but PCP was his drug of choice. Prior to hospitalization he had been heavily involved in dealing, gang violence, and street life. For him, like Jan, onset had been in middle school after having been a polite, compliant, passive child. As Bob reported it, his family had taught him middle-class, Christian values that emphasized appropriate and polite behavior and family closeness. As a result of lead poisoning while Bob was an infant, his mother had continued to exercise a great deal of control over him. She had attempted to create on the military bases where they lived a safe, serene, and structured world that she felt she had while growing up in a small town in Kentucky. Bob entered middle school in Hawaii, however, and his parents had enrolled him in a school where Caucasian and other "mainlanders" were in a minority. As a polite, compliant, passive child, he was a perfect target for abuse and intimidation. His family's mode of living did not provide him with guidance or structure to deal with this situation or with the biological demands of the onset of adolescence (Laufer and Laufer 1984), so Bob turned to drugs and the secure, but negative identity it offered. Like Jan he rejected all aspects of himself that existed before the onset of substance abuse, as he put it, "I hate that wimp, I want to be a badass."

The other two cases, Sean and Jim, came from very different background. This was Sean's fourth hospitalization. He had been quite violent in previous hospitals and had assaulted at least one of his therapists. He had grown up in a single parent family home in public housing in Baltimore. He had begun using alcohol and marijuana at age five, given them initially by his mother's younger sister. His father had left his mother when Sean was 2, and she had then been involved with a series of violent, abusive men, several of whom were drug dealers. Sean had developed into a large, powerful-looking, and intimidating man. He had engaged in thefts and other crimes to support his drug habits. His drugs of choice were crack and PCP.

Jim Kirby has had two previous hospitalizations. He had been introduced to drugs when he was 6 by an older brother. His family had lived a very chaotic existence, with one of his mother's husbands committing suicide by shooting himself in the family home, and another threatening the family with guns after experiencing a schizophrenic break when Jim was a child. Jim's primary drugs were alcohol, marijuana, and LSD.

The technique of the naive observer worked especially well with Sean. After a brief period of trying to intimidate me by telling me how he had beaten up previous therapists, Sean moved into trying to impress with his toughness, the crimes he had committed, and dangerous escapades. These war stories prompted me to inquire as to what he had to prove. His hypermasculine stance covered passive longings, dependency cravings, and shame. He was then able, in about the sixth week of treatment to be able to talk about incidents of sexual abuse by a babysitter and about the disorder, chaos, and intimidation that he had lived with for most of his life. He asked "Do you think I screw so many girls to prove I'm not gay?" He had begun using alcohol and marijuana at the age of 5. Sean spoke as if the only way he could relate with other people was to get together with them and do drugs. Now PCP and crack were his drugs of choice.

Initial family sessions, like the initial individual therapy sessions, also focused upon containment. These families were characterized by denial, splitting, verbal abuse, and repetition of stereotyped arguments. In all of these families the father was either absent or emotionally uninvolved in the initial stages of treatment. In general the mothers sought "control," focusing on some aspect of the adolescent's pre-hospitization behavior such as friends, music, or clothing style, while the adolescent demanded independence or autonomy ("It's my life").

Thus, it was apparent that the family structures as they existed could not contain the negative projective identifications or the ambivalence. "Projective identification" here refers to the process where ambivalent feelings are denied in the self, and the unaccepted feelings are split off or disowned and projected into another. Projective identification has little concern for the person who is the object of these projections; in its essence projective identification aims at dominating the object without concern for the cost to the object (Joseph 1987). Indeed, in many ways projective identification seeks to manipulate or coerce the object into accepting the projection and becoming an extension of the person doing the projecting. As Joyce McDougall (1985) describes it: "They use people . . . resulting in exploitation. . . . Unaware that they are using others as stand-ins . . . for their inner psychic world, they fear annihilation if others do not fulfill their expectations . . ." (p. 10). Instead they engage in stereotyped, repetitive verbal attacks spoken with anger and bitterness. It was readily apparent that the aim of these was domination of the other and projection onto the other to obtain control.

Individual sessions with each parent were scheduled to delineate developmental history and the representational world (Sandler and Rosenblatt 1962), and to learn how the adolescent functioned as a transformational object for the parent (Bollas 1987). These sessions revealed a common element among the families: they had not been able to provide a holding environment or secure base (Bowlby 1988, Scharff and Scharff 1987, Laufer and Laufer 1984, Minuchin and Fishman 1981, Stierlin 1981) that would allow the adolescent to meet the challenges of adolescence. Instead, two family patterns emerged: (1) the rigid family, where the developing child had been so controlled and dominated that he or she had not developed the skills to be successful in the out-of-family world, and (2) the chaotic, out-of-control family, where the developing child, had been exposed to deviant norms and role models, disorder, and had received, covert or overt sanction for chemical dependency and/or delinquent behavior.

## *Rigid Families*

Two families (Jan and Bob) exemplified the rigid modality, the central elements of which are (1) an overinvolved mother, (2) an absent or emotionally unavailable father, (3) reinforcement to the child for remaining dependent, and (4) avoidance of peers by children who feared being rejected, beaten up, or ridiculed and who lacked the relational skills to survive in peer group (Stierlin 1981, 38). The rigid modality further expressed itself in these two families with the development of family systems that did not provide support or guidance for functioning in the out-of-family world. These family systems prescribed socially appropriate and polite behavior in a ritualized and stereotyped manner. This was done, however, to please the parents or adults, so it did not provide the children internalized guidance in new or difficult situations or allow for modification. Thus, the rigidity was a mask, almost a "false self" (Winnicott 1965) that covered a lack of personal and psychological development.

Jan's mother, Mrs. Hull, focused initially on how hard she had tried to be a "good" mother, providing a stable home that taught values and appropriate behavior. In sessions with Jan, Mrs. Hull often focused on how her daughter had let her down by not writing to Mrs. Hull's parents. In therapy we were able to weave together these two themes (good mother, contact with mother's family of origin) and the historical data of Mrs. Hull's feelings about the death in her family of origin of six children, several of them males, in infancy after her. When asked for a phenomenological description of her experience of carrying the love and expectations for her lost siblings, Mrs. Hull was able to talk of how she felt she was a disappointment to her father. Her hope had been to give him a grandson; unable to do that, she had disowned her own ambivalence and set about making her two daughters, Michelle and Jan, into perfect children to fulfill that unconscious project (Mahler, Pine, and Bergman 1975).

As a result of this, Mrs. Hull had supervised almost every aspect of her daughters' lives. She chose their clothes, did their hair, fixed nutritious snacks and supervised them constantly. Polite, well-mannered, and "appropriate" behavior were her goals. Her husband, an Air Force pilot, had gone along with this rather passively until the family had moved from Texas to the Washington, D.C. area; he then rather abruptly moved out and sued for divorce. With the advice and help of the father's new girlfriend and Jan's outpatient therapist, Jan maintained a diary of her mother's "craziness," which was used to get the father custody and, in the family's words, to have the mother declared "unfit."

In the Schaffer family both parents had grown up in small-town Kentucky. That social milieu had maintained traditional values. As an Air Force family, the Schaffers had lived on base and attempted to recreate that small-town atmosphere, seeing the military as an extended family. As an infant, Bob had suffered lead poisoning, and his mother had to worry about him constantly. Indeed, she had worried so much that she had come to treat him as if he had a defective immune system, and that only she stood between him and death.

## Chaotic Families

With the other two families (Sean and Jim) it was stormier. As noted above, both Sean Shotruff and Jim Kirby had grown up in extremely disruptive, indeed chaotic families, where there had been domestic violence, negative adult role models, deviant norms, and lack of protection for the developing children from exposure to overwhelming disorder and trauma. Not surprisingly, in these families the hierarchy had been undercut to the point that the adolescents' treatment of their mothers tended to be abusive, demeaning, cruel, and manipulative. Sean, to give one example, demanded that his mother bring him a constant supply of snacks, soft drinks, new clothes, and demand items. When his mother arrived, he did not greet her or ask about her or her life, but instead wanted to know what she had brought him.

Not surprisingly, also, family sessions in these families quickly disintegrated into shouting matches, with the adolescents' demanding immediate discharge and threatening either to run away or hurt someone if their demands were not met. Individual sessions were therefore emphasized.

Mrs. Shotruff had married early, actually pregnant with Sean. After the birth of her third child, the father left, and she had to move into a public housing project in Baltimore. One neighbor told her "Honey, you ain't going to make it." Mrs. Shotruff had a succession of live-in boyfriends. They tended to be drug dealers and to physically abuse her; they also physically abused Sean who was also, as we discovered later, sexually abused by a babysitter. Mrs. Shotruff told this in a rather matter-of-fact way. Her own developmental history showed considerable substance abuse and antisocial behavior in her family of origin. All of her brothers had become chemically dependent and several had been in prison. Interestingly, Mrs. Shotruff reported that her family of origin was still in denial about the chemical dependency of her brothers.

Sean's father reluctantly came to a couple of interviews. These required rather extraordinary efforts on my part since, he was unable, due to work commitments and other obligations, to come to the hospital other than after 4:00 P.M. on weekends. He emphasized to me that he did not "believe in long-term treatment." Sean's father was able to tell me that there was a significant history of alcohol abuse in his own family of origin and that he himself had "gone crazy" and started drinking alcohol excessively and begun to have extramarital affairs when Sean was 2. Interestingly, for Mr. Shotruff the precipitant here was the death of his own father. He reported that, even as an adult, he had feared his father and behaved himself in socially appropriate ways so as not to incur his father's anger. When his father died, that removed the external control, and Mr. Shotruff began to drink heavily and have affairs. He had also been unable to grieve the death of his own father.

Jim's mother initially emphasized the maintenance of family "secrets." There were a lot of them. Jim's father had been repeatedly hospitalized for chronic paranoid schizophrenia, and in Jim's early childhood he had often physically threatened family members and been constantly verbally abusive. Mrs. Kirby's first husband had committed suicide. Jim's two older brothers had become heavily involved in substance abuse and had almost "initiated" Jim into drugs when he was 6 years old.

Thus, the first phase of treatment used individual therapy with parents and adolescents to delineate the lines of struggle and to create a therapeutic holding environment. A major element of this was to move out of projective identifications and splittings and let individual family members see themselves as products of their own histories. Treatment also included concurrent chemical dependency counseling and the long-term structure of the Residential Treatment Center.

MIDDLE PHASE OF THERAPY

The middle phase of therapy consisted in moving the individuals and families from ambivalence to ambiguity. *Ambiguity* is here defined as the ability to confront squarely the contradictions that exist in oneself and in others (Merleau-Ponty 1964). Treatment involved (1) healing the splits, (2) taking back of the projective identifications, (3) aiding the internalization of AA/NA beliefs and value and, (4) aiding the family in becoming a source of help, strength, and power.

Each of the adolescents settled into treatment at a different time: it was the third month for Jim, the fourth for Jan, the fifth for Bob. As we shall see Sean never really settled into treatment.

Three of the four (Bob, Jim, and Jan) were, in relation to peers and staff, almost too cooperative, compliant, and agreeable. In many ways they had therapeutically regressed to a latency age stance of being polite, compliant, orderly, and somewhat passive (Sarnoff 1976). This therapeutic regression allowed for the integration of that part of their personality. Interestingly, Jan, Jim, and Bob each now seemed to reclaim their own developmental history; each began to remember and reclaim that aspect of themselves that had been disowned when they moved into chemical dependency. Even more, each of them came to see how chemical dependency, the negative identity of a drug user, and the gang structure of the "druggies" provided a developmental dead-end, which gave the illusion of freeing them from meeting the developmental tasks of adolescence. Each came to see that the drugs and the gang demanded little in the way of personal development. Indeed, to fit into the drug culture, all one had to do was use the drugs, wear the black clothing or whatever other uniform was prescribed, and listen to the music. The gang came to function as a home away from home, providing almost continuous gratification and "support" and sanction for all sorts of self-indulgent and self-destructive behavior. The gang or peer group also lent strength to them to break away from the infantile objects, use the gang and drugs as containers for the positive feelings, and externalize the denied, split-off parts of the self. Negative parts of the self were then projected onto environmental figures. They came to see how interpersonal relationships regressed to the exploitive, need-gratifying part-object level. The final element that emerged was how cruelty, brutality, intimidation, and bullying of nongang peers and family members was used to externalize the split-off parts of the self onto others.

Family therapy now sought to consolidate the gains made in the individual work. The individual work had delineated how the family systems had collapsed, either early in the children's lives or at the onset of puberty. Now family therapy sought to help the families hold and contain the feelings and ambivalence and to become a source of strength for all the members (Bion 1967, Bowlby 1988, Minuchin and Fishman 1981, Scharff and Scharff 1988).

We began by acknowledging the pain and hurt each person had

suffered, pointing out how angry outbursts covered pain and desperation and, indeed, unwanted feelings in others. The preparatory individual therapy seems to have made it possible to be vulnerable in family therapy.

Jan's mother was able to acknowledge her mistakes and speak of the burden she had carried of not being the son she thought her father had wanted. Jan's father was not able to do as much. He was able to see how his long and frequent absences from the home as an Air Force pilot had prevented him from exercising much of a role in Jan's life. In effect, he had abdicated much responsibility for his daughter. When he divorced his wife, he had not had much contact with Jan until he wanted her to help him fight her mother; then he encouraged her to maintain a diary of how "crazy" her mother was. Initially, his new wife, Ruth, refused to attend any sessions, claiming that she was too "burned out" on Jan to have anything to contribute. When Ruth did attend, she was able to articulate how cut off she felt in almost all aspects of her life. She felt this most strongly in relation to her own family of origin, from whom she felt considerable estrangement. As the therapy progressed Ruth was able to see that she had felt unvalued as a female in her family of origin.

Bob's mother was able to acknowledge how she had worried constantly over Bob. Family members were all able to acknowledge how they had used issues of control and autonomy as their only ways to interact with each other. We were able to reframe much of the parents' attempts at control as desperate attempts to save the life of their child. We were able to help everyone see that Bob had been attempting to build an identity for himself that worked in the out-of-family world. As the family began to be able to talk together, Bob's father talked about how much he disliked his military career and how much he wanted to retire and settle down in a small town in the Midwest. He was able to acknowledge that in many ways he had been emotionally "dead" for years. The family was moving to create that reality for themselves, rather than attempting to pretend that it existed for them in the confines of an Air Force Base.

For Sean, it remained more chaotic. He made it difficult, very difficult, for his mother to create a holding environment. And she remained cut off from external support systems. She was largely alienated from her own family of origin and her relationships with men tended to be codependent. It was as though she had no one from whom she could borrow strength to deal with Sean. He continued to attempt to control her with his anger and demandingness, and sought constantly to undermine any aspect of her parental authority. The absence of Sean's father or of another father figure hampered Mrs. Shotruff. In family therapy she tended to continue to placate Sean, joke with him, and be unable to set limits. When she did set limits, she undercut them by laughing or pretending that Sean's acting out and chemical dependency were some sort of adolescent shenanigans. She seemed to want me to do the work: "Maybe he'll listen to a man like you." This and further individual work with her clarified how multiply determined her relationship with Sean was. He expressed and acted out her anger over not being taken seriously, he embodied many of the qualities of men who had abused her; and she displayed with him, at the emotional level, the same denial and belle indifference that her parents had held toward her brother's chemical dependency and acting out.

For Jim, progress was much more dramatic. In family therapy sessions with his mother he was able to explain the constant sense of fear and disquiet that he felt at home and ask her to help him understand it. As a result of the outpatient work she had done herself, Jim's mother was able to tell him the story of her life and of his family. Especially important had been the tragedy of his father's mental illness. That freed Jim to ask that his father come to Richmond and talk with him. The impact of this was substantial. It released a great deal of previously denied material and allowed Jim to look clearly at his previous hypermasculine stance. He almost immediately formed a very strong positive relationship with his chemical dependency counselor. When he himself announced that he wanted to become a chemical dependency counselor, he was alluding to the strength of that relationship. Jim's mother, freed from having to maintain these secrets, entered into couples therapy with her new husband, who was able to provide her with support, and began to seek treatment for her other sons.

## FINAL PHASE OF THERAPY

The final phase of therapy focused on integration and preparation for discharge. This occurred in the sixth or seventh month for Jan, Bob, and Jim. Sean was discharged in the fifth month, long before he had made the necessary therapeutic gains. Key elements in this phase of treatment were the internalization of the AA/NA philosophy by the patient and his or her family and the consolidation of the family's ability to provide the holding environment and safe base that each of the patients needed. For Sean, things did not go so well. His father had never fully supported the treatment and the insurance company continuously pressed for discharge. While Sean said the right things about addiction, they did not have the ring of heartfelt sincerity. Indeed, the insurance company terminated treatment for him before he had internalized the AA/NA philosophy and the therapeutic gains he had made to that point.

For the other three families, major structural reorganizations took place: Bob's father made the decision to retire from the Air Force and move to the small town that he and his wife had dreamed about. Bob's mother, for the first time in her life, sought full-time paid employment. Jan's father, while deciding to remain in the Air Force, took an assignment that allowed him a great deal of free time. This meant that he had to give up his "hard-charging" style and the hope of further advances in rank. Ruth, His second wife, began to reclaim her Jewish heritage and reconcile with her own family of origin. As soon as she did that, she was able to both confront her husband and Jan that she was no longer going to be a minor player in the melodrama that was going on in their family. It was almost as though Ruth needed that powerful connection with her heritage and with her higher power in order to have the strength to deal with her new family. Jan's mother began to bring her new husband to family sessions and to integrate her new husband into her child's life. Jim's mother made the decision to remarry and got his older brother into the treatment he needed. It was only in Sean's family that no major structural changes occurred. Each of the other families was able to develop the strength and cohesiveness that was needed to be able to be a source of strength to their members.

Two major issues dominated individual therapy with the adolescents in the final phase: (1) relapse prevention and (2) integration back into thc family and mainstream school system. The biggest issue to be dealt with in relapse prevention centered on how the adolescent would find the support system he or she needed to not relapse. That meant that the peer system which the adolescents had previously been a part of had to be given up. Interestingly, the three "successful" cases

(Jan, Jim, and Bob) reported that most of the members of their group had gone off to treatment facilities or left the area. According to Sean, no change had taken place in his gang. Each of the adolescents and their families sought some way to continue the treatment. Two of the families decided to continue to maintain a relationship with the therapists and treatment facility; one, which was moving to the Midwest, asked for help to find a therapist who could continue the work in the same way. In the case that did not do well, that of Sean Shotruff, a number of factors intervened. First, although Sean's father had come to a couple of sessions, he had not invested emotionally in being a part of Sean's treatment. It later became apparent that the father was providing Sean with some covert approval for not engaging fully in the treatment. Second, Sean had, of all the patients in the study, the most significant family history for chemical dependency and antisocial behavior, so it is likely that genetic elements played a role. And finally, Sean had the longest history of chemical dependency, having begun at about age 5, so that it was the most ego-syntonic for him.

CONCLUSION

The results of this clinical study suggests a number of conclusions. The first is that the onset of severe chemical dependency in these cases occurred in two patterns: either at the onset of puberty, when the internalized family norms failed to provide guidance and support or even got in the way of normal adolescent development (Jan and Bob); or earlier in life, under the impact of the emotional flooding of disorder in the home, lack of appropriate adult role models, negative adult role models, and parental chemical dependency (Sean and Jim).

The result in either case was a collapse in the psychic structure of the developing child or adolescent and in the family's "holding" capacity. That, combined with the regressive and disinhibiting aspects of the chemicals, produced massive regressions and fixations. With the predominance of denial, acting out, splitting, and projective identification as primary modes, a pathological characterological structure began to emerge. The family moved from being a holding environment to individual family members to becoming a repository of split-off and denied aspects of the self.

The second is that chemical dependency and the ready-made "druggie" identity provided a pathological resolution to the identity dilemma. A false self (Winnicott 1965) that claimed adult privileges without adult responsibilities emerged. A peer group, the gang, provided sanction for the false self and for deviant, although highly ritualized, norms.

Likewise, each of the families we examined had developed its own personal pseudoreality that failed to provide the container and stimulus barrier which the developing child or adolescent needed. In the chaotic families (Sean and Jim) the family denied the abuse, disorder, and chaos in which they lived. In the rigid families (Jan and Bob) the rigid systems had prevented the developing adolescent from making real contact with the out-of-family world.

In none of these families had the father or father surrogate been available emotionally. In no case had the father served as a "wedge" to lessen the pathological enmeshment between mother and child. In the chaotic families the father and subsequent father surrogates had either abandoned the family or provided quite negative role models of appropriate adult behavior. In the rigid families the father had played a largely passive role. Regarding the mix between individual and family therapy, it appears that in the initial stages of treatment individual therapy with each of the family members is the optimal approach. These families were too enmeshed and there was too much emotional abuse to allow family approaches to be productive. As noted above, the interactional patterns tended to be dominated by splitting, projective identification, acting out, and denial. Interactional patterns tended to be repetitive and ritualized, with each member dealing with the other in a ritualized and stereotyped manner. The individual work allowed each individual to claim his or her own identity and at the same time the initial family work was critical to identifying interactional patterns and identifying the specific transference/countertransference patterns that obtained. Further, it was apparent that it was a mix of both individual and family therapy that provided the space needed to detoxify family processes to the point that real family work could occur. To have attempted it in the initial stages would have been destructive. The middle stage of treatment began at that point when individuals could profit from family therapy and internalize the AA/NA philosophy. This pattern provided a holding environment and source of external strength that the individuals and families could use to support each other through the process. Especially important was the ending of denial, splitting, and projective identification. As noted above, the effects of these pathological defenses were an impoverishment of the personality of each family member and a reduction of family members' interactions with each other to rigid and stereotyped patterns. The family and AA/NA were sources of strength that allowed each member to rediscover his or her own full humaneness. Individual therapy tended to flow from the family therapy and be enriched by it.

The final stage of therapy, preparation for discharge, moved along nicely for three of the four cases. None of these families had been able to provide the flexible structure, boundaries, and holding environments or safe bases the developing child or adolescent needed. Neither group of families had been centered. This lack of centering showed itself in the rigid families in the fixed and invariant ways they dealt with issues and problems. In the chaotic families it showed itself in the episodic and disorderly pattern of responses. In the rigid families there had been an attempt to create a separate family reality that collapsed because it did not provide guidance and support for the developing adolescent. In the chaotic families the collapse of the family system had taken place earlier in the lives of the identified patients. The fathers had been unwilling or unable to provide holding for the mothers; and neither of the parents had been able to call family, friends, or social agencies or other support systems to create the holding. Indeed, in each of the chaotic families there had been a developmental collapse in both the mother's and the father's family of origin, so that mother and father had entered adulthood without the internalized support of their families.

The rigid families had created a family system that was "too good to be true" and that which did not provide support and guidance to the developing adolescent. Chemical dependency and the gang structure provided an alternative false self (Winnicott 1965) that gave the illusion of adult freedom with childish dependency. The chaotic families had collapsed much earlier and the characterological false personalities had emerged in early latency. These were characterized by a hypermasculine stance, coupled with the dependency expressed through anger and demanding, domineering behaviors.

The utilization of concurrent individual and family therapy provided a modality to allow the disinvestment in the false selves, the ending of the ambivalence, healing of the splits, and reintegration in both the individual and the family.

# PART THREE

# OTHERNESS: APPLICATION OF THOUGHTS ON PROJECTIVE IDENTIFICATION TO UNDERSTANDING OF GROUPS

# 7/ Clinical Decision-Making in Groups, Countertransference, and Projective Identification

*Howard F. Stein*

> The symbolic elements in life have a tendency to run wild,
> like the vegetation in a tropical forest;
> —Alfred North Whitehead (1927, 61).

This chapter presents the story of what takes place in clinical *groups* of decision-makers and its consequences for the work of the group. Emphasis is placed on subjective, largely unconscious contributions to clinical group decision-making (biomedical and otherwise), and the role of projective identification in "cementing" group perception and action is noted. There has accumulated by now a sizable literature on the dynamics of the dyadic doctor-patient relationship, doctor-family relationships, and the culture or social organization of medicine (Balint 1957; Bowen 1978; Crouch and Roberts 1987; Fox 1959; Freud 1912/1958; Gerber and Sluzki 1978; Katz 1984; Parsons 1951; Stein 1985g; Stein and Apprey 1985, 1987). That is, there are "micro" and "macro" or global studies both written about medicine and used within medicine.

Virtually absent, however, are studies of the middle ground, so to speak, of local, relatively small medical groups in which crucial clinical

An earlier version of this chapter was presented as the Faculty Lecture at the University of North Carolina at Chapel Hill on 8 January 1986.

187

decision-making occurs. This chapter argues that the group dynamics of clinical decision-making, while little investigated, deserve to become part of the forefront of medical and residency education, since they have significant consequences for the process of diagnosis and patient care. I use the phrase "clinical decision-making" in the widest possible sense, however: to include diagnosis, treatment, and referral of individual patients and families, medical case conferences, grand rounds presentations (lecture or case-review format), curriculum committee meetings, tumor conferences, quality assurance meetings, medical faculty meetings, physician-nurse hospital staffings, and so on. In this chapter, I shall first offer a brief, selective review of pertinent literature on group dynamics, then illustrate how unconscious factors in the life of clinical groups affect decision-making and (through projective identification) often are projectively played out in the clinical content.

I wish to make clear at the outset that I do not construe this topic to be either of purely academic interest or to be principally relegated to behavioral science. Both of these compartmentalizations displace attention from the ordinariness, indeed universality, of group-dynamics issues that merit attention in all clinical group contexts. By understanding the group dynamics of authority and leadership, identification, role allocation, "groupthink" (Janis 1982), and of the "basic assumptions" (Bion 1959) by which groups are regulated, we discover some surprising answers to the question: How do medical students, residents, and faculty decide which diagnoses, laboratory tests, procedures, medications, techniques, even curriculum items to select? This chapter thus examines in a preliminary fashion *the group psychology and group logic of choice itself in medicine*; it explores emotional investments in the group, and their consequences for decision-making and medical action.

Further, I wish also to make clear from the outset that I introduce "group dynamics" not as yet another "new subject" to vie for time in the already densely crowded curriculum of medical education; it is not, in my thinking, a distinct, separate subject but instead is intrinsic to all medical subjects where groups are involved in thinking and acting together. In group decision-making it would behoove us to ask, rather than simply assume, "What is this meeting all about?" One begins to approach an answer by considering the language of discourse used by the group, together with its underlying meanings, of medical group decision-making (see, for instance, Stein 1986a). Given the fact that this language is often not limited to the biomedical model that constitutes medicine's official worldview, it is necessary to explore medical standards of evidence in day-to-day episodes of decision-making, rather than only in relation to the explicit biomedical ideal. Metaphors serve as powerful organizing principles in this implicit group or cultural model (Stein and Apprey 1987).

A content analysis of medical meetings reveals that much of emotional consequence for patient care bubbles beneath the surface of the official and prescriptive biomedical model. For instance, consider the following statements taken from a variety of recent medical conferences: (1) "You ought to fire him (the patient) if he doesn't follow orders" (business metaphor); (2) "Sometimes you'd like to drop-kick a patient into the end zone, but you can only make a lateral referral to somebody else's service (sports metaphor); (3) "He tackled the real difficult patient. He handled it aggressively. But he got shot down (by a faculty physician) a couple of days later" (sports and war metaphor); (4) "In the clinic, I hit her with everything (antibiotics), but she still came in the hospital door" (sports/military metaphor); (5) "We're either going to be a gatekeeper of medicine or become part of the food chain" (business metaphor; projected oral-aggressive impulses); (6) "We've got to get in there and blast away with the biggest guns of steroids" (war metaphor); (7) "It's cheaper to keep a person healthy than to fix him after he's broken" (mechanical metaphor); (8) "This resident has the skills of plugging into people" (electrical metaphor). The central point to be made is that, while all these metaphoric statements are often rationalized as mere figures of speech, they indeed articulate underlying—if disavowed—agendas and implicit ways of viewing the subject matter of medicine (see Burnside 1983, Caster and Gatens-Robinson 1983, Hayden 1984).

## GROUP PROCESS THEORY

In a study of "the double-bind between dialysis patients and their health practitioners," Alexander (1981) argues that "case conferences, staff meetings, patient forums and exchanges are all presently characterized by detailed itemizations of persons' proclivities, symptoms and character, rather than by consideration of the interactive structures that occur in clinical environments" (p. 323). In this chapter, I investigate the group *psychological dynamics* of this group labeling process and of the interactive structure in clinical environments. In an overview of "the social labeling perspective on illness," Waxler (1981) writes that

> illness labels are created in social negotiations between several parties, including professionals and the troubled individual, and they occur within institutional and social contexts that play an important part in the negotiation. Ideologies and organizational procedures as well as the relative power and interests of the negotiating parties contribute to the label of illness (p. 296).

Later she argues that

> even the information from hospital or clinic records that we tend to think of as "hard" data can also be conceived as the product of social processing. Labeling theory suggests that facts such as diagnosis, length of stay, prognosis, may tell us much more about the social character- istics of selected patients and the workings of the treatment system than about a biomedical process (p. 302).

The language of discourse of medical group decision-making, together with the standards of evidence revealed by that discourse, often suggest the presence of medical "explanatory models" (Klein- man 1980) that deviate considerably from the naturalistic biomedical one (see Stein 1986b). For example, at medical teaching conferences, the presenting physician and other participants (faculty, residents, interns, students) may stigmatize a particular patient as a "troll," "albatross," "crock," "jerk," "dirtball," and the like. These images might alternately designate a patient who has failed to be compliant on medical regimens, a patient who has not been found to have an organic lesion (equated in the medical lexicon with "real disease"), a patient who has been especially difficult or demanding personally, or one who seems to be virtually identical with patients previously seen who occupy a disdained category (e.g., Veterans Administration patients who are dependent, manipulative, demanding, etc.).

Often the effect of the stereotypical label "troll," for instance, is for the physician or clinical group to presume that they know more about the patient than is warranted by actual experience with the patient. This in turn may lead to the possibility that the physician will overlook or dismiss complaints, symptoms, perform a more cursory physical exam, omit the ordering of laboratory tests, and the like. As a result of overlooking the possibility that a more serious disease process might be present, the physician may miss a medical diagnosis because it has been superseded by a metaphorical one. The converse of this is also common, as in the medical argot which describes a person as "the gall bladder in (hospital room) 276." Here, the biomedical diagnosis is correctly made, but expands and in turn reduces the ill person to a metaphoric image of a diseased organ. In both cases, the ill person is reduced to a metaphoric image: in the first example, a stereotypical metaphor which dehumanizes; in the second example, disease itself becomes the metaphor which dehumanizes. In both instances, the purpose of the metaphor is to increase social distance between doctor and patient, a process which is rationalized and enhanced by group consensus.

Although there is a considerable literature on the influence of unconscious distortion upon the dyadic doctor-patient or analyst-patient relationship (Freud 1912/1958; Katz 1984; Stein 1982d, 1983a, 1985g; Stein and Apprey 1985), there is a relative paucity of research on what can be called *group countertransference* to patients, families, medical institutions, diseases, theories, and so on. Metaphors are useful vehicles for expressing thought and feeling; however, in group medical decision-making as in other "corporate" activities, participants often fail to examine the truth value of these expressions, and hold them to be true, absolute, and necessary. That is, metaphors may take on the group psychological function of defenses and thus serve as resistances to further knowledge. Diagnosis and treatment—and the patient—unwittingly may be used to confirm the "reality" of the metaphor.

To "listen" to group dynamics in clinical decision-making, one identifies, in Bion's (1955) words, "the emotional states which find an outlet in mass action of the group in behavior that seems to have coherence if it is considered to be the outcome of a basic assumption. . . . Emotionally the group acts as if it had certain basic assumptions about its aims" (p. 476)—for instance, that members are trying to fulfill dependency wishes through one another, that they wish to find oneness or unanimity or merger with each other, that they hope to give birth to a messiah or redemptive idea, that they are bracing for flight or fight, and so on.

It is thus not to be automatically assumed what purposes are served by thought, decision-making, and action in groups (see La Barre 1951). In distinguishing between the pragmatic, task-oriented level of group functioning which he labels "work," and the symbolic, unconsciously driven level of group functioning which he labels "basic assumptions," Bion (1955, 1959) affirms that both are concurrent:

> I do not believe that we are dealing with two different kinds of group, in the sense of two different aggregates of individuals, but rather with two different categories of mental activity co-existing in the same individuals. In work group activity time is intrinsic: in basic assumption activity it has no place. . . . [Moreover,] the more the group corresponds with the basic assumption group the less it makes any rational use of verbal communication (1955, 463, 473).

I do not question that medical groups (e.g., case conferences) perform genuine work-group activity (e.g., learning differential diagnosis and choosing among treatment plans). However, such rational, purposive learning often serves the deeper purpose of fulfilling the group's basic assumption activity. Stated differently, patient care, curriculum content, administrative policy choices can all readily become means toward fulfilling unconscious ends, rather than be evaluated in terms of their own merits. In groups as well as individually, physicians can use patient care as a forum if not battleground for quelling their own unvoiced anxieties (see Katz 1984, Mold and Stein 1986, Stein 1985h, Stein and Mold 1988). If, as teachers or as clinicians, we conflate the "patient's (or resident's) problem" with our problem, we are doing a disservice to the very person(s) we purport to help.

In *Group Psychology and the Analysis of the Ego* (1921), Freud noted that groups are organized by emotional ties to one another and to the leader. Often in groups the individual "ego ideal" is replaced by an external object; that is, individual judgment is ceded over to the leader. In group decision-making, including medical decision-making, participants may often seek consensus—that is, "sensing" together, unanimity of vision—in order to not have to "sense" separately, independently. In medical decision-making groups, such borrowing of authority and emotional consensus often leads to the distortion of the subject matter under scientific scrutiny. Much as medical professionals pride themselves on independence of judgment, group decision-making often becomes a way of ceding and suspending that critical, individual judgment in favor of merger with the group.

In his study of American civilian and military policy-making groups, Janis (1982) revealed that beneath the surface picture lay a deeper agenda, which he called "groupthink." In this frame of mind, group participants secure morale and diminished anxiety at the price of critical thinking; loyalty and commitment to the group and to its leader is purchased at the price of reality testing. Among the characteristics of "groupthink" which Janis identifies are the illusion of invulnerability, the assumption that one's group's position is moral, stereotyping about one's own group and out-groups, group pressure on dissent from policy, self-censorship to avoid deviating from consensus by voicing misgivings about policy, the illusion of unanimity (the unwarranted assumption that silence=assent), the search for policy validation only within the group, and the emergence within the group of "mindguard(s)" who "protect" the leader from adverse information that might shatter consensus.

In his corporate consultations, Jaques (1955) came to realize that organizational groups unwittingly use group relationships and roles as defense against shared persecutory and depressive anxiety. Kafka and McDonald (1965), and before them Brodey, Hayden and Krug (1957), discovered that conflictual relationships among health-care and administrative group members often are a recreation or reenactment, via identification, of relationships in the family of the patient. If this parallelism is not analyzed by group members, but is instead acted out, the patient's and family's problem will be perpetuated. Here, the group response becomes a metaphor for understanding or misunderstanding the patient and family. In a similar vein Foulkes (1948), Abse (1974), and Volkan and Hawkins (1971, 1972) observed that in teaching a group of psychiatric residents about psychopathology, the group would by identification reenact aspects of the patient's symptoms or family history. By helping the group to understand its own emotional response to the patient, group members could be more empathic in therapy. A clinical group's emotional response in the process of data gathering, diagnosis, and decision-making about treatment can thus clarify or distort members' abilities to understand the patient.

More recently, Kets deVries (1984) has edited a volume of psychoanalytic studies in management, which shows how management style and group dynamics affect decision-making. Stein and Fox (1985) likewise showed how the metaphor of the "family" affects interpersonal relations and decision-making in medical and nonmedical environments. In *The Psychodynamics of Medical Practice* (Stein

1985g) as well as in "The Culture of the Patient as Red Herring in Clinical Decision-Making" (Stein 1985d), I have described and analyzed how the medical group process affects clinical judgment. And Stamm (1987) recently describes the disruptive role of individual and group countertransference in psychiatric hospitals.

In all forms of group decision-making unconsciously motivated agendas often fuel, if not altogether supersede, the ostensible agenda of "getting the job done." Stated differently, from the point of view of the group dynamics, the underlying "job" may override the official one, although it is commonly performed in the name of the latter, which rationalizes it. Often the organization utilizes the official task as a medium, so to speak, by which to achieve the underlying agendas which cannot, or may not, be verbalized except through metaphor (see for instance, deMause 1982, Stein 1985b).

R. H. Hook (1979) writes that "Freud discovered that the latent content, the *real* meaning of the dream, can best be understood as a reflection of wishes or ideas which can only be tolerated when expressed in a suitably disguised form" (p. 269). One may transpose this observation into a statement about *group functioning* as well: in medical decision-making groups, the latent wishes or ideas can only be tolerated when expressed in the subtly disguised form of (a) the official, ostensible agenda or task, and (b) metaphors and similes that are further rationalized as "mere" figures of speech. The formal agenda thus has the group psychological function (in addition to its conscious function) of serving as the manifest content of the group fantasies and wishes; that is, it represents them while at the same time diminishing anxiety and guilt by displacing attention from them (see also Boyer 1979).

In an essay on psycho-geography, I wrote that

> members of groups imagine their group and other groups to be *human bodies* which protect and menace one another; groups can thus be born, mate, give birth, age, die, be male or female. In the group-process of corporate, academic, medical, military, and religious committees (or organizations) alike, one commonly hears: "We've got to . . . present a united fron . . . protect the rear . . . guard our flanks . . . protect both our fronts . . . launch a frontal assault . . . conduct a two-front war . . . they're bleeding us to death . . . make sure the enemy doesn't get a chance to come in the back door." While these expressive or symbolic statements take place in the context of instrumental or reality-directed

activities, they convey what Bion (1959) termed the "basic assumptions" about what it feels like to be a member of a group (see also
deMause 1977, 11), which in turn adds impetus to the work, goal, or
task-oriented behavior (Stein 1984, 37; see also Stein 1980b).

Whatever else a clinical department or medical conference *are*, they
are *not* a human body with a powerful yet also vulnerable "front"
and "back." However, when in groups, under the influence of powerful
fantasies and shared sense of endangerment, we quickly come to feel
and think and act *as if* (although concretely, not provisionally) our
group had become a single human organism whose "front" and "back"
are endangered and which we must at all costs protect (see Stein
1980b). The most important agenda of the group unwittingly becomes
the defense of the body, not the project all had originally and ration-
ally gathered to undertake.

Decision-making in medical groups can thus be founded on the
paradox that strict objectivity is the official rule, while participants
unwittingly appropriate reality (secondary process) to fantasy ends
(primary process). In the logic of primary process, there are no
negatives, time and space are distorted or altogether negated,
omnipotence of thought and wish-fulfilling fantasies reign undeterred,
the part may represent the whole; or a thing may be represented by
its opposite, and ideas and wishes may be displaced and condensed
in symbolism (Freud 1900a/1953).

In a paper on organizational diagnosis, communities, and political
units, Brocher (1984) writes that in groups

> it is possible to destroy or divert individual insight and to prevent
> reality perceptions by creating social dependency needs, thereby forc-
> ing the individual into primary process operations through collective
> regression in the interest of collective unconscious drive needs and
> satisfaction (p. 374).

Kernberg (1984b) poignantly notes that

> understanding organizations in depth can be painful; at times, such
> awareness does not improve the effectiveness of staff members; but
> understanding always makes it possible to gain a more realistic,
> even if painful, grasp of what the future probably will be. The parallel
> to the painful learning about aspects of one's unconscious in the psy-
> choanalytic situation is implicit: there are similar pathological de-
> fenses against becoming aware of reality in the place where one works
> (p. 44).

I am not arguing that the official content (e.g., differential diagnosis, treatment plan, curriculum choice, leadership choice, and so
on) is of little "real" consequence for the group that is considering
that content. Rather, I am arguing that this content is often the "foil,"
"vehicle," or symbol of other, deeper agendas that are rarely addressed,
but are instead acted out *in the name or guise of that content.* The
group dynamics are "really" about both—all—levels, although groups
act as if the only reality that is permitted to be acknowledged and
addressed is the official topic of the content under consideration. There
are ominous consequences for group morale, medical education, and
patient care when participants remain unaware of all the "parameters" (levels of agenda) involved.

At worst, the underlying dynamics *use* the official, conscious agenda
to displace attention from their emotional investments and meanings
in the group. Such subjective involvements remain an unanalyzed
case within the case, so to speak, and profoundly influence the kind
of work the group undertakes. The value of devoting attention to
group dynamics within medical meetings of *all* types (case conferences, administrative, curriculum, and so on.) is that as participants
become able, in a nonjudgmental setting, to identify underlying
conflicts, fantasies, wishes, fears, and the like, participants will have
both greater access to and control over them. The process of the work
group will thus be facilitated and liberated rather than contaminated.

## UNCONSCIOUS AGENDAS IN CLINICAL GROUPS: BRIEF EXAMPLES

From curriculum to directly clinical decision-making in medicine,
groups can play out unconscious agendas along subgroup and individual role divisions, as well as by consensus. In medical training
settings, for example, the male physician director will often be
perceived by his colleagues, residents, employees, students, and so
on, as wise, fair, decisive, kindly, thoughtful, and the like; in short,
as a "good" father figure. Contrariwise, the male administrative director
will often be perceived by the same group as aloof, manipulative,
unavailable, inconsiderate, coldly calculating, rejecting, and the like;
in short, as a "bad" father figure (similar splits in the armed services
are well known).

In a paper on physicians' proverbial unease discussing *financial* matters with patients (Stein 1983b), I described and analyzed a common geographic and emotional distinction in clinics and hospitals between "the back," where medical care is delivered, and "the front," where patients are asked for their money. Although both are subgroups of a larger single group with, ostensibly, a single mission, they are at chronic loggerheads with one another over priorities. Each tends to view itself as "good" and the other as "bad," that is, each allocates to the other subgroup disavowed characteristics of its own perceived role, if not of its members' personalities. Both groups may even respond to this view of self and other by various strategies for undermining the other.

Consider also the potential dynamics of *generational succession among second-and third-year residents* in their group. Many years ago, one astute resident, upon assuming the third and final year of his training, referred to his subgroup as "old dogs" and to the second-year subgroup as "young pups." This image crystallized my impression of a family-style sibling rivalry in residency training. Residents, who throughout their second year had been in all aspects of decision-making cautious, deferential, quiet, unobtrusive, even meek, may seemingly undergo a dramatic personality change in their third year, becoming assertive, more self-assured, outspoken, decisive, bossy, even obnoxious. What I had initially mistaken to be a sign of "personality" change I came to see as reflecting different role transitions in the medical hierarchy. These role positions pervaded diagnosis, management style, and administrative behavior alike.

One common group teaching technique in medical education is known as "pimping." Widely used in military training as well, it is based on intimidation as an instructional style. The demonstration of knowledge is placed in the service of defending oneself from public humiliation. "Pimping" is often explained by resident or faculty physicians as a method for sharpening a young physician's or medical student's skills in diagnosis, test ordering and interpretation, and patient management. Concurrently with these, however, it also teaches the student, intern, or resident the utter necessity of being right, the conviction that there is a single correct answer to a medical problem, the belief that one must always appear certain in order to avoid being "one down" to another. To be right is to save face in the faculty's eyes and in those of the group and oneself; to "miss something" or to be wrong is to be utterly humiliated, to lose face, and to be perceived and come to perceive oneself as unprofessional (see Stein 1985b, 1985e, 1986a).

In the technique of "pimping," the teaching physicians bombard the resident, intern, or medical student with a volley of questions, probing not only for what the latter knows, but seeking out some vulnerable spot, hoping on the one hand to expose it, and on the other hand to provoke the one being questioned to show his or her mettle by holding up under fire. To "win" one must avoid being ridiculed. The conflict is openly acknowledged to be highly gendered. For instance, one male physician expressed gratitude for being able to come away from an interrogation "still feeling like a man," while another dreaded the incessant questioning as a concerted effort to make a "pussy" out of him. Similarly, many female physician trainees aspire to be accepted as "one of the guys" or "one of the boys," going so far as to have their hair cut short or "put up" (in a bun), and not wearing make-up, so that they will look more like males. During pimping rituals, they feel most degraded if they are brought to tears— that is, if signs of gender "weakness" override professional "strength."

In my experience, this method of teaching is done more in groups than in dyads, for the presence of the group of learners is vital for magnifying and intensifying the effect: the teacher and student, for instance, are the "drama" for the audience, who quickly learns the moral of the tale by identification both with the "aggressor" and the (potential) "victim." What is learned in these "pimping" rituals is both specific biomedical content (differential diagnosis, laboratory tests, the latest literature, choice of procedures, and so on) and the need to shore oneself and the group by certain defenses (projective identification, identification with the aggressor, displacement, and so on). Throughout medical education and practice, biomedical content becomes the battleground for the shoring up of these defenses.

From my experience in both urban and rural health-care training, I have noted that resident and faculty physicians often rely upon consultations/referrals with specialists in other roles to perform mental functions that they include only with difficulty in their own role perception or self-image. That is to say, the division of labor between various biomedical and psychosocial specialists serves emotional as well as practical purposes. In the two family medicine residency training settings with which I am familiar, residents spend their second and third years of postgraduate training in a community-based rural setting, following an internship spent at an urban tertiary care center. On several occasions shortly after moving to the rural training site, residents would say to me with chagrin, "Where is my medical social worker (or clinical psychologist, or family therapist, or home health nurse) to take over when I'm through with the patient?"

Such a question reflects the difficulty many physicians have—a difficulty that is institutionally supported by a rigid division of labor in urban training centers—in integrating the more personal aspects of patient care (personality, family situation, economic-employment condition, and the like) into the doctor-patient relationship (see Eisenberg and Kleinman 1981, Katz 1984, Stein 1985g, Stein and Apprey 1985). Local and institutional group dynamics formalize and sanction a splitting of mental functions into official clinical roles. Young doctors moving to more rural environments relinquish this splitting of roles with great difficulty—or else, as is more often the case, avoid the sense of threat altogether by attempting to conduct a strictly biomedical practice.

*Group dynamics can unwittingly appropriate virtually any subject or topic*, while participants ardently believe that they are above such subjectivity. The group, for example, can suddenly become fascinated with the patient's "exotic" or different culture as a means of deflecting attention from their sense of uneasiness over how they have managed the case (Stein 1985d). Case conference participants can quickly stereotype an elderly patient as suffering from a chronic illness condition, when in fact the patient had only recently become acutely ill (Stein 1985g, 21–23). Physicians can "transfer" powerful, aversive past medical experiences inappropriately onto current ones (Stein 1986b).

In my experience, tumor boards or oncology conferences often proceed according to a formula whereby the patient is presented as, say, "a 52-year-old white, married female," and the remainder of the discussion of cancer staging and treatment proceed as if there is no person, only a disease "the oat cell carcinoma in (hospital room) 205." Such group-sanctioned defenses as depersonalization and rationalization are employed to keep the painful feelings of identification, fragmentation, and decay "off limits" to the discourse (Stein 1985g, Stein and Apprey 1985). Group anxiety can trigger a "cascade" of action more designed to quell the clinicians' anxiety than to actually help the patient (Mold and Stein 1986, Stein and Mold 1988). Medical faculty (M.D. and non-M.D. alike) frequently impute to residents a sense of "threat" or "anxiety" that may be more projected than actual. Further, through residents' subsequent identification with faculty anxiety, a self-fulfilling prophecy may be created. Group outrage against categories of patients—alcoholics, drug addicts, those with AIDS, overeaters, the sexually promiscuous, the medically noncompliant—can lead to "treatment" being scarcely disguised "punishment." At issue is not only the patient's agenda, but also the group's own forbidden dependent, aggressive, and sexual impulses as projected onto, and now "managed" in, the "bad" patient (Stein 1982a, 1985a, 1985g; Stein and Apprey 1985).

In a wide variety of case conferences I have attended over the years in many medical disciplines, the official and ostensible goal of patient care is often superseded by a group dynamic whereby the *medical specialty strives to reassure itself of its identity status in contrast to competing medical specialties.* One family physician/family therapist presiding over a teaching case conference, expressed relief that the patient did not choose to go to a psychiatrist. An internist at a similar conference shared his satisfaction that the patient had not sought care from a surgeon. Diagnosis and patient care can become the battleground, so to speak, for expressing interprofessional boundary conflicts and for shoring up professional group identities.

The teaching of specific surgical, prescribing, counseling, or family-therapy skills often has the implicit agenda of affirming the group's identity and its members' sense of security. "This is what *we* do" is often conveyed by means of contrast—often with ridicule and contempt—with "That is *not* what we do" or "That is what *they* do." The ordering of certain tests and procedures is thus often used as a group ritual to affirm the rightness and sanctity of professional group boundaries. In essence, the group is saying: "What is good for us must be good for the patient." One often hears a senior resident or veteran physician (of any number of specialties) adamantly say: "I do it the way I was trained in internal medicine, the City, the Medical Center, Dr. X's service, and so on." The authority behind one's choice is thus overdetermined in the psychological sense, not simply the result of scientific considerations (see also Katz 1984).

The question of what is good for the patient may thus inadvertently become secondary to what confirms the integrity of the group's identity: stated differently, patient diagnosis and treatment may become a means of achieving group identity resolution. The defense mechanisms of "splitting" and "projective identification" often can be seen as regulatory mechanisms for clinical group behavior: keeping the sense of "goodness" inside, and expelling any "badness" outside. The unconscious group agenda thus may become the affirmation of the rightness and integrity of the group itself *via* the official content or agenda (e.g., patient care, curriculum, and so on.).

Psychiatrist Casper Schmidt (1984) writes that

> the capacity of effective working-through of emotional conflicts within groups is restricted. [W. R.] Bion [1961] has shown how groups have great difficulty in performing real work, and how insidious and predominant are those emotional positions which he called basic assumptions (where fantasy solutions hold sway over realistic ones). The commonest pathway for the discharge of dammed-up group tension, historically speaking, is recourse to action (p. 40).

In medicine as in other institutions, reality and technical know-how are often manipulated to serve fantasy ends. Striving and purporting to conduct "patient care," medical conferences frequently use the process of assessment, diagnosis, treatment, and prognostication also to "treat" their own anxieties—evoked by the patient during the diagnostic and treatment process.

Clinical consensus in a group is sometimes a dangerous blinder to important clinical data. Such consensus, however, tells us much clinical information about the culture of the group. Any case conference can turn into an unconsciously orchestrated group defense against fears evoked by the patient and/or the patient's family. At one such conference some time ago, for instance, a resident hurriedly discussed a patient with a recent myocardial infarction (M.I.), and devoted the remainder of the conference to diagnostic considerations, complete with a virtuoso review of electrocardiogram (EKG) readings, virtually omitting the biopsychosocial interplay. Although discussion of multiple levels of factors was part of the conference's official agenda, diagnosis occupied center stage; prognosis was openly tabled. I was puzzled by the virtual group taboo on discussing personal and family aspects of the M.I. A relative newcomer to these conferences, I felt awkward in making a comment at the time and remained silent.

Afterwards, several colleagues and I discussed the group process of the conference. The conference speakers felt to me to have been in something like a trance: as if they only *could* talk about EKGs. The very denial that characterizes patients with M.I.s, and that makes it difficult for physicians to diagnose M.I.s in patients, also makes it difficult for a roomful of physicians and medical educators to discuss mortality and mutually shared risk-ridden Type-A behavior. The doctor-patient and doctor-patient-family relationships can be therapeutic only insofar as the physician can avoid using doctor-physician colleague-staff relationships as a bulwark against painful self-knowledge—and in turn, painful clinical knowledge of the patient and family (see Stein 1985g; Stein and Apprey 1985, 1987).

I wish to conclude this chapter with a more extensive medical group case in which the members of the group became projectively identified with the infant who was a patient of one of the group members. It vividly illustrates how group countertransference, fueled by projective identification, can influence diagnosis and treatment alike. This specific case parallels the clinical content (maternal-infant relations and the role of projective identification) of cases presented by Dr. Apprey in earlier chapters.

## CASE EXAMPLE: "I KNOW SHE'S ON COCAINE"

Taken from a consultation I had with a medical corporation in early 1987, this case illustrates how concrete a metaphor or symbol (here the patient, her infant, and their significance to the group of physicians) can be. The example further illustrates that, no matter how symbolic an event may appear in the interpretation of an outsider, to many group insiders it is—and for them is adamantly defended as—their *reality*, one which they will staunchly, even violently, defend. Such symbolization must be taken literally and not seen as representative of or meaning "something else." The theme of "medicine-as-war" will quickly become clear.

The following events took place at a regular weekly medical corporate meeting on physician-patient and physician-corporation relationships. Beforehand, there had been rumblings among some of the (resident and intern) junior physicians that there was a major conflict with administration. When the meeting began, the Chief Executive Officer (CEO), a male authority figure in the group, sat at the head of a long open oval with the interns, residents, and myself. Next to him sat Dr. Y, a woman, who acted as facilitator and began the session by asking whether the group wanted to talk about any administrative issues before we started in with a difficult case. There were no takers.

One of the junior physicians then presented a passionate account of a recent encounter he had had with a woman and her five-month-old baby during a "well baby" visit. The physician said he had been forty-five minutes late for the appointment (physicians at this facility often being considerably behind on their schedules), and had apologized to the patient. In response to his questions, the patient said she felt depressed. She also said that she had to be somewhere else soon, and could not stay for a long appointment. The physician felt frustrated because he had wanted to explore her depression and its etiology more, but that she left before he could do so. When he asked her whether she was taking drugs—he suspected cocaine—she replied no.

As the conference continued, the presenting physician, then many of the participants including the CEO of the medical group, were convinced that the woman was addicted to cocaine. They discussed that it was often necessary and justifiable to deceive addicted patients into making a "confession." The CEO, who smoked used the example of working with patients whom he wanted to persuade to quit smoking: "You listen to their chest with the stethoscope, and even when you can't hear any unusual sounds, act and talk as if you do, to pull their bluff, saying, for instance, 'It sounds pretty bad. You must smoke pretty heavy,' to get them to admit their addiction and be frightened into quitting smoking."

The presenting junior physician, and many of the group, often referred to the baby as a "victim" of the mother's probable neglect and abuse, and did not trust the mother to take good care of her child if she was high on cocaine. Shortly thereafter, many of the group members escalated the discussion and virtually pushed the presenter to do more and more to rescue the baby from the bad, victimizing mother. When I briefly commented on how we might have jumped to conclusions about the mother's "addiction," since we had so few facts, the group continued unanimously as if it were an undisputed, indeed, indisputable *fact* that the bad mother was endangering the life of her innocent infant. The group had identified with the victim-child fantasy, and saw themselves as suffering at the hands of an abandoning or abusing mother. The group consensus was that the woman should be persuaded to return to the clinic soon and to admit that she was on drugs.

Much of this case, and subsequent discussion, concerned the doctors' need to get control of their practice, of the patient, of the patient's addiction. Attempts to discuss difficulties in controlling patients or the reality that clinicians do not control their patients' lives were to no avail. The group almost single-mindedly branded the woman as "bad" and in need of treatment ("punishment"?) in order to ensure protection for her helpless child. The presenting physician became the perceived instrument of the group will.

The physicians then began to discuss their own mistrust and resentment about their ambiguous role in the medical corporation. The CEO had left prior to this part of the discussion. They talked about him as "father," "leader," and "Doc," often speaking of themselves as "victim" of him and his corporation, implying that he was hiding the truth from them, using them, exploiting them, and so on. (Interestingly, earlier in the meeting I had imagined the CEO and the facilitator to be the "father" and "mother" of the organization—group members often go to the "mother" to mediate for them, to complain of how the organizational "father" mistreats them.)

The facilitator and I both tried to help the group to distinguish between (a) what the leader was actually doing to them and (b) what they imagined him doing to them. (I knew from other conversations that the CEO had not long ago given a then-destitute junior partner an automobile, had given others money to tide them over in difficult times, and had, with his family's permission, taken temporarily into his household a staff physician going through divorce.) The group rejected this distinction, because they felt persecuted and exploited by him. One junior physician acknowledged that he loved "Doc" and that "Doc" really did have an open-door policy toward his junior partners. However, he went on to say that they really didn't feel they were treated like junior partners, but like children. The group started to vacillate between expressions of love and hate toward the CEO, rather than talking about their original hate and fear of persecution. By the session's end, the group resolved to keep discussing these things with the CEO and in the group's regular meetings.

In the final moments, the group expressed their resentment that the CEO had recently dismissed a senior physician, one whom they hoped could be reinstated. They clearly felt that the senior physician had been victimized by some sinister administration plots that the group had not been informed of. The group expressed some sadness at the loss of their colleague, that they missed him; however, they phrased this mostly in terms of his and their victimization at the hands of an abandoning and ruthless parent. At the end of the meeting, the facilitator and I discussed the entire process, and concluded that the group's overdetermined response to the "crazy" case was really a metaphor for the group issues that later emerged. The case showed how *concrete* a group metaphor or fantasy can be. Not only could it not be challenged, but, for at least the time being, it was impermeable to challenge.

Just as the junior and senior physicians in the group had talked early in the session about the need to "deceive" patients in order to get them to admit their bad habits or addictions (smoking, drinking, drugs, and so on) and in order to frighten them into changing, the junior physicians later in the session used the same word—"deceived"—in describing how they felt at the hands of their CEO. There was thus a progression in the mental representation in the group: from (a) an unconscious identification with the aggressor, turning passive into active *in behalf of* rescuing an infant with whom they had projectively identified, to (b) a subsequent conscious identification of themselves as the victim of the leader's aggression, deception, manipulation, and betrayal of trust. The final issue brought up by the group was the recent dismissal from the corporation of a well-liked senior physician. Discussion suggested that group members identified with the "victim" (as this latter physician was perceived) and were unable to mourn his loss. The group briefly explored the issue of whether he could be brought back (can the dead be brought back to life?).

The recent history of the corporate group itself may have underlain the choice of the initial case example by the junior physician and the continuous reiteration of the themes of "victimization" and "deception" throughout the two-hour discussion, irrespective of the official subject matter. The group, however, accepted no thematic link as existing between the various segments of the marathon meeting, even though the above themes clearly pervaded it.

CONCLUSION

Any unit of clinical, didactic, or research interest (chromosome, cell, person, family, culture) can inadvertently be used by a group as a blinder in the guise of illumination (Devereux 1967, La Barre

1978). And how can these blinders be acknowledged, and their meanings if not origins understood, if they are not addressed in the professional education of the group participants and not included in their later "continuing education"? For such clinical blind spots are *magnified rather than diminished* by the influence of group psychology, wherein people cede individual conscience for collective consensus, replace their personal ego ideal with the person and role of leader, and partly surrender the self in merging with the fantasied powerful collective self by identifying with group members and with the group "itself" (Freud 1921/1955). This chapter concludes that often the purpose or aim of clinical decision-making in groups is not patient care per se; instead, patient care becomes a symbolic means toward the validation and actualization of a shared metaphor, the alleviation of anxiety, and thereby the affirmation of group identity by consensus.

Every time yet another curriculum component is suggested for medical or residency education, the outcry arises from students and residents alike: "Don't we get enough thrown at us already? How will this new item help us be better physicians? Won't it detract from the really important topics we're already studying?" What, then, justifies my advocacy of attention to group dynamics in medicine and in all clinical training? Nothing less than the fact that, given our unaware, subjective investment in our groups and in the topics we discuss, such attention serves as a *corrective* to our tendency to distort the very topic we are considering. In clinical work, as in all realms of human activity, our problem is not what we know, but what we prefer to think *must* be true when, for unconscious reasons, we overextend our theories, when we impose on the subject matter what in fact belongs to ourselves—and then proceed to treat the object of our projective identifications as if the characteristics were intrinsic to it. Alas,

> Man, proud man,
> Dresst in a little brief authority,
> Most ignorant of what he's most assured,
> His glassy essence, like an angry ape,
> Plays such fantastic tricks before high heaven
> As make the angels weep.
>
> —Shakespeare, *Measure for Measure* (2.2)

# 8/ Adapting To Doom
## The Group Psychology Of An Organization Threatened With Cultural Extinction

*Howard F. Stein*

> In order to be accepted in a culture one must accept or adopt an uncritical attitude towards its customs and its fears. . . . A consequence of this is unthinking acquiescence and extinction of all possibility of solving the underlying problem.
>
> —Jules Henry (1963, 122)

This chapter illustrates the role of unconscious activities in organizations and cultures. Through a case study, it describes the interplay between organizational fantasies and organizational realities in the political life of a medical corporation. This case study is of the decline of a corporate group that has been slowly allowed by its parent company to atrophy, and of the relationship between the subsidiary, which I shall call Managed Care Affiliate (MCA), and its corporate headquarters. It explores the dynamics of grief-work and impediments to it posed by a sense of catastrophe. In this chapter I also explore my evolving role as an organizational consultant seeking to help—albeit in a limited way—the subsidiary, MCA, through its protracted uncertainty, rage, and grief. At the descriptive level, the case study interweaves (1) the narrative of an organization whose members were haunted by a sense of doom; and (2) the narrative of my role as organizational consultant, a role which both gave me access to (1) and provided conflicting expectations for my interventions on the organization's behalf.

At one level, this is a case study in cumulatively traumatic culture (organizational) change. At another level, it is a contribution to (a) the theory of culture and organizational identity; (b) the study of organizational/cultural decline and grief-work; (c) the study of the relationship between individual and group; (d) the study of the relationship between organizational fantasies and realities; (e) the analysis of the process of adaptation to the social environment; (f) the study of intergroup "transference" (projection, externalization) and its relationship to group images and their consequences; and (g) the literature on consultant roles, including the role of corporate consultant as transference object, and the opportunities and limitations of such roles. This chapter attempts to address a central theoretical issue in all social/behavioral sciences: How does the researcher/scholar avoid reifying social units or organizations (ethnic groups, corporations, nations, political parties), while at the same time doing justice to informants' or participants' own felt and constructed worlds? How does one clarify reality within worlds in which social units are invariably experienced as metaphors—images of living organisms, biological bodies, or supernaturally created entities?

At the outset I wish to identify my roles in the main office and its subsidiaries, and to explain my choice of this case study. Both in the main office and in its branches I was employed principally as a behavioral-science trainer in communication theory and skills. My official function was to offer seminars and workshops to physicians and clinical administrators on physician-patient-family-staff relationships, corporation-community networking, and cultural and religious factors in clinical practice. I actively involved community and service agencies and businesses in these training programs, including ethnographic visits to occupational sites from which some of the patients were drawn. Among my more informal roles, I also did individual and group counseling of executives, managers, and staff at all facilities. The official title of my role in the subsidiaries was "consultant."

Because of the rigidly hierarchical structure, role compartmentalization, and status distinctions at the home office, my roles there were more circumscribed, and my authority more limited, than in the smaller subsidiary companies. In the smaller, largely rural, companies people learned multiple roles beyond their job description on paper, in order to be able to fill in for one another and keep the organization functioning. Initially, my role in all these sites was defined as consultant to the manager trainees and to the manager-development program. That is, I expected to limit my interaction mostly to the physician and administrator trainees.

In the subsidiary organization, partly because of my "systems" or "contextualist" orientation, and partly because of the greater role latitude and autonomy allowed me, I quickly began to include executives, midlevel managers, trainees, and medical and nonmedical staff in my round of activities, in conferences, and in group problem-identification and problem-solving sessions. Many of the problems the trainees were having with patients or families were exacerbated by conflicts between the clinical-service and the administration or business sectors, between expectations of the laboratory and the nursing staff, between the medical and the administrative executives, and so forth. As in clinical work with families, where an "identified patient" bears the symptoms for the family, I found it advantageous to involve—at first informally, unofficially—personnel whom I had not been officially hired to train or consult. Over the years, these informal roles grew into shared expectations (although nothing had changed on paper).

There was thus an evolution from formal roles to informal (albeit explicit) roles, which included but transcended them. I was regularly enlisted by upper management at these subsidiaries to address companywide issues of "communication" and morale. Mobility in the organization gave me a sense of the larger context of problems, the focus of which might be patient behavior, payment/collections problems, or community relations. It also led to my being regularly enlisted by company members at the subsidiaries to function informally as facilitator of communication between quarrelling units, for example, or as a mediator bringing key group issues to the attention of upper management (thus permitting group members to save face, while assuring that the issues were addressed). I was on occasion humorously labeled "the Henry Kissinger of MCA." It was in this expanded role that I gradually became aware of the chronic, widespread apprehension at MCA that it was targeted for extinction by the home office.

Over several years I had noticed from my seminars and workshops, and from individual supervision of trainees and consultation with managers, that they were much less interested in and capable of devoting concentrated attention on problem patients or problem families. I gradually concluded, and corroborated from work throughout MCA, that apprehension of doom and preoccupation with "survival" made all but the most routine clinical and educational activities of lower priority than in previous years—even for some of the same managers and staff who had been ardently devoted to psychosocial and community issues. From cues such as demoralization, greater infighting, and diminished empathy toward patients, I began to pay greater attention to and inquire into (both in the subsidiaries and in the home office) the reality of the threat and the fantasies associated with the MCA members' growing sense of fatalism.

As with many of my earlier studies in medical culture and in physician-patient relationships (Stein 1985g, 1986d, 1988; Stein and Apprey 1985), I did not initially set out to conduct a study of this medical corporation. Rather, the "case" took shape during the course of my regular work as an applied anthropologist in this corporation's home office and regional subsidiaries. During the course of ordinary clinical seminars and workshops, and during informal hallway conversations, I began to notice—or to think I was noticing—the emergence of certain new patterns. Using such techniques or tools as participant observation, open-ended interviews, and naturalistic observation, I conducted ethnographic fieldwork in the course of doing my job. I began to keep detailed notes, both to document and make sense of the "pattern" I thought I was discerning, and to provide additional observational data to test and revise earlier impressions.

In the earliest years as consultant to these often rural subsidiaries, I was viewed with suspicion variously as a "Yankee" (in the southern Great Plains, with heavy influence from the Old South), as a "spy" for the home office, and as an "unknown quantity." After several years of cultural "probationary" time, I was accepted as one of "us" (at MCA), while my ties to "them" (headquarters) were acknowledged, but without contamination by the insider/outsider dichotomy. MCA personnel came to realize that I had their welfare at heart. At the beginning of this phase, the group transference toward me shifted affective poles: from distrusted stranger, who had to prove himself and his loyalty, to ally, informer on the secret deliberations of executives hundreds of miles away, and one who might even be a rescuer.

As the years of collaboration continued, these idealizations diminished, giving way to more realistic perceptions of "coworker" and "friend." With each new visit I made, personnel would invariably inquire whether I had any new information from headquarters with which they might better divine their future. Although this role of newsbearer continued, MCA members became increasingly realistic as to the limits of my "omniscience." For one thing, I was not a member of executive councils at the home office, and was thus not privy firsthand to high-level corporate decision-making (including budget). My ascribed role at MCA came to be defined in terms of such epithets as "the listener," "our shrink," and—during the course of a three-hour marathon with one manager—as "our toilet paper, who takes us as we are."

Chronic role confusion and role limitation were not unique to me. The mystification of corporate agendas and policies by the new Chief Executive Officer (CEO) at headquarters, his abrupt policy and priority shifts, and his inability to delegate authority or to share fiscal information, engendered role confusion among many at all levels in the central office and subsidiaries. In my roles both at the home office and the subsidiaries, I strived to serve as an advocate for psychosocially informed medical training and medical care, and as an advocate for group morale, founded on reality acceptance and on a concern and respect for one another's welfare. I attempted to help the members of the subsidiary acknowledge perceptions and feelings they were dreading, while at the same time I attempted (informally) to document to the corporate executives at headquarters the consequences of actions and policies that these executives would not openly acknowledge. My documentation and private expressions of concern to executives at the home office were characteristically met with reassurances that their "flagship" affiliate continued to have their unwavering support—or with discounting, incredulous smiles. Still, I staunchly advocated that executives from the home office and MCA make more frequent contact through visits, letters, or on the telephone. In sum, my advocacy was less for one side than it was for greater reality testing on the part of both.

The material discussed in the case was collected from such regular (weekly, fortnightly, monthly, quarterly) corporate activities as staff and managerial meetings (I was not privy to meetings of the highest executives in the corporate headquarters); clinical case conferences; division meetings (between nurses, managers, trainees, and business

officers); marketing meetings; and numerous individual consultations
with various organizational members over six years. The case study
is distilled from field notes, and discussed as an example of a widespread, if not universal, psychological process. Moreover, although
the organizational group to be discussed had been in existence only
fifteen years, its dynamics in the face of continuous threats to its
existence will be shown to be the same as those of tribes, ethnic
cultures, factory towns, and intergenerational neighborhoods that have
existed for decades or centuries.

## SETTING THE CONTEXT FOR THE STUDY

The medical corporation under consideration in this discussion,
together with its regional subsidiaries, can be characterized as a
bureaucracy both in the social structural sense and in the experience
of authority. Baum (1986), for instance, writes of bureaucracies as

> hierarchical organizations in which authority is centralized and respon-
> sibility is diffused. ... The authority who assigns, variously controls,
> and evaluates a subordinate usually is relatively distant, relatively
> anonymous, and more or less autonomous. This situation of being
> controlled by someone powerful but poorly visible—a situation not
> unique to bureaucracy—encourages subordinates to fill in reassuring
> details by transferring past assumptions about authority to contempo-
> rary authority. Some of these transferred assumptions deriving from
> infantile and childhood experiences, make bureaucratic authority seem
> larger, more powerful, and more punitive. ... Workers may respond
> to organizational authority associated with earlier images of the superego
> and ego-ideal (pp. 159–160).

The dynamic identified by Baum will be shown to apply not only
to individuals within an organization, but to subsidiary organizations—
subunits—of a superordinate corporation, units with which workers
(members) have identified themselves culturally as an "us" who possess
a shared fate.

Moreover, what Volkan (1980b) writes of narcissistic leadership
will be shown to characterize the leadership ambience at the home
office in our case example:

> Clinging to the illusion of being powerful among others, some narcis-
> sistic people ambitiously seek the leadership of groups, organizations,

or even nations. In their relentless search for power they use other people, discarding them without compunction whenever it seem advantageous. The success of such a person bent on leadership is obviously contingent on many variables, some of which may depend more on the psychology of the group itself than on his own. For example, a group may have undergone humiliation and defeat and be impelled on this account to seek a glorified leader who will lift them up (p. 136).

Volkan later identifies "the 'fit' between an individual's grandiose ambition and his potential followers' need" (p. 138), specifically the leader's need for power (together with his aura of power) and the group's sense of powerlessness and vulnerability (pp. 139–141).

In their psychobiography of Atatürk, founder of modern Turkey, Volkan and Itzkowitz (1984) offer a distinction in the dynamics of leadership that is especially germane to the dynamics of the relationship between MCA and its corporate headquarters. Writing of narcissism and leadership, they propose that

> narcissistic leaders can be divided into two general categories. One is the destructive leader who attempts to protect the cohesion of his grandiose self chiefly by devaluing others in order to feel superior. The destructive narcissistic leader poses a considerable danger. History shows that an excessive need to devalue a group often leads to the destruction of that group. For the destructive leader the devalued persons or groups become targets for the externalization of his split and devalued self and object images, and those people and groups have to be suppressed.
>
> The other type of narcissistic leader is reparative, and Atatürk is representative of this category. The reparative leader wants adoration from his "valued" followers and may attempt to uplift them in order to build his support on as impressively high a level as possible. The followers are idealized so that their mental representations can be fused into the grandiose self of the leader, making the cohesiveness of his inner world more stable.
>
> In some respects the distinction between the reparative and destructive grandiose leaders is artificial, since one may turn into the other under certain circumstances (p. 358).

In a bibliographic essay on "crisis cults," La Barre (1971) writes that

> simple theories of stress fail to predict anything about the quality of the response. *It is not stress* [the external stimulus or challenge] *as such but the psychic style of reaction to it that is important.* . . . Simple stress

theory as a single cause cannot predict the nature of the response also because it concentrates too largely on "outer" realities . . . (p. 23, emphasis in original).

In the case to be discussed I shall argue that the group's anxiety over the future of their organization was followed by regression, by the release of aggression that was alternately outwardly and inwardly directed, and by projection, leading in turn to the condensation of projective contents with apperceived reality, and thus to the diminution of reality testing. The case is interpreted as an example of the process of complicated mourning in bureaucratic cultures.

Freud (1917/1957), Pollock (1961), Volkan (1979, 1981), Mitscherlich and Mitscherlich (1975), and the GAP (Group for the Advancement of Psychiatry) Committee on International Relations and Stein (1987) have explored the vicissitudes of complex mourning for individuals, families, groups, and cultures. Owen (1986, 1987) and Stein (1986d, 1988) have argued that whole organizational groups need to work through the difficult process of grieving if a new organization is to emerge. In the case to be described, I shall offer an interpretation that the reaction within the subsidiary corporation is not altogether accounted for by labeling it as "victim" and its parent company as "oppressor." I shall instead suggest that there is evidence of a tacit collusion between inner and outer realms.

One who looks at the social history of the United States since the late 1970s and early 1980s is struck by the belligerent atmosphere of competitivism, commercialism, corporate groupism, rampant survivalism—in short, the renewal of a "live and let die" social Darwinism (Stein 1982a, 1982b, 1982c, 1985f). Catastrophism—from the religious to the ecological—pervades ideologies of the inner as well as the outer environment. One reads almost daily of "hostile takeovers" of one corporation by another, of numerous mergers, of the insatiably large engulfing and devouring the vulnerably small. Bank failures and closings, farm foreclosures, the virtual disappearance of the once proud and productive "Steel Valleys" of the upper Midwest and the Northeast, and the replacement of solo and group medical practices by corporate outpatient and hospital conglomerates—these are but several instances of societywide rapid transitions and losses of identity (Stein 1985f).

During the 1960s and 1970s large-scale American urban redevelopment and relocation disrupted networks of meaning, information, succor, and mutual assistance, and inspired terror in many ethnic populations for whom home and neighborhood were experienced as coextensive with the world (Stein 1980a). On a large time scale Fry (1970) and Shkilnyk (1985) have described societal disintegration and rampant self-destructiveness among Native North Americans experiencing rapid acculturation. Common Native American responses include emotional numbness, indifference, listlessness, passivity, disorientation to time and space, alcoholism and other substance abuse, random aggression—in short, what Jilek (1974) terms "anomic depression" (see also Jilek-Aall 1986).

From two decades of intermittent ethnographic field work in the McKeesport area of the Monongahela "Steel Valley," principally among Slavic-American steelworker families (Stein 1980a, Stein and Hill 1979), I have witnessed once-bustling mill towns become virtual ghost towns in which only the demoralized, the retired, and those unable to move are trapped. During twice-a-year visits to the Pittsburgh-McKeesport region, I have seen and read (in local newspapers) the same scenarios played and replayed. On the one hand, officials of USX (formerly United States Steel) have urged greater economic realism on the part of devastated communities, admonishing them to relinquish their understandable but pathetic symbolic attachments to the steel mills (for example, the "Dorothy Six" blast furnace at the former Duquesne Works). On the other, many newspaper editors have urged greater regionalism and less localism in spirit, and have pressed for a more cosmopolitan spirit of development (for example, thinking more of the greater-Pittsburgh development than of microdevelopments in individual towns along the Three Rivers). At the same time, many townsfolk are members of multigenerational families for whom mill-church-tavern-market were "the world," a way of life where symbols are never experienced as "merely" symbols.

Such attitudes as cosmopolitanism, parochialism, localism, tenacity against change, and tenacity for change, are all highly emotionally charged, symbolic operations. In all organizational policy development and planned change it behooves us to understand the dynamics of those who have "everything to lose" and those who have "nothing to lose" (see Grieco 1988 on organizational culture and conflict). For the former, the boundary of the self is not the skin but the multigenerational way of life of which mill and town are living symbol: the "death" of that way of life is the same as for one's sense of self to die, for historical continuity to be forever severed. For the latter, the boundary of the self lies in the new future that differs entirely from the past, involving a new social skin—consisting, say, of a wider geographic compass of identity (Stein 1987a) and a proud, new economic vehicle for identity ("clean" informatics, telecommunications, banking, rather than "dirty" coal and steel).

It is perhaps ironic that people at both extremes—those who cling to their past and those who fling it from themselves—are dealing with grief in ways that avoid its pain and inner growth. Those who cling tenaciously to the milltown past, who even hope for the resurrection of the steel-making way of life, avoid grieving by insisting that the old way is not really, or not necessarily, gone; by sheer denial, by angry, aggressive protests against corporate executives; or by a numbed, chronically depressed attempt to live life as usual amid the decay. Those who attempt to cast the past from their view, to efface it from memory and landscape, often seem to evince a kind of manic denial, a restless need to do and to change the outside so as to avoid feeling the loss and pain inside. Sadly, what is most needed by all participants to the calamity does not occur: that is, a public acknowledgement of the profound extent and depth of the change, and a public grieving on the part of all "interest groups," so that the past can be collectively worked through and then relinquished.

As a result, organizational retrenchment, regression, and factional splitting (e.g., between the "progressives" and the "conservatives") occur. Far from healing, the wounds become more gaping, even as business ostensibly flourishes in some sectors. When an individual or group cannot bid farewell to an era, when it is either clutched as if it were life itself or flung as if it were death itself, organizational renewal is aborted (see Owen 1986, 1987). Both sides invariably become stuck perceiving the other as "betrayer"—of progress, of change, of the once solid and good way of life.

What Kohut (1972) described as "chronic narcissistic rage" assures that constant battle prevents deep bereavement. Neither flight *into* the past nor flight *from* the past permit an organization, a community, a culture, or a region to grieve for what has been irrevocably lost. Moreover, attenuation of ties to the past becomes all the more unbearable when some external force is perceived as assaulting, if not severing, those ties. In a number of studies (Stein 1984, 1985c, 1987a; Stein and Niederland 1989), I have discussed individuals' and groups' representation of themselves and their identities in terms of place and space. Under the rubric of "psychogeography" I have described how developmental issues over separation and individuation become symbolized in terms of the fusion of self-boundaries with the spatial boundaries of culture, workplace, and social organization.

## CASE EXAMPLE: "HOW LONG CAN WE CIRCLE THE WAGONS?"

The case is an account of MCA, one of several subsidiaries of a medical corporation whose headquarters is located in the Great Plains of the United States. The corporate headquarters and its several regional subsidiaries are in the business of providing all areas of "patient care": clinical and preventive; hospital (inpatient) and clinic (outpatient); geriatric, family, adolescent, and pediatric medicine; wellness programs for the healthy; rehabilitation programs; screening, referral, and consultation. In the corporate headquarters, major programs, together with funding, are devoted to projections of future health trends, efforts to capture the market, the development of health-policy statements, the design of medical practices based on cost containment and increased profit, and the development and implementation of clinical decision trees based upon probabilistic analysis.

The board of directors of the main office recommended, and the shareholders overwhelmingly approved, the hiring of a new corporate CEO in the early 1980s, a time during which a new national consensus over cost containment, corporate competitiveness, and national social Darwinism was congealing. It was a time when corporate medicine became more explicitly profit-oriented and much less avowedly service-oriented. Kormos (1984) has labeled the era as the "industrialization of medicine." The new CEO, in tune with this emergent ethos, was seen by the board of directors who hired him as a "visionary" with a "grand vision of the future," a person who "flew high above everyone's heads, in the clouds, looking for megatrends of the future to capture the medical market." Many viewed him as a person who could rescue the company from its poor self-image and from its poor reputation among the corporations. He had been chosen among the applicants because he showed the most promise of expanding the company into greater profit, visibility, stature, and power in corporate medicine. He was hired with the understanding that he would increase the space, the local and regional influence, and the income of the company. From the outset he invested corporate money and personnel time heavily in a proliferation of building plans and models and architectural drafts, and in high-technology acquisition involving multiple computer systems, with a series of disappointing results.

Soon after the installation of the new CEO and his staff, proposals, policies, and practices all reflected a new set of polarities: among them the corporate center versus the periphery (e.g., subsidiary companies); urban (or metropolitan) versus rural (where the subsidiaries were mostly located); income generation and cost containment versus service; medicine-as-product-line versus medicine-as-skill-and-service; the new executives and managers versus the old ones ("young blood" versus "old blood"); centralized authority versus local autonomy; high technology versus personal medicine. Certain metaphors or images of medicine favored by the CEO recurred: "the automated physician" (emphasis on high-technology-mediated, depersonalized care); medical practice as a "product line" and the physician as a "product line manager"; patient care as "managed care" given by "producers" of health care to "consumers" of health care; "the bottom line" as "costcontainment" through "managed care systems." Within these perspectives the rural subsidiary organization, MCA, was devalued, despite the fact that it continued to be a reliable high-income generator utilizing the old ways of a family-service-oriented, moderately low-tech, hands-on approach to patient care.

For the first several years, the new leader at headquarters, unable to delegate responsibility and authority, repeatedly intruded into groups and projects he had assigned. He insisted on total control of the company's finances; he shared financial and development information only with a small inner circle. Although he frequently espoused an "open-door policy" for any one to "drop in for a visit," in fact he was often out of town on business visits; or when he was in his office, layers of offices and secretaries served as blockades that intervened between himself and others. Eventually, the door to his office was completely closed.

During these early years his executives, managers, trainers, and staff as a rule rationalized the already demoralizing situation and generously gave him the benefit of the doubt. "He needs to be up there [in the clouds] to see the big picture. He doesn't have time for us down on earth. But he has us at heart. It'll all pan out in the end. We just have to give him the time and the space he needs." His distance and personal aloofness inspired wonder and awe, as if he possessed some magical prescience and omnipotence. For the first several years, numerous displays of arrogance, his humiliation of managers, his driving off of junior executives and staff, his secrecy in decision-making and fiscal management, his aloofness and unavailability—all of these were excused and rationalized in his behalf by corporate members who had merged his vision with their future, and who had hitched their dependency to his often elusive wagon. When he found the current of the future, while testing the high winds, the expectation remained that he would make his corporation wealthy, famous, and powerful.

In exchange for the promised future of wealth and renown, the CEO asked for commitment and for the unquestioning loyalty of his "team players"—a term merging their interest and fate with his, and one which he and others in the upper corporate world would frequently invoke when subordinates began to deviate or rebel. (The accusation that "you're not a team player" was among the worst fates that could befall a corporate manager.) The CEO asked them to wait; eagerly anticipating the eventual payoff of the "vision," they were willing to wait.

A large turnover of junior executives and middle-level managers occurred with the installation of the new CEO. This was quickly justified by a polarization in which the old-timers were viewed as inadequate if not bad, and those brought in by the new CEO were admired as fresh and new. By contrast, MCA continued to be run by the "old guard." When many of the "new blood" at the corporate headquarters began to leave as well, this was further rationalized in terms of their having been poor "team players." Many members of the corporation did their utmost to maintain their idealization of their "visionary" leader, upon whom they had become increasingly dependent. After several years, however, they began to realize that his aggrandizement was purchased at their expense, that it was the corporate CEO who was not being a "team player."

After the transition in leadership at the corporate headquarters, numerous small events set the stage for an atmosphere of doom within MCA. Representatives of the subsidiary were often overlooked for notification of scheduling for such various corporationwide meetings as marketing sessions, strategic planning, and the development of philosophy, policy, and goals. Input from MCA members was rarely solicited about decisions that affected their company's internal functioning. Spontaneous visits to MCA by home office executives, and telephone calls from them, markedly diminished. Those few personnel from the home office who regularly consulted with, gave seminars at, or did troubleshooting for MCA found that executives in the home office consistently "forgot" to credit this time spent, tending to define 100-percent time only in terms of time spent at the home office. In short, MCA personnel felt that they had gradually become the consistent target of discounting or of "death wishes" on the part of the larger corporation.

Over a period of several years MCA saw an outflow and depletion of virtually all of those precious commodities necessary for its survival. Through the gradual centralization of decision-making and financial management, a sense of local autonomy about MCA's activities and about its fate was attenuated and virtually lost. All important medical, administrative, and financial information about the organization was computerized for management from the main office. Promotions in rank or replacement of vacant positions became notably rarer and slower at the MCA office than at the main office. Rewards for job performance were likewise far less frequent from the home office for MCA employees. Some years ago, not only did the CEO from the home office forget to bring plaques for an award ceremony to MCA, but some months later, on a visit to MCA, the Chief Operating Officer (COO) likewise forgot to bring the awards plaques for presentation. MCA has consistently been asked to make layoffs, cutbacks, and to endure hardships that the main office has not sustained for itself. The chronic experience of unequal sacrifices has made MCA suspect that the home office was growing and thriving at the expense of the affiliate.

Prestige likewise diminished in MCA, both in the eyes of local/ regional supporters and vendors, and in the eyes of the main office. Local businesses, health agencies, and the local medical community, who had long enthusiastically supported MCA, began to wonder whether MCA would survive. They wondered whether the main office was really behind its local affiliate and began to question whether the main office would honor MCA's commitments. With local confidence in MCA's future undermined, many businesses and health agencies adopted a "wait and see" attitude. Similarly, fewer managers have applied to train at MCA, applicants having heard "via the grapevine" that MCA might not be long-lived and that the main office has been in keen competition with MCA. Thus, with the decline in prestige, the *credibility* of MCA began decline both in the local organizational community and within the applicant pool which MCA counted on for its record of success and excellence.

The progression of events was experienced by MCA personnel as keenly felt, unrelenting death wishes from, and abandonment by, the home office. MCA's persistent initial response was the even more unrelenting pursuit of excellence and success, to prove to themselves and to others that they were indeed doing their job—unsurpassed by any. Yet, as Abse (1988) writes: "The very thought of having to justify one's existence is already expressive of a doubt about the right to be in the world" (p. 90). The CEO of MCA said to me with exasperation a few years ago, "We do the job we're supposed to do, and we're punished rather than rewarded for our accomplishments. What do they want of us?" The simple, frightening—and intolerable—answer, one that could only be voiced in gesture rather than in word was, to disappear. Both the main office and MCA acted as if extinction were the central agenda, to which MCA responded (for the most part) by striving all the more to demonstrate its quality, if not its indispensability. Yet MCA could not perceive and accept that "doing better" could not save it from dissolution.

During the most recent years I have served as a consultant, MCA has been living with an unrelenting sense of threat to its existence. Because of the complex, ambiguous relationship it has had with the home office, it has been impossible for MCA's officers to determine how real the threat is. The 30-member medical affiliate has been acting for the past five years as if the threat to its existence were real, and as if annihilation were not only inevitable, but imminent. During this period, the central office has not effectively acted to deny or disprove this growing conviction. Through understanding both the home office and its subsidiary, MCA, and by knowing both the fantasy systems and realities of each, and their interaction, we can better comprehend and evaluate the intense subjective feelings (rage, grief, resentment, confusion, and the like) of MCA.

A recurrent theme or metaphor used at MCA over the years has been the frontier image of "circling the wagons," a turning inward to protect the integrity of the organization. Feeling as if their very existence were under prolonged siege, members wondered how long the "circled wagons" could survive. Moreover, the anger, resentment, rage, sense of chaos that they felt dared not be directed externally— to the main office or to vendors in the local community upon whom they also depended. Instead, they came to redirect these sentiments internally in the form of organizational infighting, schisms between sectors of the organization (caregiving, laboratory, business-administrative, public relations-marketing, and so forth), increased incidence of MCA personnel illness and accidents, and widespread demoralization.

Ironically, in this corporation's history MCA had been consistently regarded by the home office and by other admiring and envious subsidiaries as the "flagship" of the institution, the most consistently productive, successful, and enjoyable work site in the corporation. Until recently, it had often been the case that the best of the corporation's applicant pool of medical and administrative personnel, managers and staff, and corporate trainees selected MCA as their first choice for where to work. Since its inception fifteen years ago, MCA's virtue has been its vice: envy and disparagement by other components of the organization have eaten away at it. MCA's successes became the home office's and other subsidiaries' failures; everything that MCA did well "made" the others look bad. At one home office executive meeting, at which recruitment of managers was discussed, an executive told a story about how he thought MCA succeeded in its recruitment: "They send one of their cute secretaries to take him [a management candidate] to a drive-in and give him a good time [the implication being sexual favors]. That's why they get them, and we sometimes lose out."

It is unlikely that there was ever an official written edict or explicit decision by headquarters to close MCA. Rather, members of MCA, and myself as well, inferred and frequently reconfirmed this conclusion through acts of omission and commission by the upper management at the home office, through its euphemisms, metaphors, and other turns of speech, and by its acts of mystification. Not-so-benign neglect characterized much of the home office's practice toward MCA. The headquarters published a lavish brochure describing and marketing all facets of their company—but omitting any mention of the MCA subsidiary, even though at a managers' meeting I had urged them to include MCA in the public relations brochure. The two most common responses I received from executives and managers at headquarters were "We didn't have room" and "We forgot."

Furthermore, at corporationwide workshops and managers' meetings (at which I was usually the only quasi-MCA spokesman present), I often reminded the group of the fact of MCA's existence when input from, or program planning for, the entire corporate "family" (as many members call it) has been under consideration. Several middle-level managers and junior executives approached me following the meeting and said, some with embarrassment, "You know, it's easy to forget the MCA even exists, they're so far away, and you never see any of them down here." "Forgetting" frequently seemed tantamount to the wish that MCA should disappear; action at corporate headquarters, to the conclusion that this wish had been activated.

Themes of powerlessness, vulnerability, and betrayal pervaded MCA members' accounts of their recent history. Trying to plan for their future, they felt they were given virtually no information, financial or moral support from the home office—support upon which strategically sound planning and emotionally sound anticipation could be based. The CEO of MCA said to me:

> I took it to heart when the chief at the main office said three Decembers ago that they were really hard up for money, and that we'd have to have some major cuts here at MCA. I'm willing to tighten the belt and share hard times all around. They said I'd need to let go of some people, and we couldn't fill several managers' and staff slots. I figured we'd all just have to put our shoulders to the wheel and work hard. During that time I was so concerned that I approached a number of community medical resources and vendors to see if we could fill the gaps that were going to be created by these losses. Then, as time went on, I saw the main office functioning as if money was available and flowing after all—but only for them. I saw new executives coming on board, new staff persons. I then felt embarrassed to have acted poor for my own people here at MCA and in the community. I felt like I'd *lied* to my own people and to the town that's dependent on our good faith. I feel hurt and somewhat betrayed, and foolish for having taken it all so seriously. A few months ago, several of my managers and staff threatened to quit. They don't want to go down with a sinking ship. Now, for the future, I'm determined just to submit requisitions and expect them to be processed and paid; I'm not going to hold back and keep tightening the belt when they're not doing the same down there on the red carpet.

For four years after the arrival of the new CEO at headquarters, many of the older members of MCA felt as if they were living in the shadow of the folding of another medical subsidiary hundreds of miles away. The mysterious circumstances of its demise, its slow decline, the simultaneous withdrawal of community support and of support from corporate headquarters—these were frequently (and projectively) referred to as "the handwriting on the wall," portents of a fate that might or might not be fended off. The CEO of MCA, together with several managers and staff, constantly attempted to assess the current status of their organization by calibrating it with the final years of their erstwhile "sibling" organization. The leader of MCA said to me, almost as if prophesying,

> Just you wait, we're being set up so that when our ship goes down, they (at the main office) will be able to blame me for sinking, just like they hold Dr. X, the former CEO at Grainton, for their company biting the dust. They're sharpening their excuses, getting ready for the kill. I'm their scapegoat. You can be damned sure that they'll make it look like there's no blood on their hands. We're being set up for the sacrifice, just like the hospital at Grainton was. Just you wait and see. I'll get the blame.

Various MCA members would stop me in the hallways and begin to tell me about serious or terminal illnesses or deaths in their families. Although over the years I had consulted and counseled many MCA members on a wide range of professional and personal subjects, never before had there been such a groundswell of thoughts on death. Our conversations would often drift onto the fate of MCA, suggesting to me that real as were these family events, they also served as displacements for the dread of MCA's organizational dissolution (cf. Yalom 1970, 115) and the loss of friendship networks and MCA identity.

The dispirited leader of MCA did his best to rally from time to time, and always vocalized mottos such as "Onward and upward," "Steadfast and determined," "Bowed, but unbroken," "We'll make it." However, his actions—largely inactions, his failure to take advantage of the promised change of policy at the home office, his increasing absences, and his emotional unavailability (wishing to be spared further "bad news")—expressed the opposite. Junior executives, managers, physicians, and medical and administrative staff of MCA alike frequently told me they thought their leader depressed, that they had to assume increasingly large numbers of his decision-making functions, which he had tacitly ceded to them.

In the form of depressed leadership and low group morale, the enemy was now as much within as without. Even though, over a period of several years, the head of MCA had clearly and repeatedly announced his wish to retire and leave MCA in good hands, both the home office and local MCA junior executives did virtually nothing to secure a replacement, further making MCA a captive of its collective sense of doom. On several occasions, I spoke with senior executives of the home office and even wrote letters and memoranda to them as a subtle form of pressure ("documentation"), urging the central organization to assist in the transition, to make more frequent contact with MCA leadership, to show a greater interest in its future, and so on.

Yet even when the home office executives would make a site visit and create a momentary stir of enthusiasm and hope, MCA leadership could rarely sustain the enthusiasm to try to save their organization. They immediately mistrusted the sincerity and follow-through of their visitors, and depressively fell back on the nostrum that the "handwriting [was] on the wall" long ago. Feeling tired, "burned out," after having led his organization through almost eight years of continuous corporate economic and political tumult, the CEO of MCA discounted the sincerity of the head of the home office in offering to provide any help he could to turn things around. Taking little of the initiative and giving few of the pep talks to his workers he once did, the CEO's refrain became "too little, too late." While not giving up on MCA in so many words, and still wanting to have a successor take over "a ship in full sail," by his actions and inactions he hastened the very fate he feared. With his refrain of "too little, too late" he externalized all responsibility for MCA onto the home office: "If they really mean business, they should come up here and talk with us. You know the old saying, 'Don't tell me,' show me.' I'm waiting for them to show me their intentions." The CEO's increasing passivity and fatalism unwittingly played right into the hands of those executives at the home office who had been passive-aggressively undermining all of MCA's functions.

Having started out appearing to be, and welcomed as, a "reparative" leader, the corporate CEO of headquarters came to be slowly, reluctantly recognized as a "destructive" one who directed group effort at targeting not only outer adversaries, but many within his corporation as well. I would characterize the head of MCA as more consistently of the "reparative" type. Further, their relationship, together with that of their respective organizations, can be identified as symmetrical (Bateson 1972) in that the more the leader of MCA sought to mend or save his operation, the more the leader of the corporate office engaged in direct or indirect aggression towards the subsidiary group, and vice versa. In effect, each provoked an escalation of the more-of-the-same destruction/reparation dialectic in the other.

The head of MCA, unable to save his company by attracting new trainees, new staff, and a replacement for himself, became increasingly (albeit subtly) destructive toward his unit. Withdrawing from his formerly optimistic, encouraging style, he became increasingly withdrawn, unavailable, and unwilling to make decisions that would involve confrontation with executives at the home office. Depressed because of his chronic impotence as leader, he often seemed through his actions to have given up hope; to be biding his time for the final axe to fall. He was unwilling to press his boss at the main office for the dramatic promises the boss had made months earlier: that henceforth money would be no object, that they could have whatever they needed to recover.

His chief operations officer, COO, long a conservative penny-pincher during the lean times, continued to act in many respects as if the subsidiary were still in dire poverty. For instance, the physicians had requested new knee-length lab coats, because their old ones were becoming thin and frayed. No sooner had the new ones ordered by the COO arrived, than several of the physicians bitterly ridiculed them as "pillow covers, they're so thin; you can tell how cheap they were. That's how much we're worth." Out of protest, several physicians refused to wear them.

At all levels of the organization, day-to-day work continued in perfunctory performance. Partly through identification with the depressed leader, many if not most members of MCA have given up on themselves as an organization; they have given up that sense of "we-ness" as too painful to try to preserve, if not recapture. If the demise of MCA becomes a fulfillment of the tacit wishes of the home office, it will for many MCA managers, trainees, and staff be a self-fulfilling prophecy, one in which they have unwittingly colluded.

## DISCUSSION: ORGANIZATIONAL EFFECTS OF ADAPTATION TO DOOM

The organizational effects of adaptation to the sense of doom in the above case example were numerous, pervasive, and have become indelible:

1. increased infighting and factionalism;
2. increased discrepancy between the group's self-expectation to perform at 100-percent efficiency and responsibility and their inability to fulfill their expectations due to absence of sufficient personnel and financial support;
3. episodes of group despondency, apprehension, self-blame, helplessness-hopelessness, resignation, outrage;
4. rallying periods of resolve and hope through the infusion of "new blood" (e.g., new junior executives, successful marketing, annual new groups of medical managerial trainees);
5. constant "patching things up" as with a trowel and plaster, while feeling that everything is being pulled or is falling apart (e.g., continuous negotiation with local and regional subcontractors and vendors for new corporate outlets and community support to shore up what has been lost from the main office);
6. sense of abandonment, conviction that MCA is victim of an outside plot, belief that annihilation is only a matter of time, that their fate is out of their hands, that the main office has no place for MCA in its future but is not telling them;
7. decrease of reality testing and concomitant regression;
8. discreet search for outside jobs by apprehensive executives, managers, salespeople, and staff, to "jump ship before it sinks";
9. sense of impotence on the part of MCA leadership;
10. merger of feared destruction with group self-destructive behavior by members of MCA; and finally
11. the proliferation of and vulnerability to rumors about firings, resignations, omens, together with a magical "watching for signs" in facial expressions and attitudes of MCA leaders and/or home office management personnel.

The concept of "projective" identification (Klein 1946, 1955) is a useful interpretive tool in understanding MCA as a shared representational system (possessing self and object attributes), and in understanding the relationship between MCA and its home office, both as realities and as objects of unconscious fantasy. In terms of the principle of multiple function, it serves simultaneously as a defense, as an unconscious phantasy, as a mode of communication, and as a vehicle for a wish (Apprey 1986, 115–116). Meltzer (1967), discussing the motives underlying projective identification, lists among the most powerful: "intolerance of separation; omnipotent control; envy; jealousy; deficiency of trust; excessive persecutory anxiety" (p. 14). Over time MCA and its home office became bound by a fateful "symbiosis" of projective identification in addition to their real-world economic, political, ideological, and training functions. Each came to embody or mirror the "worst" features of itself—with which battle was engaged with the "external"(-ized) enemy.

Ironically, many of the widespread dysphoric feelings within the main office of the medical corporation—aimlessness, leadership's detachment from the daily affairs of the members, lack of clear roles and expectations, demoralization due to unacknowledged members' contributions, fear of abandonment, and spasms of accountability for problems beyond any individual's control—are those which were induced in the MCA affiliate office. Stated technically, defense mechanisms such as displacement, projection, projective identification, splitting, isolation, and the like that are familiar in individual psychology can be used in regulating group cohesiveness, identity, aggressive and sexual impulses, "status anxiety" (De Vos 1966), and so on. Families, corporations, whole societies, and international groups can be, at least in part, governed by an affectively and fantasy-based division of labor (Stein 1986c). Roles can be based on the complementarity of induction and embodiment of dysphoric, if not catastrophic, feelings, fantasies, and wishes (Devereux 1980). In the case under discussion, the sense of integrity and safety within the home office was in part purchased by depositing the parallel sense of disorganization and danger in MCA—in fact, by inducing endangerment in MCA. Through MCA the home office could dissociate itself from dysphoric feelings, while "managing" them in a subsidiary that was at once a "part of" itself, yet "apart from" it (Stein 1987a).

Further, the home office experienced considerable ambiguity over its ideal professional identity, that is, regarding its medical caregiving and training versus profit-making and hierarchy-maintaining roles. I suggest that MCA became a "container" (Bion 1963) for the devalued aspects of the home office, attributes that were nevertheless still touted as its official ideals: emphasis on continuity of physician-patient relationships, consumer-oriented medical practice, "consumer-friendly" medical products, and contextually based medical and business relationships, rather than financially and technologically dictated corporate values (see Stein and Hill 1988). Over the years a recurrent, even fixed, set of value priorities, stereotypes, and dichotomies came to govern the mutual perceptions of MCA and the home office, and to regulate their interactions. The most salient of these dichotomies were rural/urban, low tech/high tech, personal medicine/"electric" physician, informal/formal, input from all levels in decision-making/ hierarchical (top-down) decision-making, interpersonal relations/"the bottom line," excellence in task performance/appearance-image-marketing-public relations, service to vendors/product-line management. Klein (1946, 1955), Jaques (1955), Zinner and Shapiro (1972), Kets deVries (1984), and Stein (1986c) have discussed in detail the operation of projective identification in cementing and stabilizing intrapsychic, interpersonal, familial, organizational, and intercultural relationships. Likewise, this mental mechanism was a powerful force in perpetuating the relations—and the internal mental representations— between MCA and its home office (see also Apprey 1986). For an extensive literature review on the subject of organizational dynamics, role formation, and the operation of various defense mechanisms, see Diamond and Allcorn 1986.

Over the years the psychological foundation or unconscious position of MCA gradually shifted from what Bion (1959) called the basic assumption of "dependency" (the sense of "belongingness," if not oneness, with the group, the sense that the leader(s) or that the group itself will fulfill succorance and nurturance wishes) to the basic assumption called "fight/flight" (heightened vigilance, the sense of imminent danger, alternating readiness to attack or to withdraw, heightening of aggressive impulses). Interestingly, Bion's third basic assumption, called "pairing" (wherein the group hopes for rebirth via a redeemer who is a product of the fantasized pairing of two group members, or from external parent figures), only intermittently and briefly appeared, as did the hope for new, young, permanent leadership.

ORGANIZATIONAL CRISIS AND REGRESSION

Over three decades ago, George Devereux (1955) formulated a
group or cultural psychology of *crisis*, one which I suggest is apt for
the MCA episode under discussion.

> A crisis comes into being through the following process: In a situation
> of stress, which elicits *fear*, time-tested and traditional mechanisms of
> orientation and of action no longer produce the expected results. This
> leads to a schizophrenia-like disorientation and to catastrophic behavior.
> *Fear*, which is an objective appraisal of the magnitude of a real danger,
> is replaced by *anxiety*, which is a sense of the inadequacy of one's
> resources in the face of stress. Since anxiety is harder to endure than
> fear, society rapidly becomes more preoccupied with alleviating its
> state of anxiety than its fear, and practically ceases to do anything about
> the danger which elicited fear in the first place. Figuratively speaking,
> a society in crisis clamors for "cultural bromides" rather than for tools
> and weapons. This means that an autistically evolved intrapsychic
> "*threat*" replaces the objective "*danger*," and comes to occupy the center
> of the psychological field. Society then attempts to bring into being
> in reality—to "materialize"—precisely the kind of objective *danger*
> which corresponds to the initially intrapsychic *threat*. . . . From then
> on society fights the phantoms—the Frankenstein's monsters—which,
> in compliance with its needs to project its intrapsychic *threats* into the
> outer world, it brought into being, and therefore ceases to fight the
> initial, objectively real, *danger*.
> In brief, crisis behavior is characterized by the presence of self-defeat-
> ing mechanisms, leading to a downward spiraling, ever expanding,
> vicious circle, where the very attempts to cope with the problem on
> hand only exacerbate the stress and create new difficulties (p. 147;
> emphasis in original).

In the face of chronic uncertainty over the future and continuity of
MCA, what little information MCA managers received was quickly
magnified into the most cataclysmic rumor, fueling the flames of doom
that were already quite real enough. A plausible interpretation is that
unconscious aggression was simultaneously projected onto the men-
acing outer world and was condensed with it, and *within* MCA it was
projected from one member onto another, one work unit onto another,
giving rise to endless factionalism and infighting (e.g., health care
versus administration, intramural versus extramural, training versus
medical service units).

To reduce the intolerable feelings of passivity and vulnerability, many MCA members "identified with the aggressor," and further defended themselves against the intolerable anxiety by fighting enemies now embodied in the form of coworkers. While the main office and the local/regional community were silent targets of MCA projections, the only actual fighting that MCA members could allow to occur was between themselves. Thus, virtually irrespective of the main office's actual deeds and intentions, MCA members began to create their own self-fulfilling prophecy through unwitting collusion with the home office. Although MCA members became increasingly suspicious of the enemy within and the enemy without, it was against the former that actual rage was directed, expressed, and discharged.

Many of the junior executives, managers, practitioners, marketing specialists, and staff—especially those who relied more on environmental cues than upon inner directedness—perceived the CEO at MCA as having given up, as just biding his time before eventual retirement, as incapable of saving them or their corporation. Many quarreled with one another over prerogatives, "turf," and responsibility, whereas before such issues were regarded as "petty." In the past, personal feuds had been more successfully subordinated to the group mission. While members of the entire hierarchy attempted to "do their jobs" at "business as usual," everyone acknowledged that "the old spirit [was] gone"—even as various executives tried valiantly to rekindle it at weekly and monthly organizational meetings. It is as though they felt that MCA's fate was too far sealed, and too much out of their hands, for them to try to "rally around the flag" again. MCA now lives under the shadow of imminent death, never knowing when it will happen, but waiting for the lethal shot to be fired and fully expecting that it will. Perception of the outer world and fantasies dominating the inner world have become increasingly difficult to distinguish.

The past several years' history of MCA has been collectively traumatic in the sense hauntingly described by Kai T. Erikson (1976) in his study of the 1972 Buffalo Creek (West Virginia) disaster, when the floodwaters from a burst dam inundated communities along the creek's path:

> By collective trauma, I mean a blow to the tissues of social life that damages the bonds linking people together and impairs the prevailing sense of communality. The collective trauma works its way slowly and even insidiously into the awareness of those who suffer from it; thus

> it does not have the quality of suddenness usually associated with the word "trauma." It is, however, a form of shock—a gradual realization that the community no longer exists as a source of nurturance and that a part of the self has disappeared. "I" continue to exist, although damaged and maybe even permanently changed. "You" continue to exist, although distant and hard to relate to. But "we" no longer exist as a connected pair or as linked cells in a larger communal body (p. 302).

At MCA there occurred no single event so cataclysmic as a flood. Rather, the "collective trauma" consisted of the slowly and subtly encroaching dysphoric sense that there was simply no future for the "we-ness" in which many managers, trainees, and staff had invested their very selves (not only their incomes).

In analysis of this kind, whether of whole cultures (ethnic, tribal, national) or of organizational cultures, it is easy to slip into reifications as if a group were a self-standing entity, homogeneous, a living organism rather than an association of individual people. Anthropologists and sociologists must also deal with their informants' own characterizations of their group or society as an immortal, ontological, if not supernaturally created entity. Yet, according to the model of methodological individualism (La Barre 1972, Bion 1959), groups do not exist apart from the people—and their motivations—who constitute and "belong to" them. That is, groups do not have independent motives of their own, although motives and characters may be ascribed to, projected or externalized upon, the group, resulting in reification for purposes of defense. All organizations and cultures are the creations and recreations of those who experience themselves as belonging to and loyal to "them" (Berger and Luckmann 1966).

Thus, while in one sense reification is inaccurate, in another sense it is necessary for us to assess its mental function for group members (see Shapiro 1989 for a discussion of reification of the social group as a denial of death). In groups mental operations differ from those of dyads or lone individuals; for instance, in groups there is greater proneness to regression, to the eruption of primary-process thinking and to action governed by it (cf. Alford 1988, 579). Through the oscillation of projection and introjection (and identification) the image of the group as the outer social skin of the self, the protective outpost or border for security operations, is reincorporated into the self. The group imago, so to speak, becomes an idealized object, the representation of which is then taken back into the self. Volkan (1980b) says of the leader that "The identification with idealized external objects creates an illusion that supports its [the self's] cohesiveness and stability" (pp. 138–139). I would slightly rephrase the sentence to read, with respect to groups, that the identification with idealized, mutually shared externalized objects creates an illusion that supports group members' cohesiveness and stability. Representations of groups, corporations, and cultures often play the shared fantasized roles of external outposts of the self and one's defensive organization. They are the mental castle walls and moats, so to speak, that people use to give themselves boundaries and distinctiveness, pride and unique-ness, separation and enclosure. These are a distal safeguard for what and who are contained within.

Discussing what binds people (in)to a group, Alford (1988) first quotes Freud (1921/1959) who defined a group as "a number of individuals who have put one and the same object in the place of their ego ideal and have consequently identified themselves with one another in their egos" (p. 48). Alford (1988) continues with a succinct discussion of the leader and the group "itself" as representation:

> It is apparent that what binds the group is not love (at least not love for one another, object love), but narcissism. Individuals identify with one another, they feel bound to one another in some way, because they share a common ego ideal, represented by the leader. It is because of the shared common ego ideal that the group is bound together by narcissistic ties, understood as a self-love that extends to others because— and only because—they are like ourselves. It is also apparent that it is not an illicit abstraction, a reification, to speak of a group ego and group ego ideal. Both exist, in the form of attitudes and emotions directed by individuals toward the leader (who embodies the group ego ideal), and other group members (who together embody the group ego) (p. 579).

In the case discussed above, it was argued that such defenses as identification and externalization lead to the reification of the insti-tution and to a merger of one's fate with that of the corporation (see also Diamond 1984, 1988; Diamond and Allcorn 1987). Moreover, I suggest that when the ability of the group to accomplish its missions and reach its goals is impeded by a threat to the very existence of the group, its self-esteem will be undermined and various emergency maneuvers to restore it will be undertaken.

## INTERVENTION AND ITS LIMITATION

My roles as behavioral scientist, consultant, and facilitator have been complex, and often ambiguous, throughout this case. My central informal role came to be what Rhodes (1986) has called an "institutional analyst," one whose task it is to understand and emotionally encompass an entire institution and thereby to help the organization understand and help itself (see also Stein 1987b). Although at the main office and in the other branches, I was able to move freely among workers and middle-management personnel, I was unsuccessful in my efforts to effect change by conveying to upper management at the home office (whether through memoranda or through meetings with corporate vice-presidents and treasurers) the sense of chronic urgency felt by MCA. As a result, there was little communication between upper-management at the home office and MCA, leaving a void filled at MCA by greater persecutory anxiety. Over the years MCA members relinquished their initial hope that I would be able to intercede for them at the home office and thus be able to "fix things." If I could not accomplish these wished-for things, what then could I *do*?

From individual counseling sessions, to executive and managers' meetings, to monthly meetings attended by all MCA personnel, my function became to listen, to help and allow them to tell their stories, to help them understand the meaning of their stories, to help them— insofar as it was possible for me to do so—compare their stories with the realities or official stories available to me from the home office, to help them listen to each other with less condemnation and greater attentiveness and compassion, and thus, to help empower them do whatever problem solving and decision-making were within their compass. In my rescue fantasy, I had once wished to be able to "sound the alarm" or "blow the whistle" at the main office, or even outside the organization. However, neither alarm nor whistle were audible at the top levels of the organization and even outside it. The fate of MCA, and of its members' mental and physical health, thus rested entirely with themselves. Our individual and group discussions gradually helped to diminish their projections and projective identifications into one another, to decrease infighting, and to increase group morale and productivity, by helping members have the courage to look at reality as directly as they could bear.

They often vacillated as a group between what Melanie Klein (1946) called the "paranoid-schizoid position" (of mistrust, mutual suspicion, recrimination, withdrawal) and the "depressive position" (sadness, wish to make reparation to the one who has been hurt), and both individual and group sessions helped diminish the persecutory anxiety and retaliation within MCA. Often taking flight from grieving by fighting, they courageously came to face their predicament over time as a group. One of my evolving roles within MCA was that of mediator, one who was given access to the stories and accounts of the various subgroups (as well as of individuals within them), and who helped these warring factions listen to one another, to try to understand the other's position. Thus, I functioned not only as a welcome ear to their plight, but also initially as a bridge between adversaries, and eventually as a facilitator of direct communication between them (see also Stein 1987b).

During one meeting of the entire MCA corporate group, members of various units were hurling accusations about how others had made their own work difficult to accomplish. Shorthanded, one work unit asked another to take care of obtaining business codes and signatures on requisitions and accused them of refusing to honor the simple request. The second unit fired back that they were overworked and did not have the time or the authorization to do this additional paperwork. And besides, it was not their job to do other people's tasks. Yet another group of managers complained that community liaisons and public relations people were spending too much time outside the MCA offices when they were needed to coordinate efforts inside.

As the acrimony escalated during the meeting, I raised my hand and was recognized by the chief nonmedical administrator. Here (roughly) is what I said:

> These are terrible times for us all. We all feel bad that we cannot do better at our jobs and for MCA. People are doing their best. I think that everyone believes that. Don't point fingers, because no one *isn't* giving 100 percent. It's difficult to prioritize values when we're so short-staffed, yet have a full complement of physicians, executives, and managers, who are all trying to do their jobs and get their work done. They're supposed to be in the office, out in the community, and traveling all over the region at the same time. Everybody is busy. In order to keep MCA afloat, at least as I understand it, we don't have the luxury of stopping doing such and such, or cutting back on something else.

> Everybody here knows we're walking a tightwire. Maybe if we can all realize that we can't prioritize our values at least for a long while, and if we accept that we can't live up to our goal of efficiency for a while, we will not be so hard on ourselves and on other coworkers, who are trying as hard as we are.

Several members of the group, hitherto having verbally attacked others and having fended off others' criticisms, had tears in their eyes. The group, I believe, felt listened to, heard, and acknowledged, rather than punished. The "solution" that there were numerous problems that could *not* be solved under the present circumstances was received as a relief to all. They no longer felt "bad" and accused as the source of their problems. The remainder of the meeting proceeded in a respectful, accepting, even warm tone.

Neither this meeting, nor other similar individual or group meetings, resolved matters once and for all. Indeed, one of my main points in the meeting was that disruptive, dysphoric, catastrophic feelings were inevitable for anyone who elected to continue business as usual in the present situation, and for whom the people and culture of MCA meant something more than "just a paycheck." My task went beyond "normalizing" the disturbing feelings and premonitions felt by the group: rather, I consistently acknowledged and interpreted what we all feared to acknowledge. Many in MCA came to realize that an instant solution was impossible. Labeling me as "the listener," and identifying with that *function* with which they had imbued me, they began to listen to each other.

In a recent paper on "The Ego and the Mechanism of Adaptation" (1987), Paul Parin writes that

> As the identification with the role is the chief instrument of the adjustment of the adult to social demands and compulsions, so the analysis of these identifications (whether exchangeable and short-lived or lasting) is an irreplaceable instrument of emancipation. In other words: The person is not master of his own home. The analysis must make him aware not only of these forces from his repressed material to which he is subject, but also of the powers of his environment that automatically dominate him because his ego, mostly unconsciously and through diverse role models, has identified with them (p. 116).

In the context of Parin's argument, at MCA I had been trying to interrupt and interpret their automatic adaptive responses that led to identification with their environment, that is, with the role they were expected to play vis-à-vis the central office. For example, I had speculated aloud whether much of the numbness, infighting, internal scapegoating, apathy, "waiting for the axe to fall," passivity (and its manic opposite, frantic activity to "save the ship") might express an identification with the role of the dead or doomed, as well as identification with the aggressor. Such interpretation was often welcomed as liberating, sense-making, and led to a more realistic appraisal of both the internal MCA and external (home office, local community, and so on) situation.

MCA personnel came to understand that they were acting as if they were supposed to be dead, or at least in the process of dying and eventually disappearing. In separating—albeit incompletely and impermanently—their individual and collective "self" representation from the home office as an "object" representation, they were able to exercise greater choice about their future. At least, they were not as ready to become accomplices in their own destruction.

At a regular monthly managers' meeting, the full force of MCA's jeopardy was suddenly realized. Managerial trainees, middle-level managers, and upper-level administrative division heads usually participated in these meetings. On this occasion both the subsidiary's CEO and COO were absent. No one seemed to know where the CEO was, and vicious humor about the COO circulated through the group. One item on the agenda was recruitment of trainees and managers. The group of current trainees noted that there was little interest in transferring to MCA among junior trainees at the home office. One member of the MCA group had recently announced that he was transferring back to the home office. At headquarters a junior manager who earlier had planned to complete his training at MCA had expressed to MCA trainees serious second thoughts about relocating to MCA at all: he feared that there would be far too much work to do among the diminishing managers and trainees at MCA.

There was much talk about continuous "bad news," and the repeated reiteration "We don't want to talk about bad news." But then soon afterwards: "What if there's only three of us here next year? It's not all our responsibility to recruit. ... It hasn't hit us, that if we don't beat the bushes we won't have jobs. The CEO's gotten so passive, and the COO's so stubborn and so afraid to spend any money that our hands are tied when we try to make changes. How do we counter that apathy?" The group then divided up the job of approaching potential recruits in various states: each trainee would take one state and contact the appropriate institutions in it. "How do we break the ice in these places?" one manager asked. Another said with resentment: "MCA has never been actively promoted by our CEO, the COO, or the other top management. I don't know where to go, who to talk to. We've been resting on our reputation."

The previous several weeks at MCA had been characterized by frenetic activity (recruitment, business-as-usual). Many MCA members recited in the halls the words of a popular song, "Don't worry, be happy," in a stereotypic, ritualistic manner. By the time of the managers' meeting, what could be seen as the "manic defense" had all but collapsed. Despair was everywhere felt and fought.

I keenly identified with and felt the managers' frustration, their sense of impasse, yet their need to do something quickly. I shared with them my fantasy of their being the "kids" of alcoholic parents, or of parents who had emotionally abandoned them, leaving the children to fend for themselves. I urged them to try to remember that the "kids" cannot be the "parents," much as the group of managers would like to try to help one another, if not to salvage MCA from annihilation. I interpreted the managers' manic plans as attempts to escape the profound depression and despair that had come to the surface. Many members of the group nodded their heads in assent; they felt understood rather than criticized for not being "good enough" kids. They concluded that the apathetic, resigned attitude of "I don't care" was the major problem at MCA, that they would do their best, but that they also realized that there were limits to their authority and power. They resolved to try to help the survival of MCA, but with their eyes open to reality-testing actual opportunities and limitations. They became appropriately (in my view) depressed rather, than continuing their manic flight into action and ritualized optimism.

On a technical note, during this emotionally pivotal meeting, I imagined for a time that I was functioning as a play therapist (in the Melanie Klein tradition). I was witnessing both the process of play and the crucial play disruption that signals underlying anxiety. The moment of "disruption" occurred as the group realized with dread and despair that their frenetic activity might be to no avail, that they could not accomplish their heroic rescue alone. This feeling triggered in me the concomitant feeling of abandonment anxiety, which in turn I interpreted to the group.

Some four hours later, the group of medical managers and trainees attended a seminar/workshop on death and dying and hospices (organizations that work with the terminally ill, and prepare the patient and the family emotionally for the death). The conference and guest speaker had been scheduled months in advance. As I later discussed with several group members after the guest presenter had left, the conference was deeply upsetting and uncannily "too close to home" emotionally for the participants from MCA. The topics presented included the following: patients' and families' need to finish, to bring closure to, their lives prior to death; the patient's being sent home to die, and the family's and the physician's inability (denial) to truly "hear" that; the family's oscillation in and out of denial; the frequent conflict between the patient's need and wish to die and the family's and physician's need and wish for a cure and for a fight to the end; physicians' feelings of helplessness in the face of issues of mortality and their wish to counter these feelings by "doing something"; the emotional reactions evoked in health-care workers by the proximity to death and by the passive (as contrasted to the biomedically ortho- dox "aggressive") approach to death; and the issue of whether to make predictions as to how much time the patient has left to live.

Throughout the conference, the usually attentive and respectful participants made numerous sardonic outbursts. One protested, "I don't want to die"; another declared, "I'm not going to die." During a discussion of the use of butter suppositories, with ground-up medi- cation, for patients who no longer can take medicine orally, one trainee snapped, "Parkay the rectum" (Parkay being a brand of margarine), this phrase being followed by raucous laughter in the group. The participants went through a miming and exclaiming of "Shake the patient!" One manager proposed that, if the patient lived longer than the 6-month limit set by hospice, the physician should tell the patient, "You're going to die" (spoken as a command). Many members of the group erupted into laughter after this brief role-playing. During the discussion of prediction of death, a manager cracked the joke, "It's OK to be dead wrong in hospice!"

I felt that it would have been inappropriate to bring up internal group issues while the guest speaker was present, so afterwards I discussed the group dynamics with several manager/trainee participants and with the chief trainee. They unanimously reported that they, or others, had been "flaky" and "definitely not in the mood to hear this." The topic had coincided with their worst fears about the group itself and its future. I interpreted this to mean that since they had identified their very selves and futures with MCA (that is, its representation or inner image), the discussion of the patient's death became linked to the repugnant idea of their own death, via the death of MCA. Although the group's manic denial had earlier lifted somewhat (and only momentarily), group members were not emotionally prepared to consider the possibility of grieving for their organization.

They had translated (emotionally transferred) the hospice issue of death and dying onto the dying and death of MCA. Earlier that day, the "mortality" of MCA had dawned on them. They acknowledged that they were not ready to go further with those disturbing feelings. Stated differently: they emotionally knew where they were not yet prepared to go. At the same time they knew that I was available to listen and help them process their feelings and perceptions about the complex relationships between themselves as individuals, and as members of MCA, and MCA's relationship to the home organization. I thus both interpreted the resistance and acknowledged that they still might need it.

Over time the group became more often resilient and rallying than regressed. That the episodes of rallying attested to genuine creativity, productivity, and even intimacy, rather than to a "manic denial" of reality is suggested by the greater degree to which MCA members verbalized to one another (as well as to me) and expressed their feelings about living with a foreshortened sense of time. What could not be changed at least could be openly acknowledged: the taboo that had kept the dread shrouded in secrecy had been lifted. MCA managers, trainees, and staff begun to talk openly about group death, of the possible limits to, if not futility of, their still valiant efforts.

Several members expressed sadness over the recent loss of one manager-trainee who had returned to the home office. Others voiced resentment that he had "abandoned" them, thereby creating more work for those who remained. One manager even angrily demanded that the "defector" be required to commute periodically to MCA and bear the burden of his own work load (i.e., acknowledging but attempting to undo the traumatic loss, symbol and harbinger of even more ominous losses).

An executive secretary openly talked with me about feeling "dead," using the metaphor of violent weather:

> It's like we're in the eye of a tornado or— you know what I mean— in the eye of a hurricane, not knowing whether we're going to be hit and blown away or whether it will go around us. It's really hit us lately, that we could be gone this time next year, that we might not have our jobs then. We try not to think about it, but it's there. We try extra hard at our jobs.

Using poignant medical metaphors, one physician-manager said with quiet foreboding: "The pulse is weak," and later wondered aloud in the group: "Is it time for DNR?" (i.e., a "Do not resuscitate" order, often used with terminally ill patients).

The inability to plan for longer than a several-month stretch, or, differently stated, short-term planning rather than the customary long-term planning, became more openly accepted. That MCA could dissolve within six months or a year was still profoundly distressing to all its members. However, they now showed greater resolve and commitment to "give it their all" for as much time as there remained. Genuine sadness—rather than the erstwhile frenetic activity to seal over the unspeakable dread—began to show. There was a sense among MCA employees that they had somehow managed to take at least part of their fate into their own hands.

## CONCLUSIONS

The contribution of unconscious dynamics to human social organization was studied through a case example. The group psychology of an organizational culture (MCA) gripped by a sense of imminent destruction was described and interpreted. The oppressive sense of foreboding among MCA members was shown to be inseparable from an interplay of (1) real likelihood of organizational demise; (2) home office's (at least many of its highest executives') conscious and unconscious fantasies about MCA and themselves; (3) MCA members' own fantasies about chronically and increasingly ambiguous circumstances, about their own depressed leadership, and about their home office after a phase of dramatic transitions there; and (4) dynamics and history of political succession (leadership) in both the home office and the subsidiary company. The paucity of contact between MCA and its distant home office, together with the type or character of the contact when it did occur, amplified both groups' fantasy systems and defensive organization.

The case was placed in the larger context of widespread closures, mergers, rapid culture change, and catastrophism. My multiple roles (and role ambiguity) as participant observer, consultant, counselor, and facilitator simultaneously gave me access to many facets of the unfolding institutional narrative, permitted a degree of psychological intervention, and limited my ability to affect structural change within the larger organizational environment that underlay the apprehension of doom.

It is hoped that this study will stimulate further research into other organizational cultures, and into larger ethnic or national groups wedged in uncertainty over their future, if not oppressed by a sense of disappearance as a group. The dynamics of grief-work over the anticipated and actual loss of culture remain a still little-explored frontier in human development, in the psychology of groups, and in applied behavioral science. Finally, in examining the role of unconscious processes in bureaucratic organizations, this chapter has contributed toward building a conceptual bridge between individual, group, organizational, and cultural psychology.

# 9/ Beneath the Anger
Projective Identification in the Depths of
Meaning of a Physician-Patient Relationship

*Howard F. Stein*

It has become widely recognized that the physician-patient relationship is the keystone of all clinical work: assessment, diagnosis, treatment, outcome (E. Balint 1974; M. Balint 1957; Scheingold 1988; Smith and Stein 1987; Stein 1985g; Stein and Apprey 1985, 1987, 1990). Conversely, distortions within that relationship quickly, albeit often subtly, come to undermine if not sabotage all clinical work (Davidson 1986; Freud 1910/1957; Heimann 1950; Kernberg 1965; Reich 1951; Smith 1984, 1985, 1986; Stamm 1987). Using a case example drawn from a family medicine faculty/resident Balint group, this chapter will discuss the process by which that out-of-awareness distortion (countertransference) occurs, how its interference with clinical judgment comes to be recognized, and the emotional/personal/family sources of this distortion. My intent is less to extol the merits of Balint seminars per se in medical training and practice (M. Balint 1957, Scheingold 1988) than to describe one group process through which the unwitting distortions were discovered. In illuminating the power of projective identification in regulating a physician's response to his patient and the group's response to him, this single case study also serves to illuminate the unconscious dynamics of clinical and other groups (Stein 1985g, 1990; Stein and Apprey 1990).

In the Balint seminars which I coordinate, interns, residents and

243

faculty have the option of making spontaneous, oral presentations, or beginning with handwritten or typed one to two-page formal cases, which are distributed and read at the outset of the group. In the example to follow, an abbreviated summary of the resident's formal case is first given. This is followed by a description of the group dynamics that processed and enacted the case. Finally, I enumerate key issues in how practitioners' unconscious agendas and unresolved conflicts can inadvertently contaminate clinical work, and how they can be recognized and addressed.

## CASE OF DR. A: "WHY DO I CALL HER SO MUCH?"

Ms. M.L. is a 50-year-old white female who came to my office for sinusitis, after receiving months of treatment from Cardiology for a sudden onset of congestive heart failure. I offered her a complete Health Assessment (pap smear, cholesterol check, and so on) and told her I was very worried about her smoking so much, especially in view of her heart disease. I treated her sinusitis, requested some lab tests, and scheduled her for follow-up.

On her return visit I expressed that her lab results had been surprising. They indicated that she very likely was diabetic, based on her markedly elevated fasting blood sugar (230). She mentioned that she may have been drinking a lot of water recently but she had "forgotten" to tell me. She started crying and expressed frustration over the medications she had been required to take from her Cardiology treatment. She said, "All these bad things the same year" and "I'm not going to take more medicines. *Old* people take medicines."

She asked me if she could stop her cardiac medications, since her heart doctor had already said that he may discontinue them on her next visit. I said clearly to wait until she saw him again. Further lab tests continued to indicate diabetes. She asked for a glucose tolerance test (GTT) to prove she did not have diabetes. I explained to her that two markedly elevated fasting blood sugar levels were diagnostic, and that she needed no further testing. She questioned my conclusion and left the clinic with doubt in her mind about my judgment. I later called her and told her to start a sugar-free diet and other recommendations and gave her an appointment for two weeks. She did not come in. I called her and left a message with her son. She phoned to express concern about her blood pressure and to report that she had stopped taking most of her medications and felt fine. I encouraged her to come in for an appointment so that I could check her as soon as possible.

During our next visit, our communication appeared to have deteriorated. In the interim she had complained to my attending about a sinus headache that she had not mentioned to me. She had implied to him that I had allowed her to stop her medications. After a consult with my attending, I presented her with a treatment plan. She did not want to take any medicine. I told her this problem could kill her in the long run. She stood up and said that if it was going to kill her, "What the heck am I doing here?" I explained that I meant if "untreated," but that there was treatment: the pills and diet. She told me I was very "lousy" explaining things to patients. She tolerated instruction on how to take blood sugar readings at home. Then she insisted that we schedule a GTT.

I called her two days later. All her sugars were normal. She said, "I told you my diet is good." She had not filled her prescription. "I think I forgot to tell you I have had this high sugars due to stress, and the GTT proved I'm fine every time." I bowed my head and told her I truly believed she had diabetes, but I had to concede that I didn't understand what was going on and that she could be right. I called her again that night after talking with my attending. I am scheduled to see her again and to review her BS [blood sugar] records.

At the end of his narrative, Dr. A posed a series of questions that vexed him about his relationship with his patient:

1. Why do I worry so much about this patient?
2. I feel she really "shakes" my confidence badly, but I can't help wanting to keep her as a patient.
3. Why does she misunderstand everything I tell her? What I told her came back to me so different from what I said.
4. Am I trapped? What I see myself doing in this case is calling this lady a lot (three or four times) rather than her calling me.

## DESCRIPTION OF THE GROUP PROCESS

After Dr. A concluded the formal presentation, he added sarcastically: "You'll notice that the BS is underlined. The 'BS' stands for blood sugar, but also for bullshit! I didn't know what to believe." A member of the group asked him why he phoned her. "Her increased *risk* factors. Maybe I didn't make it clear enough to her. Her passive-aggressive antagonism [Dr. A pounded the couch arm with his right fist as he said this]. She had a lot of denial."

Another member asked him, "What does she look like? How does she behave in the room with you?" He replied: "She's 50, but looks like 45. A real cowgirl. Not seductive. The first time she looked disheveled, but after that she came in nicely dressed, attractive, cowgirl clothes. She said to me: 'I'm upset with you!' But she changed her mind."

A senior physician insistently asked, at times as if lecturing:

> What was her chief complaint? What was her real agenda? Why did she discontinue her meds? She didn't believe she's sick, but taking medicines like an old lady. What are her finances? What were her expectations? There were crossed physician/patient expectations. What is important to the patient? Find out her real agenda. Things you did interfered with her life. Her stress level was already high. Your new information increased her stress. She sought to make you fail.

Dr. A nodded his head in assent: "Before surgery, she smoked three packs of cigarettes per day. Later, she went down to a halfpack per day. Now she's back to a lot more cigarettes." A resident added: "You were going to take away her control, and she was going to show you she's in control. She wants to be in good health for the open market on marriage." A faculty physician questioned:

> What are we assuming? It's an issue of language and communication: "I said" versus "she heard." There's barriers, different agendas. Hers is still hidden. How do you record this disparity of agendas on the medical chart? What did the patient expect from a particular visit?

Dr. A, having sat diligently through this avalanche of advice, looked overwhelmed, and courteously replied: "I couldn't agree more." Then, speaking as if a defendant, he added: "There were different channels of communication."

The senior physician continued, "You should try to comfort her, saying 'We're not on the right track. What am I misunderstanding?'" A faculty behavioral science member asked Dr. A: "What would it be like for you to communicate *your* frustrations with the patient?" While pounding the arm of the couch, Dr. A acknowledged: "The part I can handle the least is her telling me she doesn't have a problem. She threatens my personality, also my knowledge" (still pounding the couch emphatically). Serving as group leader, I asked him: "What does the pounding of the couch feel like? What are you saying and feeling or meaning as you do it?" A faculty behavioral scientist followed up with the question of whether it was difficult for him to be angry with patients.

Now quietly, no longer adamant and pounding, he replied: "In my family, my father's a physician; you don't get angry with a patient. You keep your quiet, your calm. In my family, anger toward patients just didn't exist." A faculty member interpreted: "You do well in the presence of the patient, then you get angry after she leaves. You're running away from the *anger*; she's running away from recognizing she's got *problems*. You're both defensive." Dr. A said thoughtfully: "It made me upset when she said I said what I didn't say. I say 'I'm sorry,' but I feel like squeezing her neck! It's a time bomb in me." A faculty physician added: "Maybe she wants to *talk* to you, not just for you to treat her. Who are you treating? The diagnosis? The chart? You gotta treat the illness [emphatically]. For example, patients who come for a pap smear; the pap smear may just be the ticket they use for some underlying agenda. She wants to be healthy and go to rodeo! Deal with her illness *behavior*."

A resident added: "There's a distinction between the view that as a physician, you're calling all the shots, versus how you approach the case as complex from the outset." A faculty physician stated: "She unloaded all this stuff on you. If you open her, you've got to close her. She's barren, bare, defenseless; you cannot leave her open," he said adamantly. "Never take away the hope. As a physician, you're her ally and friend." A female behavioral scientist asked: "Could you *fire* [discharge] the patient? When there's a threat, do you fight or flight? What do you want to feel worse about? Hanging in there in a dysfunctional relationship?"

Dr. A responded: "I shouldn't get angry with any patient. I expect myself to be on top of all my emotions." A behavioral scientist challenged him: "Is it realistic to expect yourself to work well with *all* patients?" Dr. A emphatically replied: "Not being the mean doctor is very important to me." Several members further pushed Dr. A to recognize his equation of "anger" = "being disrespectful." One physician commented: "The group expects you to *feel* angry toward your patients! So what do you *do*? Can you say to her 'That *statement* you made makes me angry'?" Dr A said with urgency. "How would you recommend my following her up when I see her next? You've all been helpful, but I've got a time bomb waiting for me, and it's ticking. I'm anticipating a negative experience. She always comes in very nice." A faculty physician asked him: "What is your role? You should be a *consultant* to her health, but she's in charge of her health." Dr. A said: "Everybody with an elevated cholesterol doesn't have a stroke. She sees herself as a young lady, and doesn't want to act like an old lady."

At that point, I wanted to offer an interpretation that I feared might be "off the wall." I had tried to listen attentively both to what had been said and felt, and what had seemed to remain unsaid. I said something like

> Dr. A, throughout your case, and throughout our group discussion, the issue of her being, or wanting to be, young, and her fear of becoming or acting old, keeps getting raised. Yet, of all the things we've talked about, we never stick with it. I wonder whether you've ever addressed this issue directly with her, about her self-image, about the meaning of where she is in life in relation to what we're calling symptoms and diseases. Can you talk with her about it?
>
> Some other thoughts come to me from the discussion and from your presentation. Your anger and frustration come out as you repeatedly pound the couch. And look at us, we're kind of pounding or pummeling you with advice, with "shoulds," and you sit there and take it. It's as if we as a group are reliving and reenacting all you and your patient have been through. You're now her, and we've become you.
>
> I keep wondering "Why her?" and "Why now?" Is there anything else going on in your life that makes *her* so especially hard to deal with? I keep wondering, "How old are your parents? Is there something you've not said happening to your family so many thousands of miles away?"

Dr. A's eyes had become tearful, and his posture, tense and braced for battle up to then, became very relaxed. The group, too, became less militant. Looking at me with eyes riveted, Dr. A. said:

> I think you're onto something, though I'd rather not recognize it. My dad now has "something" medical for the first time in his life. Blood pressure or cholesterol, I'm not sure. He's about her age, and it really scares me. I try not to think about it. My father is a doctor, always sure of himself, always taking charge!

The group atmosphere too now had "softened" considerably. Reviewing the emotional trend of the group, I wondered aloud: "Maybe you're trying to cure your dad through this lady. You might be blurring him with this patient, trying to make him young by trying desperately to keep her young. You keep wondering why you call her on the phone so much. Are you calling her in order not to call your father in New York?"

A female behavioral scientist asked: "How long does she expect to live? What is her time-line? Maybe a genogram of her family could help you get a sense of how long people generations above her lived, and where her expectations of her own longevity come from." Dr. A said: "I'm *really* worried about her not doing what I said. She's got me in doubt even in the medical sense. I keep rationalizing and justifying." Another physician added: "She's making you doubt." Dr. A replied: "That's why I keep calling her back."

A senior physician admonished him: "Make your clinical decisions in concert with the patients. Don't just try to control her, but take her reality into account." I somewhat whimsically interrupted, and commented to the group:

> I think that we just rang the bell in the boxing ring and started "Round Two," pounding Dr. A with advice again, trying to make him do to her what he can't do so far himself. I think we're playing out his relationship with her. I don't want us to lose that pearl that was said a moment ago, about the time expectation of death—"How long do you think you'll live?" or "When do you think you expect to die?" That's a profound question about somebody's vision of what they imagine their life to be.

The group having run out of time, I concluded by wondering aloud about the possibility of "displacement" of painful personal family issues onto clinical ones, and of inadvertently treating the wrong patient. I added that in Balint groups we also believe—as in family medicine—in "continuity of care," and the group would welcome follow-up on this case at a later Balint seminar. After the group had disbanded, Dr. A, obviously moved, approached me privately and said pensively:

> There's even more that you made me think about. When I talked with my father several months ago, he said his cholesterol was within the normal range. But now the latest research on cholesterol has revised the upper normal limit, so that it has me worried that he might be less healthy than I assumed. It's the first time I ever thought I could lose him. He's always been so gung ho, enthusiastic, a hard worker, that

it's scary to see such a strong man look weak. What can I do to help
him from here?

I speculated aloud that he might be displacing his fear, worry, wish
for control, and telephone calls from his father to his patient, who
was the current focus of his own suffering. I asked him: "How can
you know you're treating the patient when you blur your father with
her?" I then asked: "When did you last call your father? Maybe calling
her is less scary than calling your father because she's 'only' a patient."

Dr. A resonated with this. "You manage to get underneath and help
us to see what's really going on," he said with both gratitude and
sadness. I added: "Today, you pounded the couch, and we hounded
and pounded you with advice and demands about how you should
take her life seriously. Our group 'acted out' on you the drama you
had enacted with your patient. Sometimes one set of feelings can keep
other ones at bay. Maybe that's what happened with you: your zeal
for control, your frustration, anger, might prevent you from feeling
scared, sad, worried about your father and yourself." Dr. A thanked
me for going beyond the battle lines.

I concluded our brief visit by saying that I did not have any particular
advice for him as to how Dr. A. should "manage" this patient. However,
if he directed attention to his family and sorted out what were his
issues and what were those of his patient, he would be more ready
to listen to his patient, to respond to her, and would not be frightened off by her and made so angry by her. She would no longer
"embody" his personal, family issues.

FOLLOW-UP

In the months following the Balint group, Dr. A felt less haunted
by his patient, and less compelled to telephone her and to take control
of her life. Dr. A also spoke via telephone with his father and visited
him, tempering his own fantasy with reality. In discussions we had,
Dr. A spoke more freely about his feelings toward his father (including the sense of being helpless to do anything for him at so great
a distance), of his admiration for his father as a physician, and the
dawning realization of his own—not only his father's—mortality. This
heightened, perhaps unwelcome awareness, had emerged through his
struggle with his own ambitions. A sense of limitation now made him

reassess what it meant to be a competent physician. This episode helped—if not forced—him to rethink what it meant to be a human being and a man, not only a male physician. Over time, Dr. A became less strident and controlling and became more compassionate toward patients and medical collegues. This change cannot, of course, be entirely accounted for by this single case.

Eleven months after the Balint group process, I requested a formal follow-up interview with Dr. A. I wanted to discuss his current relationship with his patient and to inquire about developments in his relationship with his father. He agreed to meet, approaching it in the spirit of wishing to learn more about the quality of his relationships.

I have long been wary of religious, anthropological, clinical and other testimonials of enduring personal transformations from single, cathartic events such as shamanic tribal healing rites. Though I had been deeply moved by the group in which I had participated nearly a year earlier, I was skeptical about its ability to "hold" participants permanently and wondered about the nature of the change that had occurred. By talking with the chief protagonist of the original play, I hoped to recalibrate my memory and reality-test my wish that the group had been profoundly transormational—at least for Dr. A and for myself, as listener.

Dr. A spoke openly about the topics I wanted to explore. I was cautious about my own countertransference potential, and I expected that Dr. A's report might be filtered through his own transference as he might wish to say what would please me as a quasi-parental authority figure. I was pleasantly surprised to find that we did not play out these unconscious roles. I asked Dr. A to first update me on his contact with his patient.

> I met with her again a couple of weeks after that group. I had no tension from her at all. I was prepared to plan to approach things from her view. She was becoming [well-attired, attractive—qualities Dr. A always notices in his female patients, something we often privately discuss], talkative. She took her son's medicine. Her son had a heart attack a few years ago, when he was around 38. He took Nicotinic Acid, over-the-counter medications he had heard about on TV. She increased her meds for her cholesterol and triglycerides. Those are the problems she's most concerned about. She and I got to joking about her smoking. I try to talk her out of smoking. She gets very seductive about smoking, saying "You know I'll never quit smoking. You don't

need to give me all that bull shit." She really says "bull shit," but she's very playful now. My major aim was to get her to quit smoking. Her major aim was cholesterol. I've seen her on an infrequent basis. Her wish is to get a hormone shot without having to see me. She comes in once a month for her shot. I see her maybe once every three or four months.

I saw her again six months after the group. She wanted her cholesterol checked again. It was slightly lower than before. She wanted to change her meds. I worked it up a different way as a consequence of our group last year. I asked her what she wanted, what she heard and read about cholesterol-and triglyceride-lowering medicine. She said a neighbor took Lorelco [generic name: Probucol). This time she was different; she wanted to know what I thought! I told her my favorite drug is Gemfibrozil [generic]. We got out my *PDR* [*Physicians Desk Reference*]. We went through it and agreed my choice was best. She would have had to readjust her anticoagulant too much, so she went for Lorelco. She comes in twice a month or so for sinusitis.

I feel much more at ease with her now. I'm not concerned with myself, or with convincing her I have to do the right thing. She actually makes decisions that *make sense* to me. Before, I would have said that she was making decisions that were wrong. Now I call them decisions that don't appeal to me. I've changed my approach to her. She's always felt all right. It was me that didn't feel all right.

I then asked Dr. A whether anything had changed about his relationship with his father and his feelings toward him. Dr. A smiled, and as he spoke, became a bit tearful.

I got to see my father in May. It had been a year since I saw him. That's a long time, since I saw him every day for 25 years. Earlier in 1990, I knew I was going to see my father that May. If the person is close to you, you get more concerned about him. [I asked him to clarify.] The closer the time got to when I could see him again, the more concerned I grew about him. I didn't realize it was the case until after the fact. I saw my dad in May and he looked great.

I asked him whether he contacts his father by phone or letter, and how frequently.

We're not fond of the telephone. My mother *loves* the telephone. But the last three months, Dad and I talked and talked on the phone about the practice position I'm applying for. He's always been hesitant to give me direct advice. He's been a real pain about it, saying "I don't know; I don't care." It's not that he really didn't care, but he didn't want to impose himself on my decisions. He wanted me to make it on my own. He now feels that we (my brothers and I) have grown enough to make our own decisions, so he feels comfortable to give us advice.

I talked with him last night on the phone. It was his birthday, he's 56 years old. In our culture we do what we're told to do by authority. My dad refused to do that. My dad and I had a close relationship; we always talked a lot. Yesterday he said on our Christmas visit he'd give me advice on selecting a place to practice medicine. [Now Dr. A's voice was very animated and raised in pitch, and he spoke faster.] It was the first time in my *life* that he told me he was going to give me some advice! His writing is different from his speech. In his speech, he's much warmer: we talk about life, sex, medicine, everything; in his letter, there'll be just a few lines, but he is emotional.

At this point, Dr. A needed to leave for another meeting. As he left, however, he asserted that the Balint groups had allowed him to learn much about himself. I felt deeply affirmed, even as I had sought through this meeting to affirm Dr. A's growth. I was convinced that his greater capacity for intimacy—and, for want of better word, lightness—was emotionally symmetrical to his deepening relationship with his father. Moreover, if I had been of help to him, he likewise had helped to stretch me to be more empathetic than I had thought I could be. If relationships (from pairs to groups) are healing, it is because the healing—a making more whole—occurs for all who participate in them.

## DISCUSSION AND CONCLUSION

The above case has attempted to offer ethnographically a "thick description" (Geertz 1973) of the complex texture and depths of meaning latent in a single physician-patient relationship. The case was selected to highlight the fact that these complex psychodynamics and group dynamics are evoked as much in cases of what is often called "real medicine" and "organic disease," as in cases that we culturally label "psychiatric," "psychosocial," "marital," "family," "contextual," "sociocultural," or "community." The case illustrates the process by which, in Balint and other groups (e.g., clinical work groups such as health-care teams, hospital/clinic staff meetings, curriculum committee meetings, continuing education conferences, utilization review groups, quality-assurance committees, tumor boards, case conferences, grand rounds, and so on), the physician-patient relationship literally comes alive anew via the group itself and can here be worked through. In the above case, the process of enacting the "actual" clinical case both preceded and supplied material to set the stage for a degree of working through the presenting physician's painful life situation.

The defense mechanism of "projective identification" was central both to the drama of the physician and patient and to the drama of the group response in which the group earnestly pounced on the physician in their effort to help him. A term introduced by Melanie Klein (1946), *projective identification* refers to the complex mental process by which an unacceptable affect and fantasy-driven idea is first split off from conscious awareness, projected onto another person, and finally perceived and responded to as though this other person were its source as well as its embodiment. As Apprey (1986) discusses this complex concept, one of its principal functions is to attempt to avert painful separation by the unrelenting control of another person. To put the case into something of a formula: Dr. A had projectively identified with his patient his own feelings toward, and image of, his father; in parallel fashion, the group had treated Dr. A as if they had "become" him, and he had "become" his hapless patient.

Although this chapter is not written primarily as a validation of, or brief for, Balint groups, it supports the recognition that Balint seminars, as well as groups where self-reflection is *not* the central agenda, become settings in which the group reenacts disturbing material through projective identification with "the case" (Abse 1974, Foulkes 1948, Stamm 1987, Stein 1985g, Volkan 1984, Volkan and Hawkins 1971). Members of health-care teams and other medical groups can be encouraged to explore their difficult relationships as a means of assessing relationships in the patient's family and wider network. Kafka and McDonald (1965), for instance, write that Brodey, Hayden, and Krug (1957)

> have observed that the "intrateam" reactions in a clinic may be a reduplication, diminished in intensity, of the significant family conflicts. These observations have been confirmed in our setting, and our permissiveness toward the development of multiple combinations has permitted us to observe the parallelism of patterns of avoidance within the family and within the hospital staff. For example, in one situation where the father was ignored by the mother and patient, the administrator

seldom met with the social worker and therapist. Furthermore, we have noted that a family in which the internal power structure is being tested by the family members may also test the power structure of the hospital staff in a parallel way. For instance, a family, in which the father's power was being questioned, repeatedly tested whether or not the Medical Director of the hospital would or would not overrule the decision of the unit administrator. Members of the hospital's administrative hierarchy were informed of this family pattern. The resulting approach interrupted the family's long-established pattern of moving the patient after brief hospitalization from one institution to another (pp. 174–175).

In a similar vein, Volkan (1984) discusses the literature and clinical experience that demonstrate how clinical groups unconsciously identify with and enact aspects of patients' psychopathology, and how conscious access to this fact is a means of achieving greater understanding of the patient's own dynamics:

> Following the observations of Foulkes (1948) and Abse (1974), Volkan and Hawkins (1971) noted a phenomenon that appeared in teaching a group of psychiatric residents the elements of psychopathology. Whenever the residents met regularly to review the psychotherapy of a patient being treated by a member of their group, aspects of the patient's psychopathology, behavior pattern, or family history were reenacted in the teaching group in what is called the parallel (or echo) phenomenon. It is as though the group itself brings facets of the patient's situation "to life" in order to identify with his problems and respond to them empathically (pp. 3–4).

This enactment can of course be empathic or contemptuous (as in frequent "gallows humor"), fostering greater or diminished understanding of the patient, respectively. Given the ordinariness and ubiquity of physicians' individual and group responses to patients and their families, if clinically sound action is to result, it becomes the task of the leader or facilitator to interpret the medical group culture to its members, a role rarely assigned or welcomed by the group. For such an activity and role redefinition to be tolerated (not to mention accepted), one must have had a "good enough" relationship with the group over time; one's confrontation and interpretation in the group must be well timed (when ill timed and in the absence of a relationship history, these will be construed as attack); and one must be able to convey the new perspective nondefensively and empathically.

The individualist image of physicians throughout American culture militates against the recognition that physicians, like all other humans, function in groups all the time—groups both in the sense of frequent interaction and in the sense of internalized norms, values, attitudes, expectations, procedures, and the like (Stein 1990). In this chapter, I have attempted to illustrate (1) the complex topography or emotional "archaeology" of physician-patient relationships via (2) the group dynamics of a clinical group in which those affective undertows not only surfaced, but were themselves addressed, through projective identification, as part of the clinical "material." In conclusion, it is my hope that this brief case will sensitize medical practitioners, educators, and researchers to the role of out-of-awareness factors in all facets of clinical decision-making, and to the role of groups as places in which those unconscious issues are not only played out, but in which they can be identified and their wounds, at least to a degree, healed.

# Conclusion

"Otherness" is no simple matter—perceptually, emotionally, or relationally. This is the conclusion toward which we are compelled by an array of evidence, ranging from the experience of anorexia nervosa, and a pregnant woman's attitude toward her unborn child, to parents' feelings and fantasies about their children (and vice versa), the group dynamics of medical organizations, and relationships between physicians and patients. The common thread that weaves these disparate story lines into a single fabric—one that could be extended to the underpinnings of international relations (GAP Committee on International Relations and Stein 1987, Stein 1987a, Stein and Niederland 1989, Volkan 1988)—is the perspective of projective identification. Through this process, the otherness of individuals and whole groups can be obliterated, violated, controlled, denied, and heavily contaminated. Projective identification is, in a sense, an unconscious social glue that cements if not seals human relationships, preventing the emotional rebirth or differentiation of the other in the name of preserving the relationship ("tie").

Although this "other" may well be cognitively recognized to exist as a being distinct from oneself (or one's group, from corporate to ethnic and national), at the deeper, intersubjective level, this "other" ceases to exist at all. The other becomes role, cipher, foil, container, target, cliché. Relationships—e.g., parent to child, clinician to client, analyst to analysand, family members to each other, ethnic groups to one another, and so on—play out the dangerous, yet anxiety-allaying drama of embodiment and disembodiment, interiorizing and exteriorizing. The vicissitudes of projective identification, as extensively documented in this volume, make our declarations of human boundaries problematic. They also make the upwelling of love, compassion, empathy, reparation and transcendence all the more remarkable and healing.

In 1 Corinthians 13.12 Paul makes a compelling metaphor of human perception: "For now we see through a glass, darkly; but then face to face; now I know in part; but then shall I know even as also I am known." His contrast, of course, is between human imperfection and divine perfection. He could, however, for all the world be describing perception and intersubjectivity polluted by projective identification, as opposed to that moved by empathy (or at least by projective identification introspectively examined, processed, and returned).

The image of "projective identification," too, might commend a different optical metaphor: not so much the translucent or opaque glass, or the prism that refracts and distorts; but the projection and the screen made flesh, wherein one casts out from oneself and intrudes upon another. The "other" is not merely tainted by the pigment in the filter. He, or she, or they *personify*, *mirror*, and *become* what we cannot avow to be a part of ourselves. Paul expects from God what he cannot expect from any mortal. To know and to be known—to be otherness and to acknowledge otherness—is at once the most crucial and most difficult developmental process for parent, infant, family, and society alike. The common root, perhaps, of what we dare expect of each other and of our deity (or deities) is the intersubjectivity of our earliest childhood years.

We wish to underscore the ordinariness of projective identification in life, its role as a kind of metatext behind numerous parent-child, family, and cultural narratives. With little imagination, it can be seen as the not-so-secret player in countless dramas. Consider, for instance, the conflict between the United States and the former Soviet Union, between capitalist and communist ideologies.

In *The Hidden History of the Korean War* (1952/1970), I. F. Stone described the "paranoid logic" that was coming to characterize Washington, D.C., on the eve of the Korean War. He described America's obsessive fear of losing Japan to Communist China and

Germany to Communist Eastern Europe, should the occupation come to an end. Stone concludes with a magnificent psychogeographic portrait of how the American lack of faith in its capitalist system and the Soviet lack of faith in its socialist revolution formed a fateful symbiosis, one that can be seen in terms of a reciprocal projective identification:

> Capitalist America's evident fear of peaceful competition testified to an ignominious lack of faith. Somewhat similar anxieties explained the iron curtain erected round the Soviet bloc lest nascent socialism look too frightfully austere beside the lush pastures of American capitalism. It was this mutual fear, itself the reflection of a subconscious unwilling admiration, which bound Washington and Moscow to each other in a cold war which brought out the worst in both, like a dreadful marriage of hate (p. 34).

The boundedness between Washington and Moscow, between capitalism and communism, like the control-ridden attachments between many mothers and their infants, and family members to one another, can be better understood through the intersubjectivity regulated by the silent tenacity of projective identification. Between parents and children, between subunits of a corporation, and between nations themselves, there is an abundance of "communication," even when diplomatic relations have been "cut off." Understanding, we have come to realize, is heavily poisoned between people and whole peoples. It is only the painful withdrawal of projections, together with a realization that they have been haunting inner presences all along, that can give birth to the human self and to authentic otherness. The essence of this new identity is a new dialogue between self and other, between the many houses within the mansion of the self. Here neither psychoanalysis nor anthropology nor political psychology (nor any discipline) dare arrogate to call itself "applied," for that would claim too much, be too unidirectional. Understanding must become true dialogue.

No discussion of the role of projective identification in life would be complete without including the in many ways parallel contributions of Jungian analysts, marital/family therapists, and scholars (see, for example, Campbell 1980, Hendricks and Hendricks 1985, Johnson 1983, Jung 1966, von Franz 1978). One of the major inner stumbling blocks to differentiation and integration, according to the Jungian view, is people's tendency to project onto others the "shadow" counterpart to their gender's dominant persona. Males project their "anima," while females project their "animus." Marital partners, family members, employers, and employees subsequently come to personify and embody these disavowed gender characteristics. In the Jungian tradition these male and female phantoms are less derivatives and mental representations of the interplay of actual parent-child relationships, than they are universal features of biological maleness or femaleness. They constitute "archetypes" that cannot be reduced to an experientially deeper common denominator; in this view, they are preexperiential. Discussing the role of projection in marital entanglements, Hendricks and Hendricks (1985), for example, write that

> one facet of projection that is almost always present in entanglements is the working out of one's internal male and female issues in the relationship. All of us, whether we're man or woman, must develop the male and female within us. Each of us must develop a healthy relationship with those traits traditionally considered feminine: feelings, intuition, compassion, an all-embracing view of life. Too, each of us must develop the masculine principle within us: the outgoing, expressive, problem-solving, specific function. A whole man is in touch with his feelings; a whole woman is at home expressing herself in the world. Most of us have a great deal of work to do to perfect the development of the male and female consciousness within us. When we are out of balance, we may try to make ourselves whole by linking up with a person who represents what we do not have. A man, for example, may need to learn to be more in touch with his feelings and needs. He may connect with a woman who is very emotional and needy; then he may complain about what he's got. It may not occur to him that she is simply a reflection of something he needs to open up to in himself. Similarly, a woman may not be willing to cultivate the assertive, outgoing part of herself that the masculine principle represents. So she may project onto the relationship and think, "He won't let me be who I really am" (pp. 62–63).

Much literature on couples and family dynamics likewise corroborates in parallel fashion our own findings about projective identification. For example, in a discussion of family roles—"baby," "the oldest," "daddy's girl," "mother's little helper," "the peacemaker," "the black sheep"—in relation to power struggles, Campbell (1980) writes that an infant's growing independence of childhood might become sidetracked (p. 37). Her formulation would be compatible with that of Anna Freud on "altruistic surrender" (1936, 136) and with Melanie

Klein's views of projective identification:

> While we as toddlers may *want* mommy or daddy to come and feed us, we no longer *need* this after a time. Still, we feel frustrated and angry when we don't get our want met. We may even attempt to manipulate the big people to treat us as if we were more helpless than we really are. We may learn to "play helpless" in order to avoid facing the fact that the environment is not always nurturing and that we must learn to "feed" ourselves. Such manipulations never work with people who are themselves independent and self-responsible, but with parents who themselves are still indulging the belief that the world should provide for us, the child may succeed considerably in his or her attempted manipulations. When a little person becomes very successful at playing on the "guilt" of big people, we say that the child is "spoiled"—tyrannical in the expectation of getting his or her own way. Thus, martyr-like parents produce tyrants as children (Campbell 1980, 35).

In such an unconscious intergenerational scenario, parents may foster an overweening sense of entitlement in their children that they later find horrifying, all the while deriving vicarious satisfaction by "living through their children" what they do not feel entitled to have or be for themselves—an attitude that constitutes the negative side of much futuristic child rearing in the United States.

In this world, no discipline—clinical or scholarly—can claim special dispensation. The road toward genuine selfhood and recognition of otherness will be built by a different attitude toward *knowing*. We live in a changing world, where knowledge no longer constitutes a truth culled from an essence, from a tradition ("bodies of knowledge"), or from a predetermined meaning. Understanding is not mere decoding. Writing of psychoanalysis as an intersubjective hermeneutics, Simon Grolnick (1987) poetically notes that

> we understand each other by understanding ourselves, and vice versa. A reflection on the misunderstandings of "the other" helps to bring about self-understanding. (Winnicott maintained that we help our patient most in working out the effects of our mistakes on them.) In other words, a misunderstanding of the object helps the subject to know himself. Both subject (and subjectivity) and object (and objectivity) are involved: paradoxically, they are inseparable (p. 138).

We need to grasp new methods and new modes of knowing in order that multiple but determinate meanings can be allowed to emerge. Psychoanalysis, psychoanthropology, political psychology—to name but three disciplines—are part of this postmodernist conversation, where we may freshly experience rather than search for some pre-determined foundational premise. If we can allow our clinical and scholarly disciplines to be part of new experiences, rather than—projectively?—structure them beforehand, they can play vital, while always subtle, roles in understanding and healing the turmoil that is our world.

# Afterword

*Maurice Apprey*

We can now imagine the existence of ontological hate that kills any sign of life across generations, not only in families of anorexics and transsexuals, but also in every human that breathes life into others. We have arrived at this point by turning around the concept of projective identification, so that instead of examining a child's projective identification with its mother, we have explicated a mother's projective identification with her child. The result is the recognition that a mother is also someone else's child and that across generations humans are in appositive relation with one another. In such a relation, every human may carry out an urgent/voluntary errand. It is urgent because an anterior other designates the deathly project. It is voluntary because a living grandchild or child unconsciously appropriates and transforms this project. In this way two sides of ambivalence are acted out, that is, remembered in action. Life is extinguished in one form, but sustained in another. Projective identification, conceived of, from the standpoint of the child, hides this tragic drama of humans from ourselves. Projective identification, conceived of, from the standpoint of a parental relation to a child, exposes the challenge that humans face in having to detoxify or, at the very least, balance the deathly errand with life sustaining projects that are less costly. Ambivalence then can be seen as a necessary human condition that humans must appropriate and transform, so that each subsequent generation will have less cruelty to contend with. The phantom

(Abraham 1988) that subserves this ambitendency of extinguishing and sustaining life is more than the construction of the living to fill gaps in history. Specifically, in the gaps that these phantoms inhabit, the human capacity to sustain life is on trial at all times. Abraham (1988) correctly links the work of the constructed phantoms to the death instinct, owing to the chaos it generates. However, the notion of urgent voluntary errands and the conception of participants in the generational drama so conceived would suggest a more *orderly* intersubjective constitution of the negotiation of how humans extinguish and sustain life. In short, the drama is *chaotic when we do not know who the enemy is* that lurks behind the phantom.

# References

Abraham, N. 1988. Notes on the phantom. In *The Trials of Psychoanalysis*, edited by Françoise Meltzer, 75–80. Chicago: University of Chicago Press.

Abse, D. W. 1974. *Clinical notes on group-analytic psychotherapy*. Charlottesville: University Press of Virginia.

———. 1988. Kriegman's "nonentitlement" and Ibsen's *Rosmersholm*. In *Attitudes of entitlement: Theoretical and clinical issues*, edited by V. D. Volkan and T. C. Rodgers, 79–92. Charlottesville: University Press of Virginia.

Aichorn, *A. 1983. Wayward youth*. Evanston, IL: Northwestern University Press.

Alexander, L. 1981. The double-bind between dialysis patients and their health practitioners. In *The relevance of social science for medicine*, edited by L. Eisenberg and A. Kleinman, 307–329. Boston/Dordrecht, Holland: D. Reidel.

Alford, C. F. 1988. Mastery and retreat: Psychological sources of the appeal of Ronald Reagan. *Political Psychology* 9(4): 571–589.

Apprey, M. 1986. Discussion: A prefatory note on motives and projective identification. *International Journal of Psychoanalytic Psychotherapy* 2: 111–116.

———. 1987. Projective identification and maternal misperception in disturbed mothers. *British Journal of Psychotherapy* 4(1): 5–22.

———. 1991. The intersubjective constitution of mother-daughter relations in anorexia nervosa. *New Literary History: A Journal of Theory and Interpretation*, vol. 22, 4, pp. 1051–1069.

Bachelard, G. 1942. *Water and dreams*. Translated by E.R. Farrell. Dallas: The Dallas Institute of Humanities and Culture, 1983.

———. 1986. *Lautréamont*, translated by R. S. Dupree, Dallas: Dallas Institute of Humanities (orig. 1939).

Balint, E. 1974. A portrait of Michael Balint: The development of his ideas on the use of the drug "doctor." *International Journal of Psychiatry in Medicine* 5: 211–222.

Balint, M. 1957. *The doctor, his patient and the illness.* New York: International Universities Press.

Bateson, G. 1972. *Steps to an ecology of mind.* San Francisco: Chandler.

Baum, H. S. 1986. Response to commentary by Cynthia McSwain. *Political Psychology* 7(1): 159–162.

Beattie, H.J. 1988. Eating disorders and the mother-daughter relationship. *International Journal of Eating Disorders* 7(4): 453–460.

Bell, R. M. 1985. *Holy anorexia.* Chicago, IL: University of Chicago Press.

Bell, R. Q., and D. Pearl. 1982. Psychosocial change in risk groups: implications for early identification. In *Journal of Prevention in Human Services* 1(4): 45–53.

Bell, R. Q. 1982. Age specific manifestations in changing psychosocial risk. In *The Concept of risk in intellectual and psychosocial development*, edited by D. C. Farran and J. D. McKinney. New York: Academic Press.

Benedek, T. 1959. Parenthood as a developmental phase: A contribution to the libido theory. *Journal of the American Psychoanalytic Association* 7: 389–417.

———. 1977. Ambivalence, passion and love. In *Journal of the American Psychoanalytic Association* 25(1): 53–80.

Berger, P., and T. Luckmann. 1966. *The social construction of reality: A treatise in the society of knowledge.* New York: Doubleday.

Bibring, G. L. 1959. Some considerations of the psychological processes in pregnancy. In *The psychoanalytic study of the child* 14: 113–121.

Bibring, G. L., T. F. Dwyer, D. S. Huntington, and A. F. Valenstein. 1961. A study of the psychological processes in pregnancy and of the earliest mother-child relationship. In *The psychoanalytic study of the child* 16: 9–72.

Bion, W. R. 1955. Group dynamics: A re-view. In *New directions in psychoanalysis*, edited by M. Klein, P. Heimann, and R. Money-Kyrle, 440–477. New York: Basic Books

———. 1959. *Experiences in groups.* New York: Basic Books.

———. 1961. *Experiences in groups and other papers.* New York: Ballantine Books.

———. 1962. *Learning from Experience.* London: Heinemann.

———. 1963. *Elements of psycho-analysis.* New York: Basic Books.

———. 1967. Differentiation of the psychotic from non-psychotic personalities. In *Second thoughts*, 43–64. New York: Aronson.

Bollas, C. 1987. *The shadow of the object: Psychoanalysis of the unthought known.* London: Free Association Press.

Bowen, M. 1978. *Family therapy in clinical practice.* Northvale, NJ: Aronson.

Bowlby, J. 1988. Developmental psychiatry comes of age. *American Journal of Psychiatry* 145: 1–10.

Boyer, L. B. 1979. *Childhood and folklore: A psychoanalytic study of Apache personality.* New York: Library of Psychological Anthropology.

Brazelton, H. 1980. *New knowledge about the infant from current research: Implications for psychoanalysis*. Presented at meeting of American Psychoanalytic Association, San Francisco.

Brazelton, T. B., and H. Als. 1979. Four early stages in the development of mother-infant interaction. *The Psychoanalytic study of the child* 34: 349–371.

Brierley, M. 1944. Notes on metapsychology as process theory. *International Journal of Psycho-Analysis* 25:97–107.

———. 1951. *Trends in psycho-analysis*. London: Hogarth Press and Institute of Psycho-Analysis.

Brinch, M., T. Isager, and K. Tolstrup. 1988. Anorexia nervosa and motherhood: Reproductive pattern and mothering behavior of 50 women. *Acta Psychiatrica Scandinavica* 77(5): 611–617.

Brocher, T. 1984. Diagnosis of organizations, communities, and political units. In *The irrational executive: Psychoanalytic studies in management*, edited by M. F. R. Kets deVries, 373–391. New York: International Universities Press.

Brodey, W. M., M. Hayden, and O. Krug. 1957. Intra-team reactions: Their relation to the conflicts of the family in treatment. *American Journal of Orthopsychiatry* 27(2): 349–355.

Bruch, H. 1974. *Eating disorders*. London: Routledge and Kegan Paul.

Burnett, C. 1982. *Hermann of Carinthia: De essentiis*. Leiden: E.J. Brill.

Burnside, J. W. 1983. Medicine and war—A metaphor. *Journal of the American Medical Association* 249: 2091.

Campbell, S. M. 1980. *The couple's journey: Intimacy as a path to wholeness*. San Luis Obispo, CA: Impact Publishers.

Caster, J. H., and E. Gatens-Robinson. 1983. Metaphor in medicine. *Journal of the American Medical Association* 250: 1841.

Ceasar, M. 1977. The role of maternal identification in four cases of anorexia nervosa. *Bulletin of the Menninger Clinic* 45(5): 475–486.

Chatoor, I. 1989. Infantile anorexia nervosa: A developmental disorder of separation and individuation. *Journal of the American Academy of Psychoanalysis* 17(1): 43–64.

Chediak, C. 1977. The so-called anorexia nervosa: Diagnostic and treatment considerations. *Bulletin of the Menninger Clinic* 41(5): 453–474.

Crisp, A. H. 1977. Some psychobiological aspects of adolescent growth and their relevance for the fat/thin syndrome (anorexia nervosa). *International Journal of Obesity* 1: 231–238.

———. 1980. *Anorexia nervosa: Let me be*. London: Academic Press.

———. 1981. *Anorexia nervosa* at normal body weight: The abnormal weight control syndrome. *International Journal of Psychiatry in Medicine* 11: 203–233.

Crisp, A. H.,, L. K. G. Hsu, B. Harding, and J. Hartshorn. 1980. Clinical features of anorexia nervosa: A study of a consecutive series of 102 female patients. *Journal of Psychosomatic Research* 24: 179–191.

Crisp, A. H., and R. S. Kalucy. 1974. Aspects of the perceptual disorder in anorexia nervosa. *British Journal of Medical Psychology* 47: 349–361.

Crisp, A. H., R. S. Kalucy, T. R. E. Pilkington, and J. C. Gazet. 1977. Some psychosocial consequences of ileojejunal bypass surgery. *American Journal of Clinical Nutrition* 30: 109–120.

Crouch, M., and L. Roberts, eds. 1987. *The family in medical practice: A family systems primer*. New York: Springer-Verlag.

Davidson, R. H. 1986. Transference and countertransference phenomena: The problem of the observer in the behavioral sciences. *Journal of Psychoanalytic Anthropology* 9(3): 269–283.

Deese, J. 1965. *The structure of association in language and thought*. Baltimore: The Johns Hopkins Press.

deMause, L. 1977. Jimmy Carter and American fantasy. In *Jimmy Carter and American fantasy: Psychohistorical explorations*, edited by L. deMause and H. Ebel, 9–31. New York: Two Continents/Psychohistory Press.

———. 1982. *Foundations of psychohistory*. New York: Creative Roots.

Deutsch, H. 1945. *The psychology of women*, vol. 2, *Motherhood*. London: Research Books.

Devereux, G. 1955. Charismatic leadership and crisis. *Psychoanalysis and the social sciences* 4: 145–157.

———. 1967. *From anxiety to method in the behavioral sciences*. The Hague: Mouton.

———. 1980. *Basic problems of ethnopsychiatry*, translated by B. M. Gulati and G. Devereux. Chicago: University of Chicago Press.

De Vos, G. 1966. Toward a cross-cultural psychology of caste behavior. In *Japan's invisible race*, edited by DeVos and H. Wagatsuma, 353–384. Berkeley/Los Angeles: University of California Press.

Diamond, M. A. 1984. Bureaucracy as externalized self-system: A view from the psychological interior. *Administration and Society* 16(2): 195–214.

———. 1988. Organizational identity: A psychoanalytic exploration of organizational meaning. *Administration and Society* 20(2): 166–190.

Diamond, M. A., and S. Allcorn. 1986. Role formation as defensive activity in bureaucratic organizations. *Political Psychology* 7(4): 709–732.

———. 1987. The psychodynamics of regression in work groups. *Human Relations* 40(8): 525–543.

Donovan, D. M. 1989. The paraconscious. *Journal of The American Academy of Psychoanalysis* 17(2): 223–251.

Eisenberg, L., and A. Kleinman. 1981. Clinical social science. In *The relevance of social science for medicine*, edited by L. Eisenberg and A. Kleinman, 1–23. Boston/Dordrecht, Holland: D. Reidel.

Erikson, K. T. 1976. Loss of communality at Buffalo Creek. *American Journal of Psychiatry* 133(3): 302–305.

Foulkes, S. H. 1948. *Introduction to group-analytic psychotherapy*. London: Heinemann.

Fox, R. 1959. *Experiment perilous: Physicians and patients facing the unknown.* New York: Free Press.

Freud, A. 1936. *The ego and the mechanisms of defense.* New York: International Universities Press, 1966.

———. 1965. *Normality and pathology in childhood.* London: Hogarth Press.

———. 1967. About losing and being lost. In *The psychoanalytic study of the child* 22: 9–19.

Freud, S. 1900a. The interpretation of dreams. In *Standard edition* 4/5: 1–361. London: Hogarth Press, 1953.

———. 1900b. The primary and secondary processes—Repression. In *Standard edition* 5: 588–609. London: Hogarth Press, 1953.

———. 1910. The future prospects of psycho-analytic therapy. In *Standard edition* 11: 141–151. London: Hogarth Press, 1957.

———. 1912. Recommendations to physicians practicing psycho-analysis. In *Standard edition* 12: 109–120. London: Hogarth Press, 1958.

———. 1917. Mourning and melancholia. In *Standard edition* 14:239–250. London: Hogarth Press, 1957.

———. 1921. Group psychology and the analysis of the ego. In *Standard Edition* 18: 69–143. London: Hogarth Press, 1955.

———. 1923. The ego and the id. In *Standard edition* 19: 3–66. London: Hogarth Press, 1961.

Fry, A. 1970. *How a people die.* Toronto: Doubleday.

GAP Committee on International Relations, and H. F. Stein. 1987. *Us and them: The psychology of ethnonationalism.* Group for the Advancement of Psychiatry (GAP) report no. 123. New York: Brunner/Mazel.

Geertz, C. 1973. *The interpretation of cultures: Selected essays.* New York: Basic Books.

Geist, R. A. 1989. Self psychological reflections of the origins of eating disorders. *Journal of the American Academy of Psychoanalysis* 17(1): 5–27.

Gerber, W. G., and C. E. Sluzki. 1978. The physician-family relationship. In *Family medicine principles and practice*, edited by R. Taylor, 216–220. New York: Springer-Verlag.

Giorgi, A. 1979. The relation among level, type, and structure and their importance for social science theorizing: A Dialogue with Shutz. *Duquesne Studies in Phenomenological Psychology*, vol. 3, edited by Amedeo Giorgi, R. Knowles, and L. Smith, pp. 81–96. Pittsburgh: Duquesne University Press.

———. ed. 1985. *Phenomenology and psychological research.* Pittsburgh, PA: Duquesne University Press.

Gordon, B. 1978. The vulnerable mother and her child. In *The place of birth*, edited by Sheila Kitzinger and John A. Davis, 201–215. Oxford: Oxford Universities Press.

Gordon, C., E. Beresin, and D.B. Herzog. 1989. The parents' relationship with the child's illness in anorexia nervosa. *Journal of the American Academy of Psychoanalysis* 17(1): 29–42.

Graumann, C. F. 1988. Phenomenological analysis and experimental method of psychology—the problem of their compatability. *Journal of the Theory of Social Behavior* 8: 33–50.

Green, A. 1969. *The tragic effect*, translated by A. Sheridan, Cambridge: Cambridge University Press, 1979.

Greenspan, S. I., and R. S. Lourie. 1981. Developmental structuralist approach to classification of adaptive and pathological personality organizations: Infancy and early childhood. *American Journal of Psychiatry* 138: 725–735.

Grieco, M. S. 1988. Birth-marked? A critical view on analyzing organizational culture. *Human Organization* 47(1): 84–87.

Grolnick, S. 1987. Reflections on psychoanalytic subjectivity and objectivity as applied to anthropology. *Ethos* 15(1): 136–143.

Grosskurth, P. 1986. *Melanie Klein: Her life and work.* New York: Alfred Knopf.

Grotstein, J. S. 1981. *Splitting and projective identification.* New York: Aronson.

Hall, A., J. Leibrich, F. H. Walkey, and G. Welch. 1986. Investigation of "weight pathology" of 58 mothers and anorexia nervosa patients and 204 mothers and schoolgirls. *Psychological Medicine* 16 (1): 71–76.

Halmi, K. 1974. Anorexia nervosa: Demographic and clinical features in 94 cases. *Psychosomatic Medicine* 36 (1): 18–26.

Hartmann, H. 1958. *Ego psychology and the problem of adaptation.* New York: International Universities Press.

———. 1964. *Essays on Ego Psychology.* New York: International Universities Press.

Hayden, G. F. 1984. What's in a name? "Mechanical" diagnosis in clinical medicine. *Postgraduate Medicine* 75: 227–232.

Heidegger, M. 1968. *What is called thinking.* New York: Harper and Row.

Heimann, P. 1950. On counter-transference. *International Journal of Psycho-Analysis* 31: 81–84.

Heinlein, R. 1967. *I will fear no evil.* New York: Putnam's.

Hendricks, G., and K. Hendricks. 1985. *Centering and the art of intimacy.* New York: Prentice Hall.

Henry, J. 1963. *Culture against man.* New York: Random House.

Hoffheimer, J. A., and M. Apprey. 1987. Patterns of socioaffective development in disturbed mothers' perception and interactions with their infants. In Nonna Slavinska-Holy, *Identity dysfunctions, the borderline and narcissistic patients in therapy.* New York: International Universities Press.

Hogan, C. C. 1983. Transference. In *Fear of being fat,* edited by C. P. Wilson, 153–168. New York: Aronson.

Hook, R. H. 1979. Phantasy and symbol: A psychoanalytic point of view. In *Fantasy and symbol,* edited by R. H. Hook, 267–291. New York: Academic Press.

Husserl, E. 1931. *Ideas*, translated by W.R.B. Gibson, London: Allen and Unwin, Ltd. (orig. 1913).

———. 1973. *Experience and judgement*. Evanston, IL: Northwestern University Press (orig. 1948).

Isaacs, S. 1952. The nature and function of phantasy. In *Developments in psycho-analysis*, edited by M. Klein, P. Heiman, S. Isaacs, and J. Riviere, 67–121. London: Hogarth Press and Institute of Psycho-Analysis.

Janis, I. L. 1982. *Groupthink*. Boston: Houghton Mifflin.

Jaques, E. 1955. Social systems as a defense against persecutory and depressive anxiety. In *New directions in psycho-analysis*, edited by M. Klein, P. Heimann, and R. Money-Kyrle, 478–498. New York: Basic Books.

Jilek, W. G. 1974. *Salish Indian mental health and culture change*. Toronto: Holt, Rinehart and Winston.

Jilek-Aall, L. 1986. Review of A. M. Shkilnyk's *A poison stronger than love: The destruction of an Ojibwa community*. *Transcultural Psychiatric Research Review* 23: 241–244.

Johnson, R. A. 1983. *We: Understanding the psychology of romantic love*. New York: Harper and Row.

Jones, E. 1985. Anorexia nervosa, bulimia, and birth. *Birth Psychology Bulletin* 6 (1): 1–6.

Joseph, B. 1987. Projective identification: clinical aspects. In *Projection, identification, projective identification*, edited by J. Sandler, 65–76. Madison, CT: International Universities Press.

Jung, C. G. 1927. *Metamorphoses et symboles de la libido*. Paris: Presses Universitaires de France, 1945.

———. 1966. *The psychology of the transference*. Bollingen Series. Princeton: Princeton University Press.

Kafka, J. S., and J. W. McDonald. 1965. The latent family in the intensive treatment of the hospitalized schizophrenic patient. In *Current sychiatric therapies* 5: 172–177. New York: Grune and Stratton.

Katz, J. 1984. *The silent world of doctor and patient*. New York: Free Press.

Kernberg, O. F. 1965. Notes on countertransference. *Journal of the American Psychoanalytic Association* 13: 38–56.

———. 1984a. Projection and projective identifications: development and clinical aspects, (unpublished).

———. 1984b. Regression in organizational leadership. In *The irrational executive: Psychoanalytic studies in management*, edited by M. F. R. Kets deVries, 38–66. New York: International Universities Press.

Kestenberg, J. S. 1976. Regression and reintegration in pregnancy. *Journal of the American Psychoanalytic Association* 24: 213–250.

Kets deVries, M. F. R., ed. 1984. *The irrational executive: Psychoanalytic studies in management*. New York: International Universities Press.

Klaus, M. H., et al. 1972. Maternal attachment: The importance of the first postpartum days. *New England Journal of Medicine* 286: 460–463.

272 References

Klein, J. 1945. The oedipus complex in the light of early anxieties. In *The writing of Melanie Klein*, vol. 1, *Love, guilt and reparation and other works*, 370–419.

Klein, M. 1946. Notes on some schizoid mechanisms. *International Journal of Psycho-Analysis* 27: 99–110.

———. 1955. On identification. In *New directions in psychoanalysis*, edited by M. Klein, P. Heimann, and R. Money-Kyrle, 309–344. New York: Basic Books.

———. 1975a. *Envy and gratitude and other works, 1946–1963*. London: Hogarth Press and Institute of Psychoanalysis.

———. 1975b. *Love, guilt and reparation and other works, 1921–1945*. London: Hogarth Press and Institute of Psychoanalysis.

Kleinman, A. 1980. *Patients and healers in the context of culture: An exploration of the borderland between anthropology, medicine, and psychiatry*. Los Angeles/Berkeley: University of California Press.

Kohut, H. 1972. Thoughts on narcissism and narcissistic rage. *The psychoanalytic study of the child*, vol. 27, 360–400. New York: Quadrangle/New York Times Press.

Kormos, H. R. 1984. The industrialization of medicine. In *Advances in medical social science*, vol. 2, edited by J. L. Ruffini, 323–339. New York: Gordon and Breach.

———. 1984. *How does analysis cure?* Chicago: University of Chicago Press.

———. 1985. *The analysis of the self*. New York: International Universities Press.

Kristeva, J. 1982. *Powers of horror: An essay on abjection*. translated by L. S. Roudiez. New York: Columbia University Press (Orig. 1980).

Kulish, N. M. 1985. Projective identification: A concept overburdened. *International Journal of Psychoanalytic Psychotherapy* 11: 79–110.

Kurth, F. 1975. Projective identification, analyzability, and hate. *Psychoanalytic Forum* 5: 313–352.

La Barre, W. 1951. Family and symbol. *In Psychoanalysis and culture: Essays in honor of Géza Róheim*, edited by G. Wilbur and W. Muensterberger, 156–167. New York: International Universities Press.

———. 1971. Materials for a history of studies of crisis cults: A bibliographic essay. *Current Anthropology* 12(1): 3–44.

———. 1972. *The ghost dance: The origins of religion*. New York: Dell.

———. 1978. The clinic and the field. In *The making of psychological anthropology*, edited by G. D. Spindler, 258–299. Los Angeles/Berkeley: University of California Press.

Laplanche, J., and J. B. Pontalis. 1973. *The language of psychoanalysis*. New York: W. W. Norton.

Lardner, J. 1983. War of the words. *Washington Post*, 6 March, G10.

Laufer, M. 1981. Adolescent breakdown and the transference neurosis. *International Journal of Psycho-Analysis* 62: 51–59.

Laufer, M., and M. E. Laufer. 1984. *Adolescence and developmental breakdown*. New Haven: Yale University Press.

Levinas, E. 1981. *Otherwise than being and beyond essence.* Translated by A. Lingis. Boston: Martinus Nijhoff (orig. 1974).

Levin, J. 1987. *Treatment of alcoholism and other addictions: A self-psychology approach.* Northvale, NJ: Aronson.

Lichtenberg, J.D. 1983. *Psychoanalysis and infant research.* Hillsdale, NJ: Lawrence Erlbaum Associates.

Liebermann, A. F., S. Wieder, and S. I. Greenspan. 1977. *Caregiver perception profile.* N.I.M.H. Technical Report.

Lomas, P. 1960. Defensive organization and puerperal breakdown. *British Journal of Medical Psychology* 33: 61–66.

Mahler, M., F. Pine, and A. Bergman. 1975. *The psychological birth of the human infant.* New York: Basic Books.

McDougall, J. 1985. *Theaters of the mind: Illusion and truth on the psychoanalytic stage.* New York: Basic Books.

Meltzer, D. 1967. *The psycho-analytical process.* London: Heinemann.

———. 1973. *Sexual states of mind.* Strath Tay, Scotland: Clunie Press.

Meltzer, D., G. Milana, S. Maiello, and D. Petrilli. 1982. The conceptual distinction between projective identification (Klein) and container-contained (Bion). *Journal of Child Psychotherapy* 8: 185–202.

Merleau-Ponty, M. 1962. *The phenomenology of perception,* translated by C. Smith. New York: Humanities Press. (orig. 1945).

———. 1964. *The primacy of perception.* Evanston, IL: Northwestern University Press.

———. 1968. *The visible and the invisible.* Evanston, IL: Northwestern University Press.

———. 1973. *Consciousness and the acquisition of knowledge.* Evanston, IL: Northwestern University Press.

———. 1983. *The structure of behavior,* translated by Alden Fisher. Pittsburgh: Duquesne University Press.

Mink, L. O. 1972. Interpretation and narrative understanding. *Journal of Philosophy* 69 (9): 735–57.

Minuchin, S., and H. C. Fishman. 1981. *Family therapy techniques.* Cambridge: Harvard University Press.

Minuchin, S., B. L. Rosman, and L. Baker. 1978. *Psychosomatic families.* Cambridge: Harvard University Press.

Mitscherlich, A., and M. Mitscherlich. 1975. *The inability to mourn: Principles of collective behavior.* New York: Grove Press.

Mold, J. W., and H. F. Stein. 1986. The cascade effect in the clinical care of patients. *New England Journal of Medicine* 314: 512–514.

Newman, L. E. and Stoller, R.J. 1971. The oedipal situation in male transsexualism. *British Journal of Medical Psychology* 44: 295–303.

Noshpitz, J. 1990. Psychotherapy versus delinquency (unpublished manuscript).

Nover, A., M. Shore, E. M. Timberlake, and S. I. Greenspan. 1985. The relationships of maternal misperception and maternal behavior: a study of normal mothers and their infants (unpublished).

Nunberg, H. 1948. The course of the libidinal conflicts in a case of schizophrenia. In *Practice and theory of psychoanalysis,* vol. 1.

New York: International Universities Press.

Ogden, T. H. 1988. Misrecognition and the fear of not knowing. *Psychoanalytic Quarterly* 57: 643–666.

Owen, H. 1986. Griefwork in organizations. *Foresight Journal* 1(1): 1–13.

———. 1987. *Spirit: Transformation and development in organizations.* Potomac, MD: Abbott Publishing.

Palazzoli, M. S. 1982. *Self-starvation.* New York: Aronson.

Parin, P. 1987. The ego and the mechanism of adaptation. In *The psychoanalytic study of society,* vol. 12, edited by L. B. Boyer and S. Grolnick, 97–130. Hillsdale, NJ: Analytic Press.

Parsons, T. 1951. *The social system.* New York: Free Press.

Pines, D. 1978. On becoming a parent. *Journal of Child Psychotherapy* 4: 19–31.

Pirrotta, S. 1984. Milan revisited: A comparison of the two Milan schools. Special issue: Integration—case studies: Mixing and switching modes in clinical practice. *Journal of Strategic and Systemic Therapies* 3(4): 3–15.

Politzer, G. 1973. *Ecrits 2: Les fondements de la psychologie* (Edited by Jacques Debouzy) Paris: Editions Socrates.

———. 1976. *Critique des fondements de la psychologie: La psychologie et al psychanalyse.* Paris: Presses Universitaries de France.

Pollock, G. H. 1961. Mourning and adaptation. *International Journal of Psycho-Analysis* 42: 341–361.

Raphael-Leff, J. 1982. Psychotherapeutic needs of mothers-to-be. In *Journal of Child Psychotherapy* 8(1): 3–14.

Reich, A. 1951. On countertransference. *International Journal of Psycho-Analysis* 32: 25–31.

Reich, W. 1945. *Character analysis.* New York: Orgone Institute Press.

Rhodes, L. A. 1986. The anthropologist as institutional analyst. *Ethos* 14(2): 204–217.

Richards, R. 1983. *Second serve.* New York: Stein and Day

Ricoeur, P. 1980. Narrative time. *Critical Inquiry* 7: 169–190.

Rizutto, A. M. 1988. Transference, language, and affect in the treatment of bulimarexia. *International Journal of Psychoanalysis* 69: 369–387.

Rosenfeld, H. 1987. *Impasse and interpretation.* London: Tavistock Publications.

Ross, J. L. 1977. Anorexia nervosa: An overview. *Bulletin of the Menninger Clinic* 41(5): 418–436.

Sandler, J. (ed). 1987. The concept of projective identification. *Projection, identification, projective identification,* edited by J. Sandler, 13–26. Madison CT: International Universities Press.

Sandler, J. with Freud, A. 1985. *The analysis of defense: The ego and the mechanisms of defense revisited.* New York: International Universities Press.

Sandler, J., and B. Rosenblatt. 1962. The concept of the representational world. *The psychoanalytic study of the child* 17: 128–162. New York: International Universities Press.

Sarnoff, C. 1976. *Latency.* Northvale, New York: Aronson.

Scharff, D., and J. Scharff. 1988. *Object relations family therapy.* Northvale, NJ: Aronson.

Scheingold, L. 1988. Balint work in England: Lessons for American family medicine. *Journal of Family Practice* 26 (3): 315–320.

Schmidt, C. G. 1984. The group-fantasy origins of AIDS. *Journal of Psychohistory* 12: 37–78.

Scholes, R. 1980. Afterthoughts on narrative: Language, narrative, and antinarrative. *New Literary History* 12(1): 207–211.

Scott, C. E. 1982. *Boundaries in mind.* New York: Crossroads Publishing Co. and Chico, CA: Scholars Press.

Segal, H. 1981. *The work of Hanna Segal.* New York: Aronson.

Shapiro, W. 1989. Thanatophobic man. *Anthropology Today* 5(2): 11–14.

Shkilnyk, A. M. 1985. *A poison stronger than love: The destruction of an Ojibwa community.* New Haven: Yale University Press.

Simon, B. 1987. Tragic drama and the family: The killing of children and the killing of story telling. In Shlomith Rimmon-Kenan, ed. *Discourse in psychoanalysis and literature.* London and New York: Methuen.

Smith, R. C. 1984. Teaching interviewing skills to medical students: The issue of "countertransference." *Journal of Medical Education* 59: 582–588.

———. 1985. A clinical approach to the somatizing patient. *Journal of Family Practice* 21(4): 294–301.

———. 1986. Unrecognized responses and feelings of residents and fellows during interviews of patients. *Journal of Medical Education* 61: 982–984.

Smith, R. C., and H. F. Stein. 1987. A topographical model of clinical decision-making and interviewing: A heuristic for family medicine teaching. *Family Medicine* 19(5): 361–363.

Sours, J. A. 1980. *Starving to death in a sea of objects: The anorexia nervosa syndrome.* New York: Aronson.

Sperling, M. 1983. A reevaluation of classification, concepts, and treatment. In *Fear of Being fat,* edited by C. P. Wilson, 51–82. New York: Aronson.

Sprince, M. P. 1984. Early psychic disturbance in anorexic and bulimic patients as reflected in the psychoanalytic process. *Journal of Child Psychotherapy* 10(2): 199–215.

Stamm, I. 1987. Countertransference in hospital treatment: Basic concepts and paradigms. Paper series, no. 2. Topeka, KS: Menninger Foundation.

Stein, H. F. 1980a. *An ethno-historic study of Slovak-American identity.* New York: Arno Press/New York Times Press.

———. 1980b. Wars and rumors of wars: A psychohistorical study of a medical culture. *Journal of Psychohistory* 7: 379–401.

———. 1982a. Ethanol and its discontents: Paradoxes of inebriation and sobriety in American culture. *Journal of Psychoanalytic Anthropology* 5: 355–377.

———. 1982b."Health" and "wellness" as euphemism: The cultural context of insidious draconian health policy. *Continuing Education for the Family Physician* 16(3): 33–44.

———. 1982c. Neo-Darwinism and survival through fitness. *Journal of Psychohistory* 10(2): 163–187.

———. 1982d. Physician-patient transaction through the analysis of counter-transference: A study in role relationship and unconscious meaning. *Medical Anthropology* 6: 165–182.

———. 1982e. Wellness as illusion. *Delaware Medical Journal* 54(11): 637–641.

———. 1983a. The influence of counter-transference upon the clinical relationship and decision-making. *Continuing Education for the Family Physician* 18: 625–630.

———. 1983b. The money taboo in American medicine. *Medical Anthropology* 7: 1–15.

———. 1984. The scope of psycho-geography: The psychoanalytic study of spatial representation. *Journal of Psychoanalytic Anthropology* 7: 23–73.

———. 1985a. Alcoholism as metaphor in American culture: Ritual desecration as social integration. *Ethos* 13: 195–235.

———. 1985b. Comment on Dundes' "The American game of 'smear the queer' and the homosexual component of male competitive sport and warfare." *Journal of Psychoanalytic Antropology* 8(3): 131–134.

———. 1985c. Culture change, symbolic object loss, and restitutional process. *Psychoanalysis and Contemporary Thought* 8(3): 301–332.

———. 1985d. The culture of the patient as red herring in clinical decision-making: A case study. *Medical Anthropology Quarterly* 17: 2–5.

———. 1985e. Portrait of a young physician. *American Scholar* 54: 485–499.

———. 1985f. *The psychoanthropology of American culture*. New York: The Psychohistory Press.

———. 1985g. *The psychodynamics of medical practice: Unconscious factors in patient care*. Berkeley and Los Angeles: University of California Press.

———. 1985h. In pursuit of maturity in the clinical relationship (Review essay on J. Katz, *The silent world of doctor and patient*, 1984). *Family Systems Medicine* 3: 486–491.

———. 1986a. "The bomb drops in 1 1/2 hours": A medical case conference as pedagogical ritual and the compulsion to repeat. *Journal of Psychoanalytic Anthropology* 9(1): 55–66.

———. 1986b. "Sick people" and "trolls": A contribution to the understanding of the dynamics of physician explanatory models. *Culture, Medicine and Psychiatry* 10(3): 221–229.

———. 1986c. Social role and unconscious complementarity. *Journal of Psychoanalytic Anthropology* 9(3): 235–268.

———. 1986d. Unconscious factors in organizational decision-making: A case study from medicine. *Organization Development Journal* 4(2): 21–28.

———. 1987a. *Developmental time, cultural space: Studies in psychogeography*. Norman: University of Oklahoma Press.

———. 1987b. Encompassing systems: Implications for citizen diplomacy. *Journal of Humanistic Psychology* 27(3): 364–384.

———. 1988. Aggression, grief-work, and organizational development: Theory and case example. *Organization Development Journal* 6(1): 22–28.

———. 1990. *American medicine as culture*. Boulder, CO: Westview Press.

Stein, H. F., and M. Apprey. 1985. *Context and dynamics in clinical knowledge*, vol. 1 of the series in ethnicity, medicine, and psychoanalysis. Charlottesville: University Press of Virginia.

———. 1987. *From metaphor to meaning: Papers in psychoanalytic anthropology*, vol. 2 of the series in ethnicity, medicine, and psychoanalysis. Charlottesville: University Press of Virginia.

———. 1990. *Clinical stories and their translations*, vol. 3 of the series in ethnicity, medicine, and psychoanalysis. Charlottesville: University Press of Virginia.

Stein, H. F., and D. Fox. 1985. Work as family: Occupational relationships and social transference. In *Context and dynamics in clinical knowledge*, vol. 1 of the series in ethnicity, medicine, and psychoanalysis by H. F. Stein and M. Apprey, 182–197. Charlottesville: University Press of Virginia.

Stein, H. F., and R. F. Hill. 1979. Adaptive modalities among Slovak- and Polish-Americans: Some issues in cultural continuity and change. *Anthropology* 3(1–2): 95–107.

———. 1988. The dogma of technology. In *The psychoanalytic study of society*, vol. 13, edited by L. B. Boyer and S. Grolnick, 149–179. Hillsdale, NJ: Analytic Press.

Stein, H. F., and J. W. Mold. 1988. Stress, anxiety, and cascades in clinical decision-making. *Stress Medicine* 4(1): 41–48.

Stein, H. F., and W. G. Niederland, eds. 1989. *Maps from the mind: Readings in psychogeography*. Norman: University of Oklahoma Press.

Stierlin, H. 1981. *Separating parents and adolescents*. New York: Aronson.

Stoller, R. J. 1968. *Sex and gender*. New York: Aronson.

———. 1973. *Splitting: A case of female masculinity*. New York: Quadrangle/New York Times Book Co.

Stone, I. F. 1952. *The hidden history of the Korean War*. New York: Monthly Review Press, 1970.

Taylor, M. C. 1987. *Altarity*. Chicago: University of Chicago Press.

Thomä, H. 1967. *Anorexia nervosa*. New York: International Universities Press.

Thouzery, L. 1984. D'un regard (ou il est question d'anorexie mentale). An outlook suggestive of anorexia nervosa. *Neuropsychiatrie de*

*L'enfance et de L'adolescence* 32(5–6): 267–279.

Volkan, V. D. 1979. *Cyprus—war and adaptation.* Charlottesville: University Press of Virginia.

———. 1980a. Transsexualism: As examined from the viewpoint of internalized object relation. In Karasu, T.B. and Socarides, C.W., Eds. *On Sexuality: Psychoanalytic Observations.* New York: International Universities Press.

———. 1980b. Narcissistic personality organization and "reparative" leadership. *International Journal of Group Psychotherapy* 30(2): 131–152.

———. 1981. *Linking objects and linking phenomena: A study of the forms, symptoms, metapsychology, and therapy of complicated mourning.* New York: International Universities Press.

———. 1984. Psychological formulations developed at the conferences on the Middle East (unpublished manuscript). Quoted with author's permission.

———. 1988. *The need to have enemies and allies: From clinical practice to international relationships.* Northvale, NJ: Aronson.

———. 1989. The development of female transsexualism. *American Journal of Psychotherapy* 43(1): 92–107.

Volkan, V. D., and D. R. Hawkins. 1971. A field-work case in the teaching of clinical psychiatry. *Psychiatry in Medicine* 2: 160–176.

———. 1972. The learning group. *American Journal of Psychiatry* 128: 1121–1126.

Volkan, V. D., and T. H. Bhatti. 1973. Dreams of transsexuals awaiting surgery. *Comprehensive Psychiatry*, vol. 14, No. 3 (May/June).

Volkan, V. D., and N. Itzkowitz. 1984. *The immortal Atatürk: A psychobiography.* Chicago: University of Chicago Press.

von Franz, M.-L. 1978. *Projection and re-collection in Jungian psychology: Reflections of the soul.* La Salle, IL: Open Court.

Von-Wallenberg, P. A. 1982. Anorexia nervosa and schizophrenia. *American Journal of Social Psychiatry* 2(1): 29–33.

Waxler, N. E. 1981. The social labeling perspective on illness. In *The relevance of social science for medicine*, edited by L. Eisenberg and A. Kleinman, 283–306. Boston/Dordrecht, Holland: D. Reidel.

Whitehead, A. N. 1927. *Symbolism: Its meaning and effect.* New York: Capricorn.

Wilson, C. P. 1983. *Fear of being fat: The treatment of anorexia nervosa and bulimia.* New York: Aronson.

Winnicott, D. W. 1947. Hate in the countertransference. In *Through pediatrics, to psychoanalysis*, 194–203. London: Hogarth Press and Institute of Psychoanalysis, 1975.

———. 1956. Primary maternal preoccupation. In *Through pediatrics to psychoanalysis*, 300–305. London: Hogarth Press, 1975.

———. 1965. *The maturational process and the facilitative environment*, London: Hogarth Press.

Yalom, I. 1970. *The theory and practice of group psychotherapy.* New York: Basic Books.

Zinner, J., and R. Shapiro. 1972. Projective identification as a mode of perception and behavior in families of adolescents. *International Journal of Psycho-Analysis* 53: 523–530.

# Index

Abandonment, 51
Abjection, 20–23
Abraham, xii
Abraham, Nicholas, 102, 111
Abse, D. W., 193, 254–55
Abstinence, 44–45
Adaptation, 236–37: to doom, 227–29
Affect, 29
Agendas, xv, 192–93: unconscious, 196–202
Aggressor, 198, 229, 233
Aichhorn, A. 171
A. K. Rice Institute, xiv
Alcoholics Anonymous/Narcotics Anonymous, 170–71, 177, 181, 183–84
Alcoholism, 64–65
Alexander, L., 189
Alford, C. F., xiv, 233
*Alien*, 157
Als, H. 31
Altruistic surrender, 260
Ambiguity, 58, 67, 69, 177
Ambivalence, 66–67, 169–84, 263: pregnancies and, 82
Anger, 243–56
Anorexia nervosa, 103: clinical findings implications, 71–74; data collection, 34–36; death fantasy, 110; definition of, 15; haunting of, 111; infantile, 27–28; intergenerational context, xi–xii; intersubjectivity and, 9–15, 15–25,

63–70; literary themes on, 28–31; literature dialogue, 56–57; maternal age and, 26; models of, 16–17; mother and, 2–3; mother-daughter relations, 31–33; projective identification and, 70–71; research and clinical findings, 25–28; sleep disorders in, 26; stealing in, 23
Anxiety, 230
Anzieu, xiv
*Aporia*, 64
Apperceptive transfer, 11–12
Apprey, M., 70, 77, 104, 187, 189, 191, 243: audiotaped data base, 87; on death fantasy, 110; on maternal misperception, 114; philosophical background of, ix, xi–xiv; and organizational wish, 228; on physician-patient relationships, 210
Asceticism, 32, 72: and maternal reluctance, 62–63
Ashbach, xiv
Atatürk, 213
Attachment-disengagement, 31
Autonomy: secondary, 111–13, 114

Bachelard, G. 7–8, 63, 107
Baker, L., 15–16, 56
Balint, E. 187, 243
Balint, M., 187, 243–56
Bateson, G. 226
Beattie, H. J., 26

Behaviorism, 16–17
Beingness, 22–23
Bell, R. Q., 62, 81–82
Belongingness, 229
Benedek, T., 83, 138
Beresin, E. 27
Berger, P., 232
Bergman, 169, 175
Bhatti, T. H., 103, 104: transsexual dreams, 105–07
*Billy Budd*, xii
Bion, W. R., 133, 178, 229, 232: basic assumptions, 188; on container and contained, x–xi, xii, xiv, 171; on mass action, 191, 192
Bisexuality, 109–10
Body as thing, 18
Bollas, C., 174
Borders, 63–64
Boundaries, 68, 69–70, 108–09, 200–01: blurred, 58
*Boundaries in Mind*, 104
Bowen, M., 187
Bowlby, J., 174, 178: child development, 24
Brazelton, T. B., 31: Neonatal Behavioral Assessment, 88
Brierley, Marjorie, 1, 134, 168
Brinch, M., 25, 30
Brocher, T., 195
Brodey, W. M., 193, 254
Bruch, H., 16, 28, 56
Bulimia, 27, 65: poisoning mother and, 23; switching from anorexia nervosa to, 43
Bureaucracy, 212
Burke, xi
Burnett, C., 32
Burnside, J. W., 189

Campbell, S. M., 259–61
Caretaker Perception Profile (CCP), 87–89, 99–101
Cartesian postulate of consciousness, 12–13
Caster, J. H., 189
Catastrophism, 214
Ceasar, M., 27
Centering, 184
Change of function, 111–17

Chaos, 43–46, 64–65, 72, 169–84, 264: dysfunctional family, xiv, 176–77, 184
Chatoor, I., 27
Chediak, C., 26–27
Chemically dependent adolescents, xiv, 169–84: final phase of therapy, 180–84; initial phase of therapy, 171–77; middle phase of therapy, 177–80
Child abuse, xv
Childbirth, 137: pain, 84–85
Christ, sacrifice of, xii–xiii
*Claustrum*, 133–34
Clinical Infant Development Program, 88
Cocaine use, 202–05
Cogito, 11, 12, 13
Coleman, xiv
Collective trauma, 231–32
Compulsiveness, 44–45
Confidantes, 58
Configuration, 140–41
Consciousness, 8, 9, 13: Cartesian postulate of, 12–13; of others, 13–14; of self, 13–14
Container, 133, 134–35, 170–71
Control factor, 47, 58
"Corinthians," 258
Cosmic hydraulic, xiii
Counteridentification, 48
Countertransference, 2, 243, 251: group, xiv, 191
Crisis: creation of, 49–50; cults, 213–14; organizational, 230–33
Crisp, A. H., 25–26, 30, 56
*Critical Injury*, 153–54
Cross-dressing, 124–25, 127
Crouch, M., 187
Cultural extinction, 207–42
"Culture of the Patient as Red Herring in Clinical Decision-Making," 194

Danger, 230
Darwinism, 214, 217
Davidson, R. H., 243
De Vos, G., 228
Death: counseling, 239–41; fantasies, 64–65, 71, 75, 110; obsession, 146–47
Deidealization, 48
deMause, L., 194
Departure-return, 31
Dependency, xv, 229
Depersonalization, 199–200

Depression: infantile, 168; paternal, 47–
48; position of, xiii–xiv, xv–xvi, 235
Destructive aggression, 72–73: maternal
case study of, 141–66; toward siblings,
143–48
Deutsch, H., 138
Developmental disharmony, 28
Devereux, G., 205–06, 230
Devil, xii–xiii
Diabetic patient-doctor case, 244–56
Diagnostic treatment, 72
Diamond, M. A., 229, 233
Differentiation: somatopsychological, 28
Disidentification, xi
Disorganization, 51–52, 95–96
Dissociation, 107
Divided personality, 66
Donovan, Dennis, 103
Doom, adapting to, 207–42
Douglas, Kirk, 105–06, 107
Dreams, 151–52, 164: as fantasies of
destruction, 145; transsexual, 105–07;
as urgent/voluntary errands, 103,
110–11
Drug abuse, xv
Duality, 50–51
Dynamic unconscious, 103, 133
Dysfunctional family, xiv

E.T., 157
Echo phenomenon, 255
Ego, 14: ideal, 192; mother's, 97–98;
young, 135–36
"Ego and the Mechanism of
Adaptation," 236–37
Ehrmantraut, xiv
Eisenberg, L., 199
Either/or thinking, xiii
Enactment, 255
Episode, 140–41
Erikson, Kai T., 231–32
Errands: dreams, 103, 110–11; urgent/
voluntary, 117
Essences, 32–33
Experience, 10: structure of, 30, 112–26
Explanatory models, 190
Externalization, 79, 80

False self, 175, 183, 184
Familial dysfunction, 30
Family conflicts: anorexia nervosa, 26

Family therapy, xiv, 178–80, 183–84:
anorexia nervosa models and, 16–17;
integrated with individual, 169–84
Fantasy, 132, 135: destructive aggression toward siblings, 143–48; transformation by pregnancy, 148–53
Fat/thin syndrome, 25–26
Fear, 230: of excess, 72
Fight/flight, xv, 229, 235
Fishman, H. C., 170, 174, 178
Formal regression, 133–34
Foulkes, S. H., 193, 254–55
Fox, R., 187, 193
Frankel-Brunswick, 66, 170
Freud, S., xiv, 187, 191, 214, 243:
ambivalence discovery of, 169; child
development model of, 24; classical
analysis of, 132; definition of group,
192, 206, 233; on dream's meaning,
194; on dynamic unconscious, 133; on
identity of perception, 135; on
metapsychological profile of, 72; on
primordal repression, 21, 71;
symbolism of, 7
Freud, Anna, 260: on asceticism, 32; on
change of function, 111–13; on
pregnancy, 85
Fry, A., 215

Gatens-Robinson, 189
Gazet, J. C., 26
Geertz, C., 253
Geist, R. A., 27, 71
Geller, xiv
Gender identity disorder, 103, 111
Generational succession, xv, 197
Gerber, W. G., 187
Giorgi, A., 33, 34, 103: on phenomenol-
ogy, 34–35; research praxis of, 118–
19, 120
Gordon, B., 27, 98
Graumann, C. F., 34
Green, A., 22–23
Greenspan, S. I., 27–28
Grieco, M. S., 215
Grolnick, Simon, 261
Grotstein, James, 78–79
Group therapy, ix, xi, xiv–xv, 187–206:
countertransference in, xiv, 191;
decision makers, 187–206; definition
of, 233; dynamics, 194, 199; dysfunc-

tional family, xiv; process theory of, 189–96; relations in, 2

Group for the Advancement of Psychiatry (GAP), 214, 257

*Group Psychology and the Analysis of the Ego*, 192

Groupthink, xv, 188, 193

Hall, A., 25, 30
Halmi, K., 26
Harding, B., 30
Hartmann, Heinz: transgeneration and, 111, 112, 113
Hartshorn, J., 30
Hawkins, D. R., 193, 254–55
Hayden, G. F., 189, 193, 254
Heidegger, M., 171: tradition, 104
Heimann, P., 243
Heinlein, R., 146
Hendricks, G., 259–60
Hendricks, K., 259–60
Henry, Jules, 207
Hermann of Carinthia, 32
Herzog, D. B., 27
*Hidden History of the Korean War*, 258
Historicity, 34
Hoffheimer, J. A., 87
Hogan, C. C., 57
Holding environment, 170–71
*Holy Anorexia*, 62
Homosexuality, 47–48, 61–62
Hook, R. H., 194
Horizontal perceptual distinctions, 57
Hsu, K. G., 30
Hunger, 16, 18
Husserl, E., 9–12, 14, 33: thought, 103

*Ideas*, 10
Immortalization, 26
Individual psychology, ix: integrated with family, 169–84
Integration, 180–82
Intentional transfer, 11–12
Interactions, body and others, 17–18
Interchangeable selves, 58
Interperceptual relations: complex of, 57–59; across generations, 59–62; mother-daughter relations, 54–56
Intersubjectivity, 56–57: abjection and, 20–23; anorexia nervosa and, 9–25, 63–70; experiences and, 10; missing

cognito and, 12; modern thoughts on, 20; in mother-daughter relationships, 19; plurality of, 68, 75; transsexualism and, 126–28
Intervention, 88, 234–41
Intrapsychic story: episode and configuration in, 140–41; fostering, 138–39; narrative and drama in, 140; and patient's history, 141–43; pregnancy and, 153–66
Introjection, xi
Introjective identification, xi
Introjects, 135
Isaacs, S., xii, 132, 134
Isager, 25, 30
Itzkowitz, N., 213
I-thou relationship, 104
*I Will Fear No Evil*, 146

Janis, I. L., 188, 192–93
Jaques, E., 193, 229
Johnson, Barbara, 153
Johnson, R. A., 259
Jones, E., 30
Joseph, B., 174
Jung, C. G., 107, 259–60

Kafka, J. S., 193, 254
Kalucy, R. S., 25–26, 30
Kanzer, Mark, 1
Katz, J., 187, 192, 199
Kernberg, O. F., 77–78, 195, 243
Kestenberg, J. S., 138
Kets deVries, M. F. R., 193, 229
Kissinger, Henry, 209
Klaus, M. H., 31
Klein, Melanie, 24, 70, 229: articulation and, 139; defining projective identification, x, xi, xiii, xv–xvi; and external reality, 131, 132–34, 135; on infantile depressive feelings, 168; Merleau-Ponty on, 66–67; on play therapy, 238; on projective identification, 76, 79, 114, 227–28, 254, 261; on schizoid-paranoid position, 235; on separation intolerance, 85; on superego, 135
Kleinman, A., 190, 199
Knapp, Peter, 1
Knowing, 261
Kohut, H., 27, 171, 216
Kormos, H. R., 217

Kristeva, J., 20–24, 70
Krug, O., 193, 254
Kubler-Ross, 150
Kulish, N. M., 70, 77: on projective
  identification, 131–33, 135
Kurth, Frederick, 1–2

Labeling, 190–92
La Barre, W., 191, 205–06, 213–14, 232
Lacan, J., 20
Lacunary perception, 11
Language, 29–30
Laplanche, J., 80
Lardner, J., 153
Laufer, M., 31, 170, 172
Laufer, M. E., 170, 172
Leadership, 212–43
Levin, J., 171
Levinas, E., 20
Lichtenburg, J. D., 31
Liebermann, A. F., 87
Liebrich, J., 25, 30
Life goals: contrary, 107
Limit setting, 52–53
Lomas, P., 138
Lourie, R. S., 27–28
Luckmann, T., 232

McDonald, J. W., 193, 254
McDougall, Joyce, 174
Mahler, M., 169, 175: on child
  development, 24
Materiality, 34
Maternal issues: age and anorexia
  nervosa, 26; entity, 22; hostility, xii–
  xiv; identification, 27; misperception,
  81–82, 114; relationship with anorexic
  daughter, 2–3, 31–33; relationship
  with child, 90–97
*Measure for Measure*, 206
Medical charts, maternal age and
  anorexia nervosa, 26
Meltzer, Donald, 1, 79–80, 132, 133,
  134, 208
Melville, Herman, xii
Memories, 9–11
Merleau-Ponty, M.: on ambiguity, 177;
  on ambivalence, 169, 170; on
  behavior's structure, 8–9, 11–14, 20;
  interview technique of, 171; on
  phenomenology, 32–34; on psycho-

logical rigidity, 65–68
Metaphors, 189, 193–94
Minuchin, S., 15–18, 56, 170, 174, 178
Mirroring, 31, 68–69, 75, 258:
  transference, 171
Misperception, 58: maternal, 81–82, 114
Misrecognitions, 29
Mitscherlich, A., 214
Mitscherlich, M., 214
Mold, J. W., 192, 199
Money-Kyrle, Roger, xi, 1
Mother-child relationship: at eight months,
  95–96; at 18 months, 96; at four months,
  90, 91, 94–95, 97; at three years, 92–
  93; at 12 months, 90, 92, 93, 96, 97; at
  two years, 90–91, 92, 93, 96
Mother-daughter relations, 19–21:
  anorexic, 2–3, 31–33; case studies,
  34–43, 89–97; interpreceptual
  structure of, 54–56; pairs, 15
Motherhood, 83: audiotaped database
  of, 87–89
Motives, 131–36

Narcissism, 26–27, 91: crisis of, 21–22;
  leadership by, 212–13; chronic rage, 216
Narrative, 140: time, 153–54
National Institute of Mental Health, 24, 87
Newman, L. E., 106
Niederland, 216, 257
Night terrors, 103
Nosphitz, J., 171
Nover, A., 81
Nunberg, H., 133

Obedience, 72
Oedipus, xii
Ogden, T. H., xi, 29
Ontological hate, 2
"Onward Christian Soldiers," 156
Oppressor, 214
Orestes, xii
Organization: doom adaptation and,
  227–29; regression and, 230–33
Otherness, 257–62: daughter's of self
  and (m)other, 46–56; at ego's expense,
  12; food as border guard, 23; primal
  repression and, 21
Overprotectionism, 52–54, 72
Owen, H., 216
Ownness sphere, 11

Pairing, xv, 11–12, 229
Palazzoli, M. S., 17–18, 56, 58–59
Paraconscious, 103
Parallel phenomenon, 255
Paranoid logic, 258–59
Paranoid-schizoid position, xv–xvi, 80
Parin, Paul, 236–37
Parsons, T., 187
Paul, 258
Perception, 9, 14, 11, 20, 57–59: daughter's of self and (m)other, 46–56; distortion of, 30; lateral, 11; mother's of daughter, 50–54; of other people's behavior, 11; of self and (m)other, 46–50
Personal risk factors, 82
Phantasy, 132–33, 135, 136, 228; destructive maternal projective identification, 141–68
Phantoms, 263–64
Phenomenology, 32–34: clinical data on, 36–37; data analysis procedure, 36; data collection procedures, 35–36; Giorgi's praxis of, 34–35; method, 118–28; parallel (echo), 255; results, 37–42; subjects and sample size, 35; transsexual dreams, 107
*Phenomenology of Perception*, 20, 32–34, 118
Physician-patient relationship, 243–56
Piaget; child development, 24
Pilkington, T. R. E., 26
Pimping, 197–98
Pines, D., 138, 169, 175
Pirrotta, S., 30–31
Pollock, G. H., 214
Pregnancies, 137: ambivalent, 82; analyses of, 138–39; clinical projective identification landmarks, 86–87; over-valued, 82; psychotherapy in, xiii, 82–85; and transformation fantasies, 148–53
Prenatal maternal feelings, 89–91, 93, 94, 96
Primal repression, 21
Projection, xii, 57, 79, 80
Projective identification, 1–3, 57, 257–59: and anger, 243–56; anorexia nervosa and, 70–71; background on, ix–xi; defense mechanisms for, 201;

defined, 24–25, 173–74, 76–81, 254; destructive maternal, 141–68; doomed organization and, 227–28; internal vs. external, 133–35; interpersonal, xi; intrapsychic, x, xiii; massive, 1–2; and maternal misperception, 81–82; and mother with child, 263; motives and, 131–36; pregnancy landmarks in, 86–87; role in transsexualism, 114, 116; violent, 1–2
*Prosopon*, 63, 75
Protentional experience, 10
*Psychodynamics of Medical Practice*, 193–94
Psycho-geography, 194–95
Psychological rigidity. *See* Rigidity

Raphael-Leff, J., 82, 138
Raskind, Richard Henry. *See* Richards, Renée
Rationalization, 199
Reaction formation, 91
Regression, 86, 133–34: maternal, 97; and organizational crisis, 230–33
Reich, Wilhelm, 111, 112, 243
Reification, 232–33
Rejection, 61
Relapse prevention, 181–82
Relationships, 257–58
Relocation, xi, 80
Reluctant mother, 61–62
Repression, primal, 21
Residency, 202–05: groups, 196–202
Retentional experience, 10
Reynolds, Debbie, 106
Rhodes, L. A., 234
Richards, Renée, 119, 120–28
Ricoeur, Paul, 140–41, 153–54
Rigidity, 43–46, 64–68, 169–84: in families, 174–76, 184
Risk assessment, 81–82
Rizutto, A. M., 29
Roberts, L., 187
Rosenblatt, B., 174
Rosenfield, H., 114
Rosman, B. L., 15–16, 56
Ross, J. L., 28

Sacrificial lamb, xii–xiii
Sandler, J., 112, 170, 171, 174
Scharff, D., 170, 174, 178

Scharff, J., 170, 174, 178
Scheingold, L., 243
Scheler, 9, 12–14
Schizoid-paranoid position, 235
Schizophrenia, 26, 133
Scholes, Robert, 140
Scott, Charles, 104
Secondary autonomy, 111–13, 114
*Second Serve*, 119
Separation-individuation, 27–28: levels, 106
Separation intolerance, 79–80, 85
Shakespeare, 111, 206
Shapiro, W., 229, 232
Shermer, xiv
Shkilnyk, A. M., 215
Sibling, destructive aggression toward, 143–48
Simon, Bennet, 110
Sleep disorders, 26, 30
Sluzki, C. E., 187
Smith, R. C., 243
Soller: case study, 108–09
Somatopsychological differentiation, 28
Sours, J. A., 15, 28
Spatiality, 34
Sperling, M., 61
Splitting, 107, 114–15, 201
Sprince, M. P., 28
Stamm, I., 194, 243, 254
Steelworkers, 215–16
Stein, H. F., xiv, 187–94, 197, 199, 202: on organization, 235; philosophical background of, ix, on physician-patient relationships, 210, 214–16, 228–29, 243, 254–57
Stierlin, H., 170, 174
Stoller, R. J., 103, 104, 106
Stone, I. F., 258
Story, fostering, 138–39
Structure, 3, 135; of experience, 30, 34–44, 122–26; mother's perceptions of daughter, 50–54
*Structure of Behavior*, 8
Subjectivity, 69
Substance abuse, 202–05
Suffusions, 104
Superego, 135: mother's, 98
Symbolism, 7–8, 23

Tansey, xi
Tavistock group method, xiv

Taylor, M. C., 20
Telepathy, 103, 110
Temporality, 10, 34
*The Texas Chain Saw Massacre*, 150
Thomä, H., 15, 56
Thouzery, L., 19–20, 26
Time dimension, 9–10
Tolstrup, K., 25, 30
Transfer, 11–12, 64
Transference, 29, 140, 199, 240
Transgenerational relations, 59–62: in anorexia nervosa, xi–xii; and haunting, 102, 111
Transitivism, 133–34
Transpersonal approach, 17–19
Transsexualism, 104, 105–07, 108–10: change of function and secondary autonomy, 111–17; dreams of 105–07; phenomenological method demonstration in, 118–28; Soller's case study of, 108–09; Volkan and Bhatti case study of, 105–07
Treatment, 73
12 (twelve)-step program, 170

Unconscious agendas, 196–202
Understanding, 261
Undifferentiation, 13
Urgent/voluntary errands, 117

Vertical perceptual distinctions, 57
Victim, 198, 214
Violence, 64
Volkan, V. D., xiv, 103, 104, 193, 212, 214, 232–33, 254–55, 257: on transsexual dreams, 105–07; transsexualism case study of, 115–16
von Franz, M.-L., 259
Von-Wallenberg, P. A., 26

Wagon circling, 217–26
Walkey, F. H., 25, 30
Waxler, N. E., 190
Weight: aberrant, 25; pathology, 30; phobia, 25, 30
Welch, G., 25, 30
Whitehead, Alfred North, 187
Wilson, C. P., 15, 56
Winnicott, D. W., x, 175, 183, 184, 261
*The Wizard of Oz*, 155–56

Zinner, J., 229

## DATE DUE